WHILE YOU WERE SLEEPING

Ewen Spencer

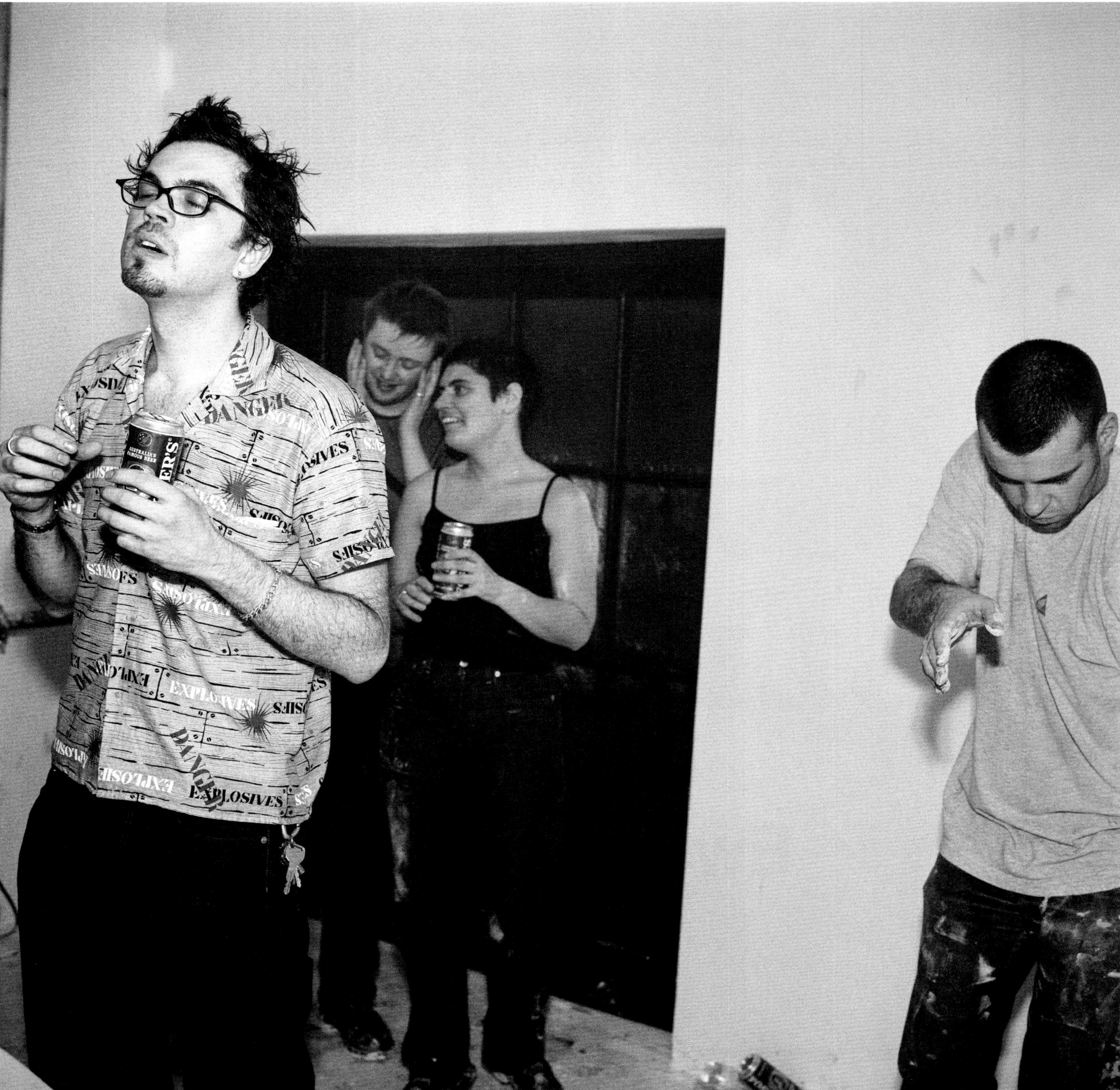
DANGER
EXPLOSIVES
EXPLOSIVES
DANGER
EXPLOSIVES

FOREWORD
Elaine Constantine

Years ago, early to mid 90's, a young man appeared in my periphery on a dance floor with a camera. Having been in the same position myself on many occasion, I studied his MO and noticed his desire to capture the spirit of the club had overcome any trepidation that situation could have induced. People don't always like to have their nights out interrupted by a stranger.

After this initial night I seemed to see him everywhere, always operating with that same fearlessness and somehow managing to stay in the thick of things without being in the way.

I've watched Ewen's impressive output over the subsequent years keenly, but I never saw the results of those early escapades until now and here they are in all their glory in a project so aptly titled, 'While You Were Sleeping'.

Ewen's lens shows us a spirit of a freedom we have forgotten. Like all good photographers, he articulates a moment in time that has irretrievably passed. This book beautifully captures the last moments where people drank and smoked in the same place as they danced; a time when everyone came together in a moment of abandonment or at least it feels this way in Ewen's pictures. As an observer I witnessed him immerse himself in the experience, with his camera always stuck to his face, he became the familiar fixture without interrupting the dance-floor rituals. For this reason Ewen's images provide us with a richer understanding of British nightlife and set him apart from the many others who photographed this subject at the time.

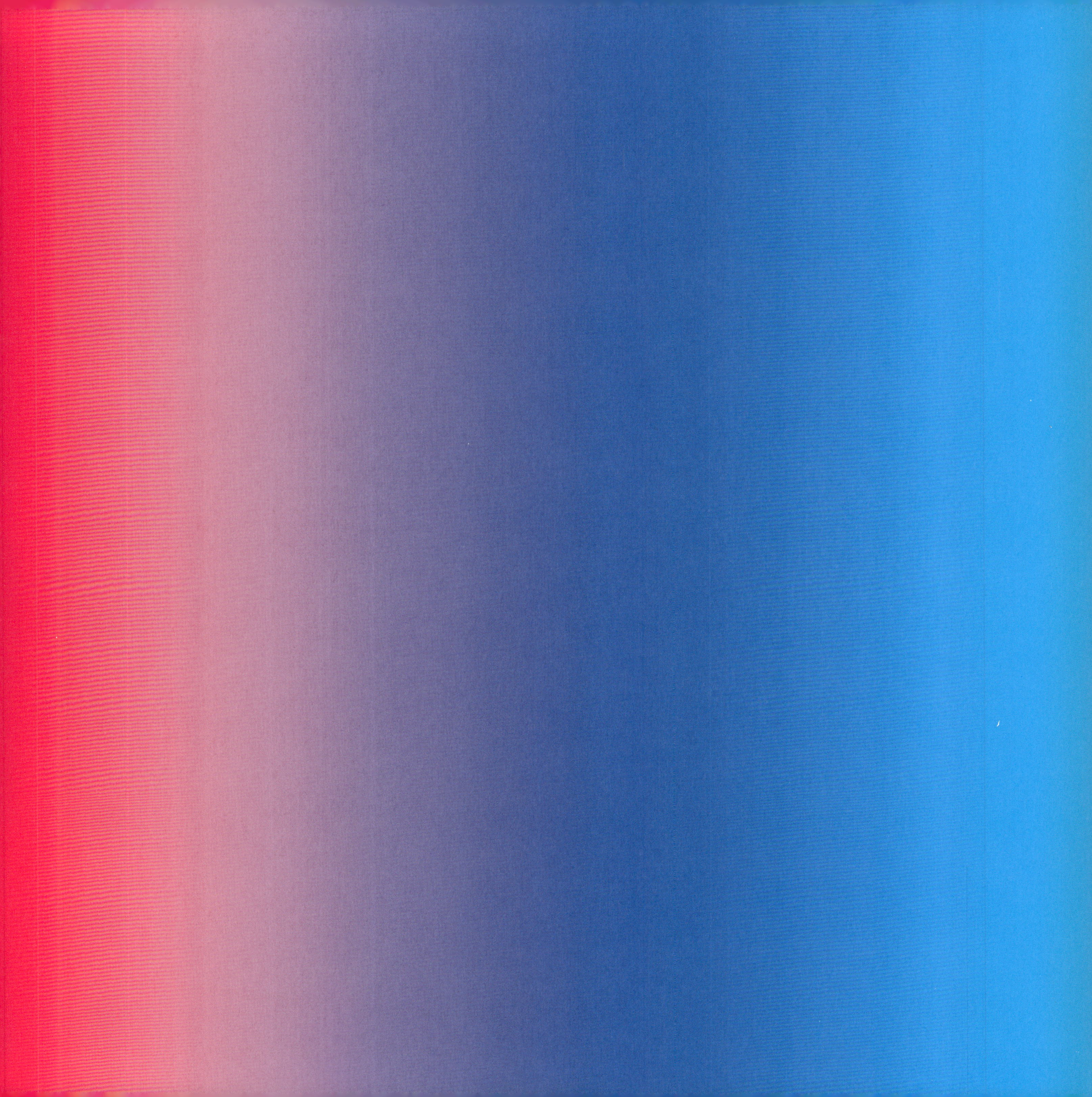

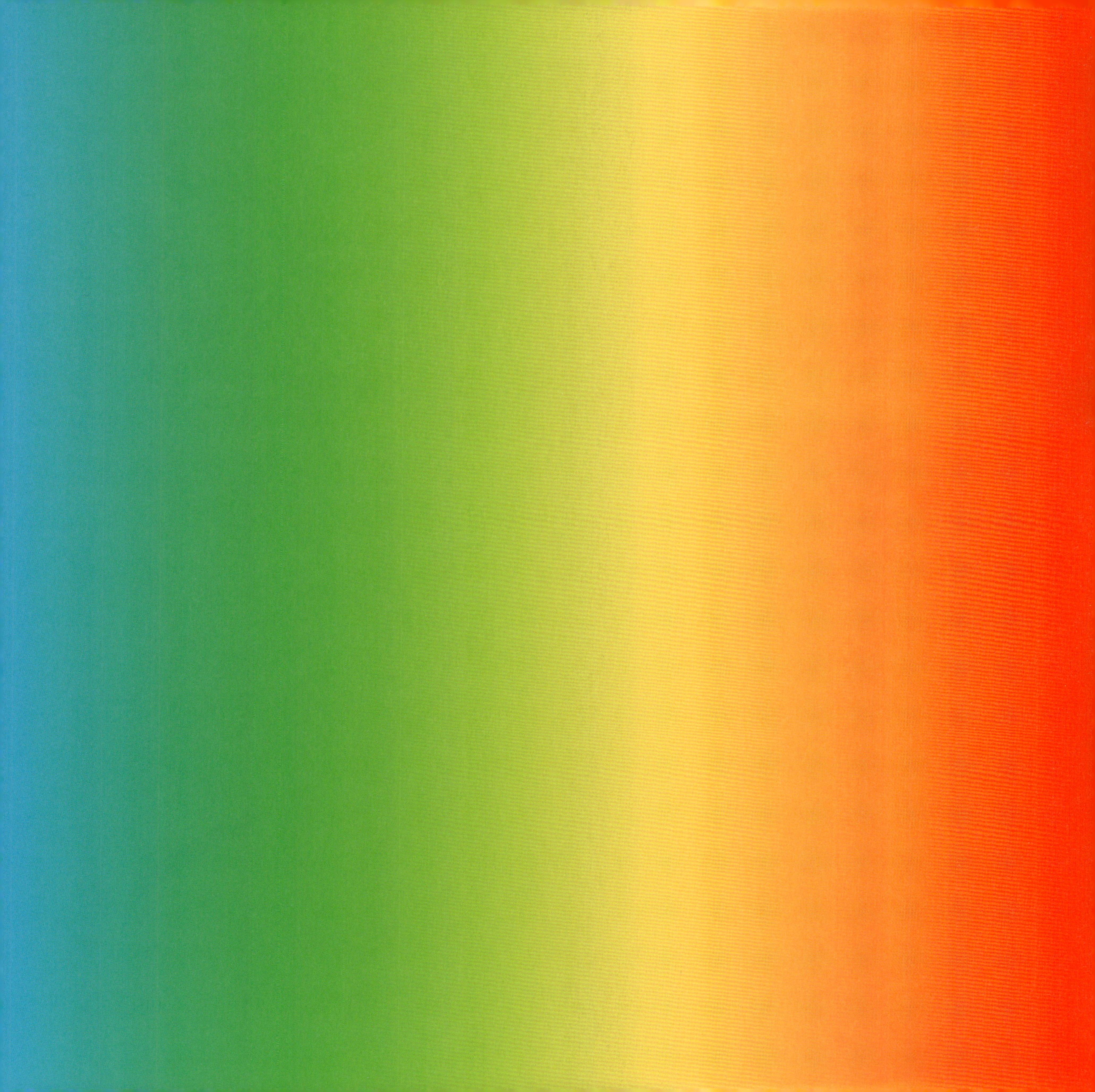

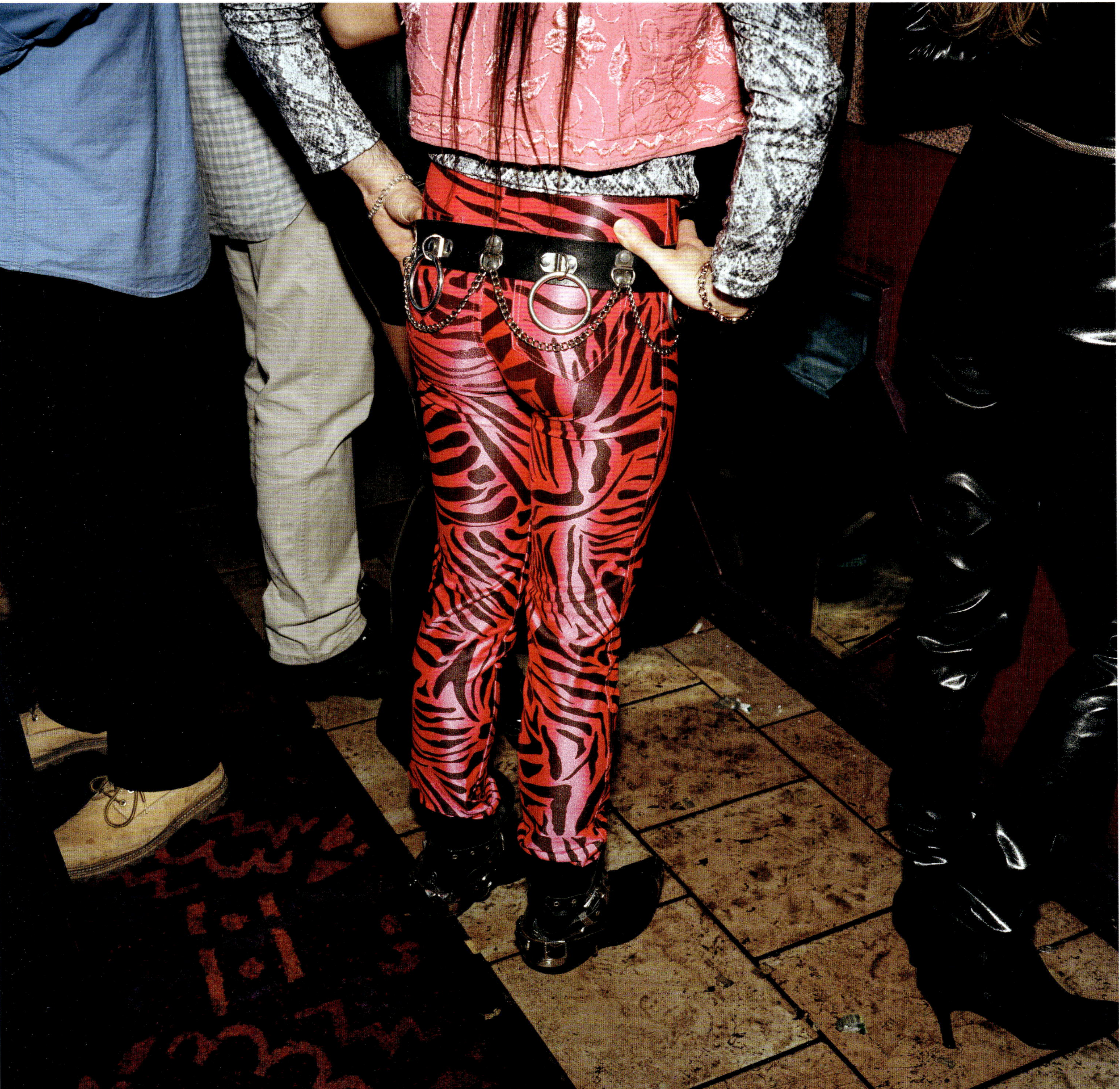

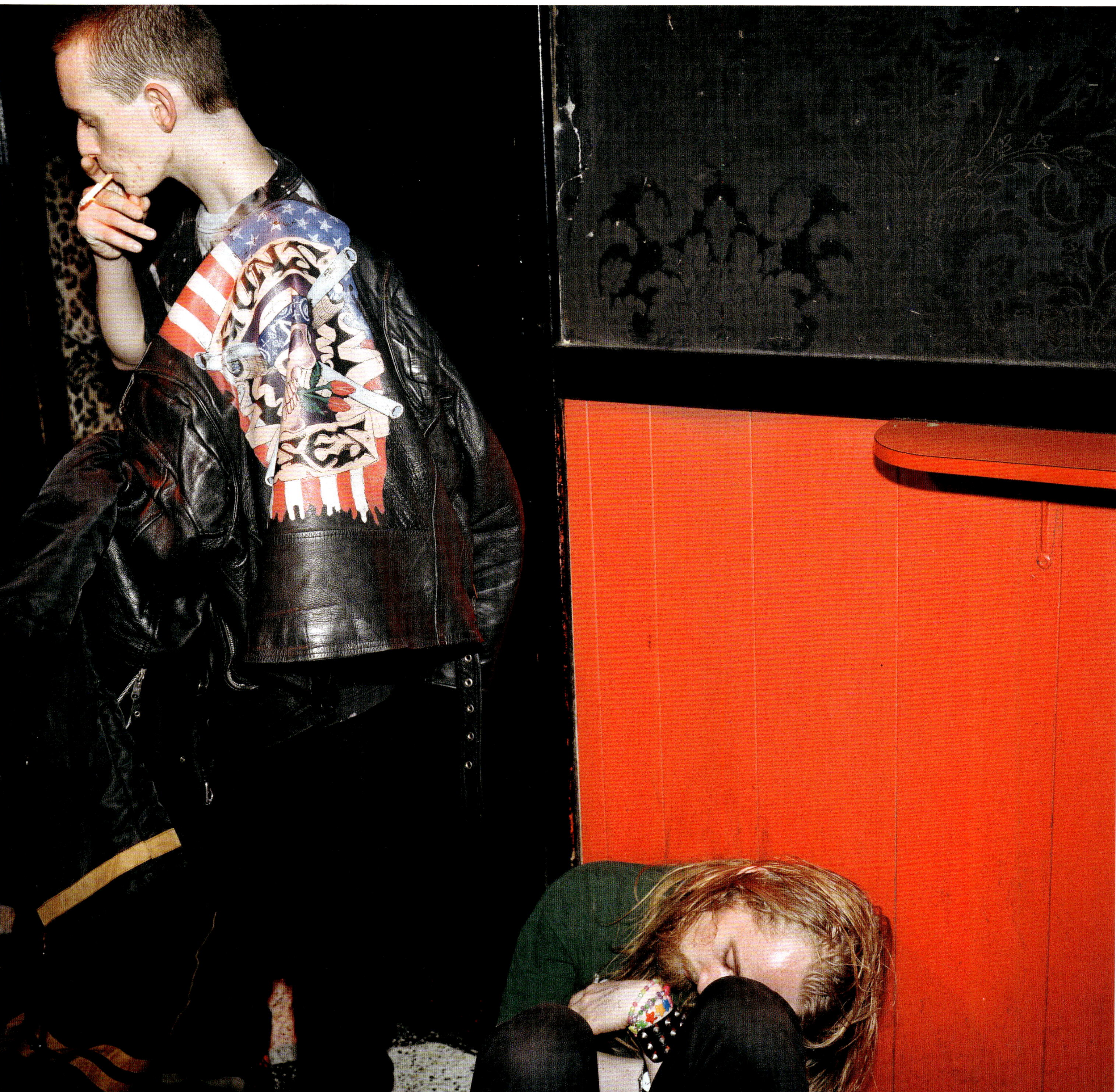

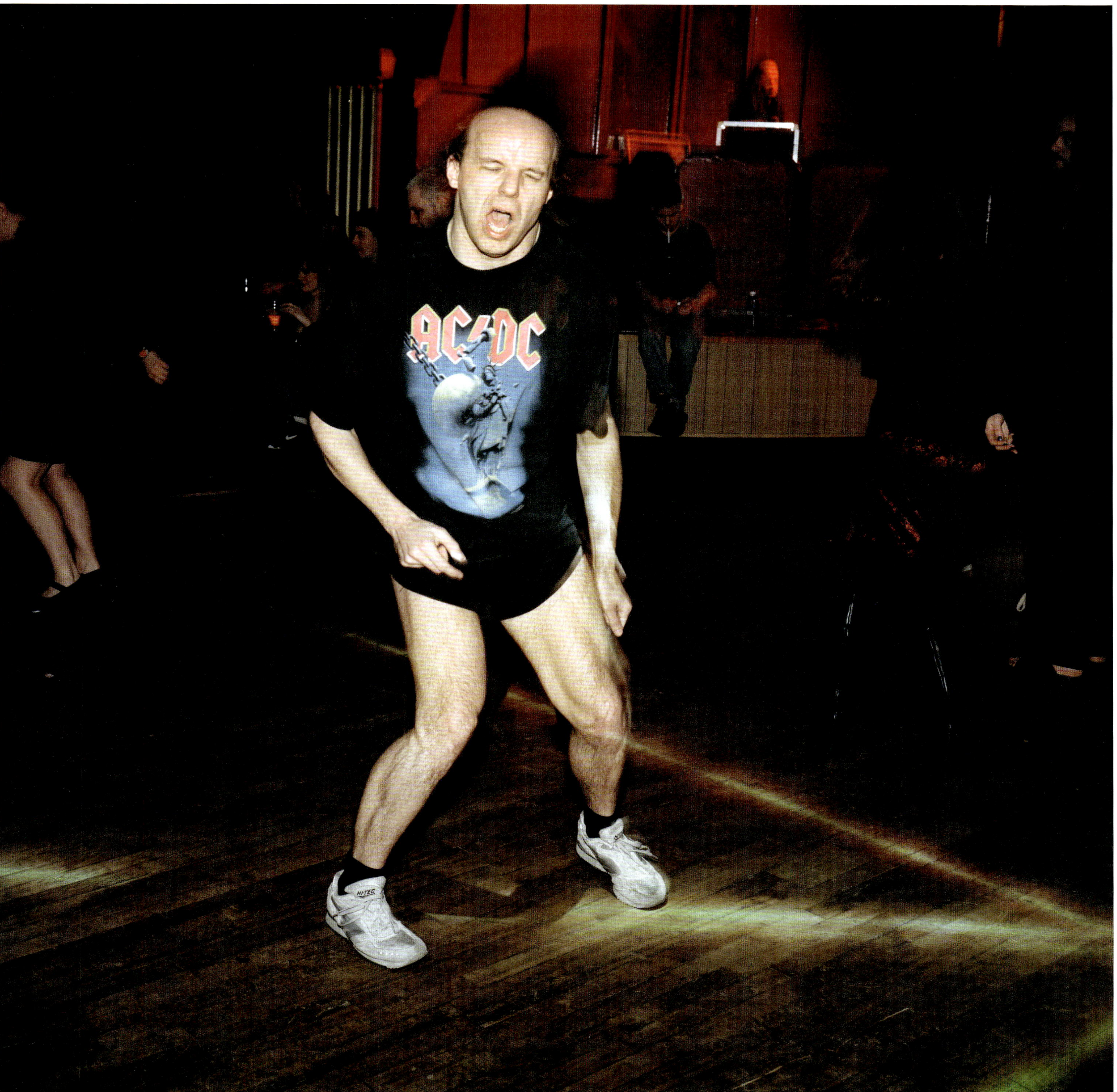
AC/DC
HI-TEC

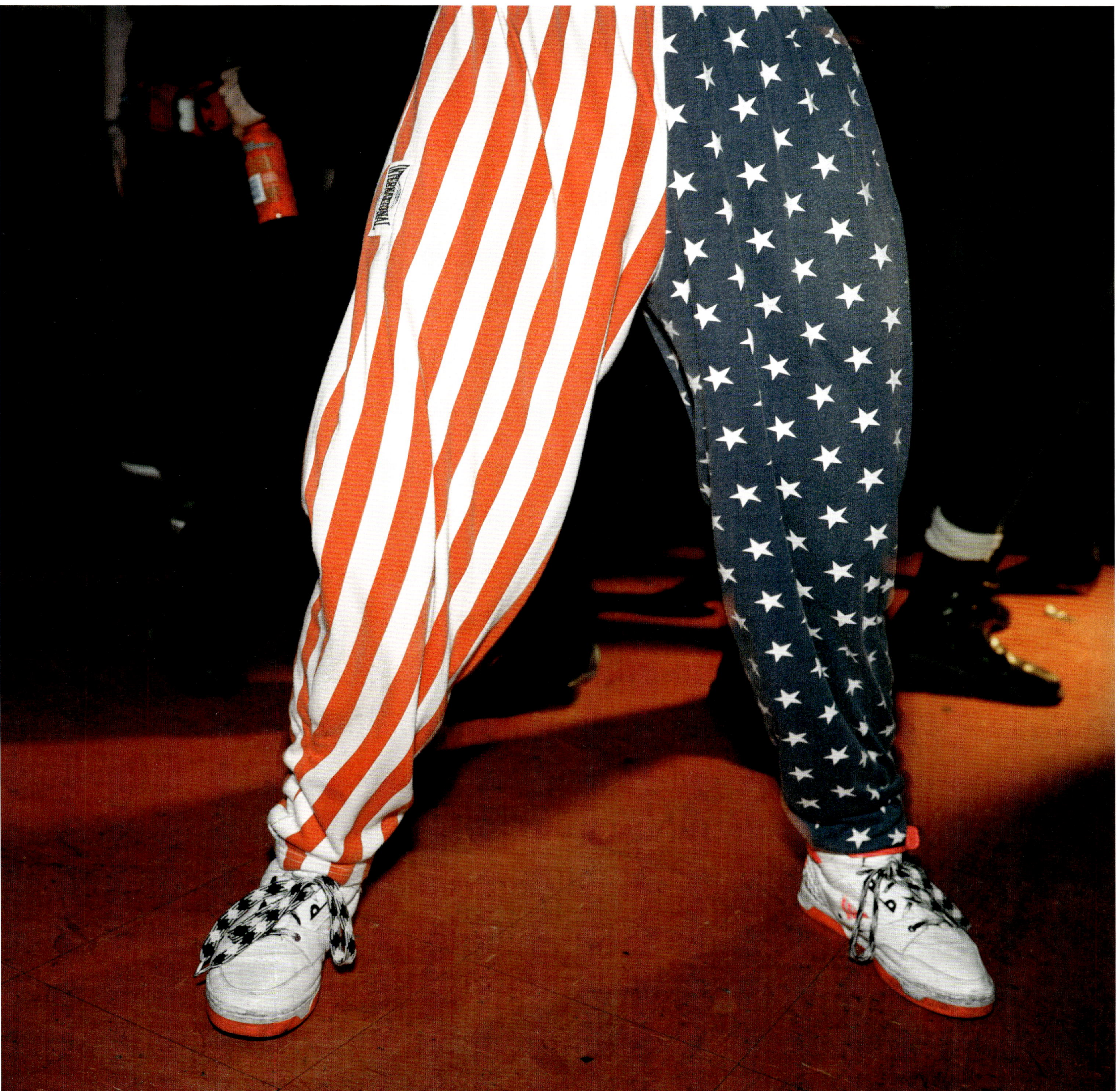

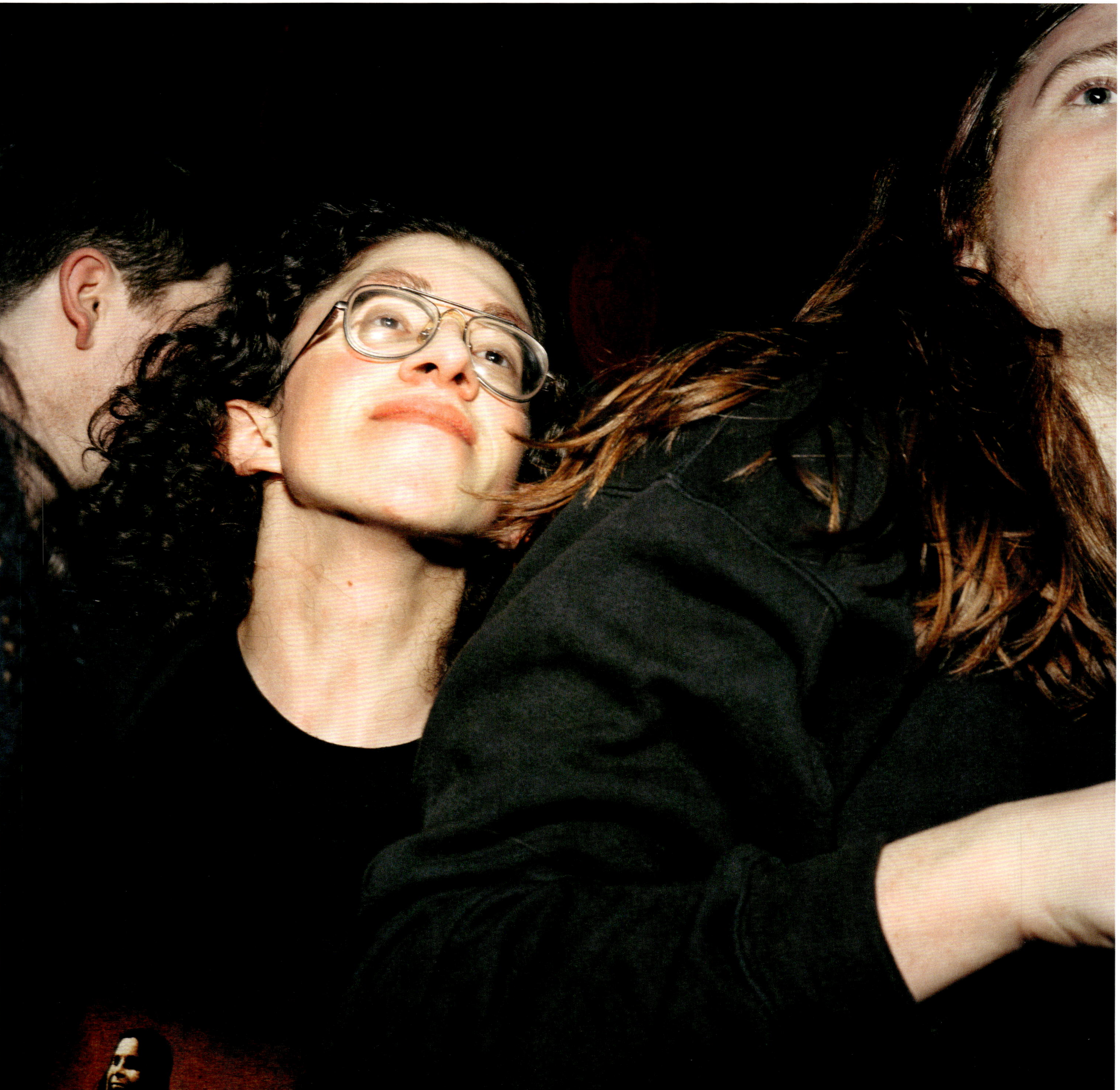

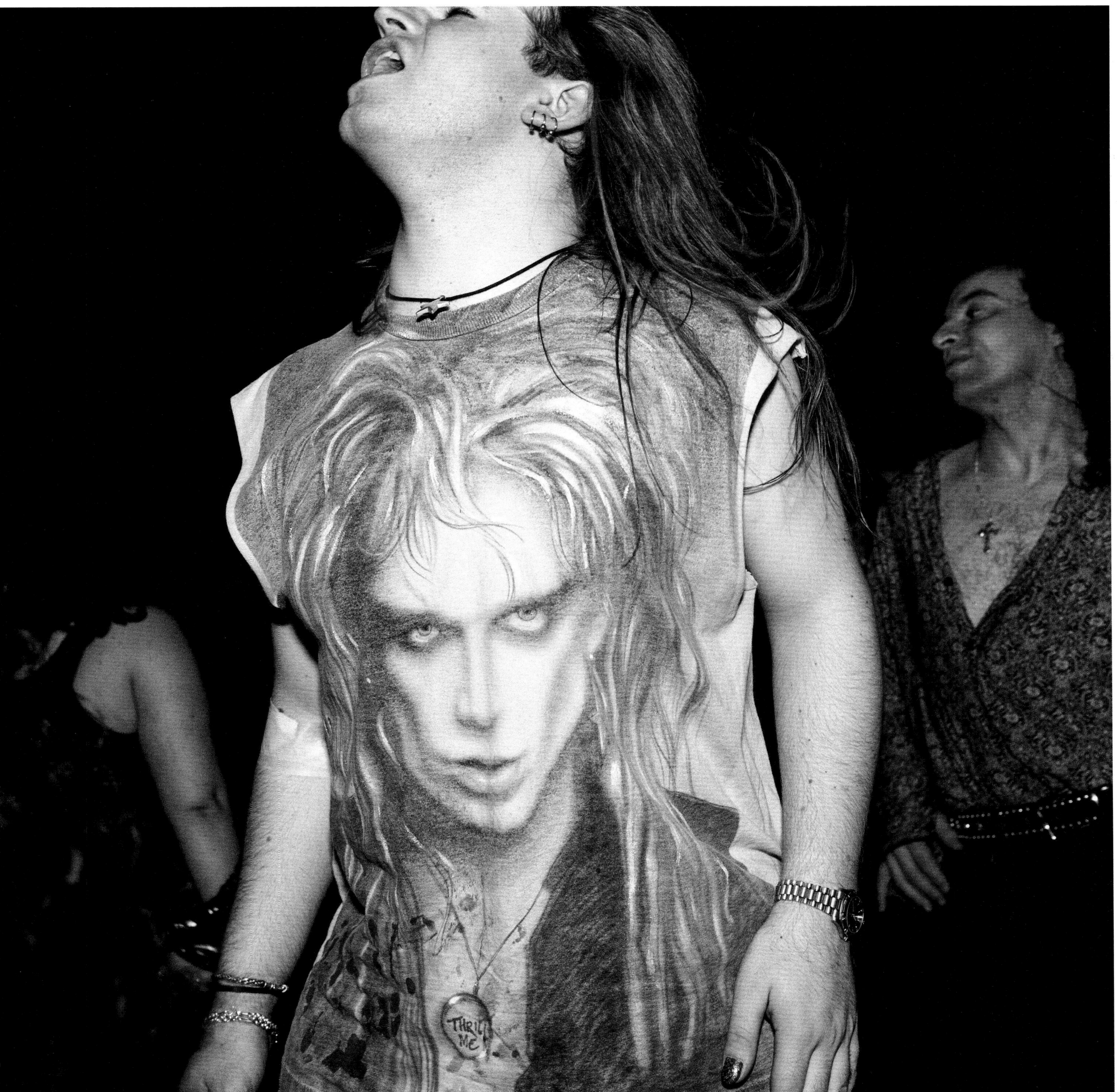
THRILL
ME

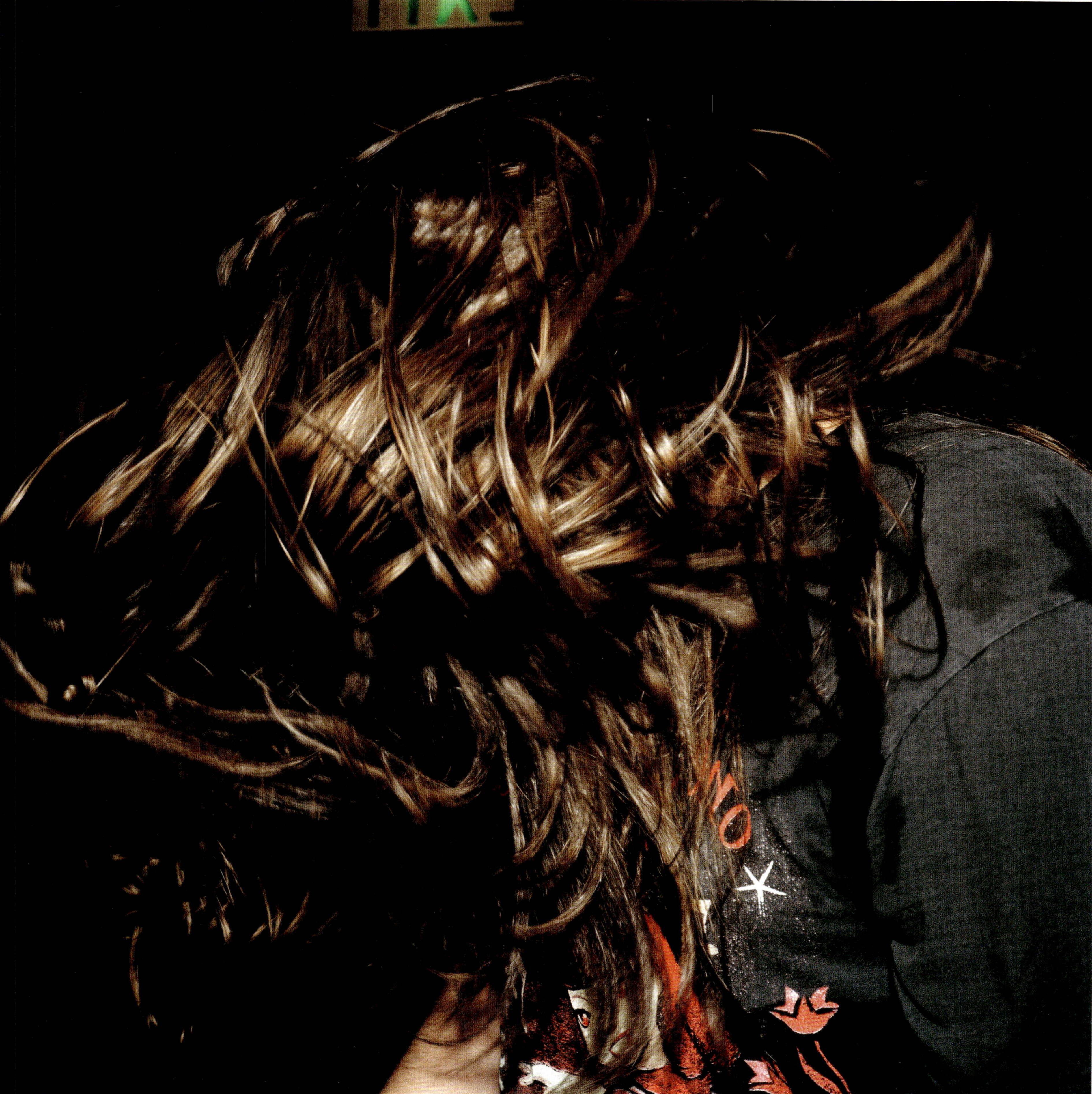

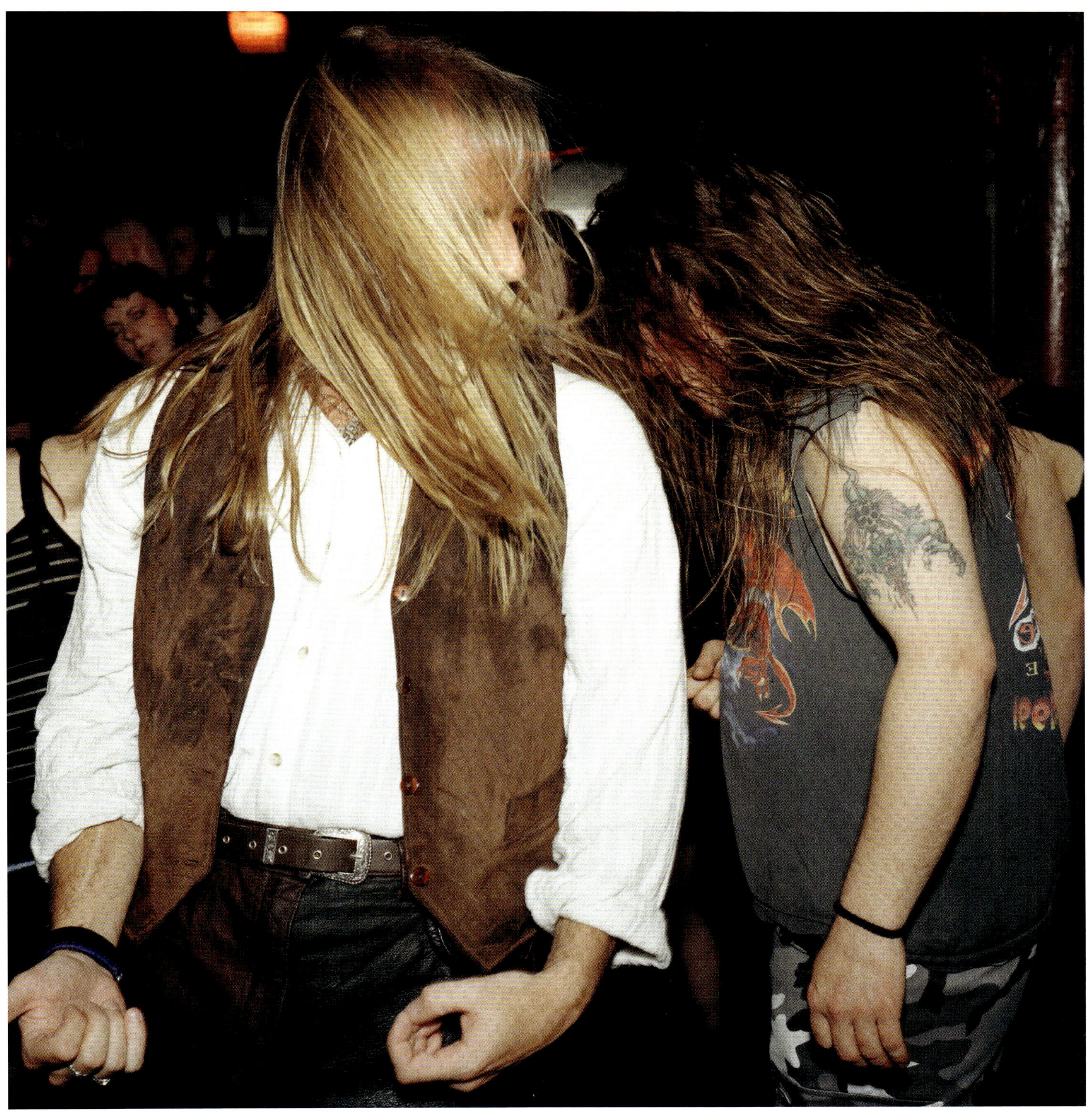

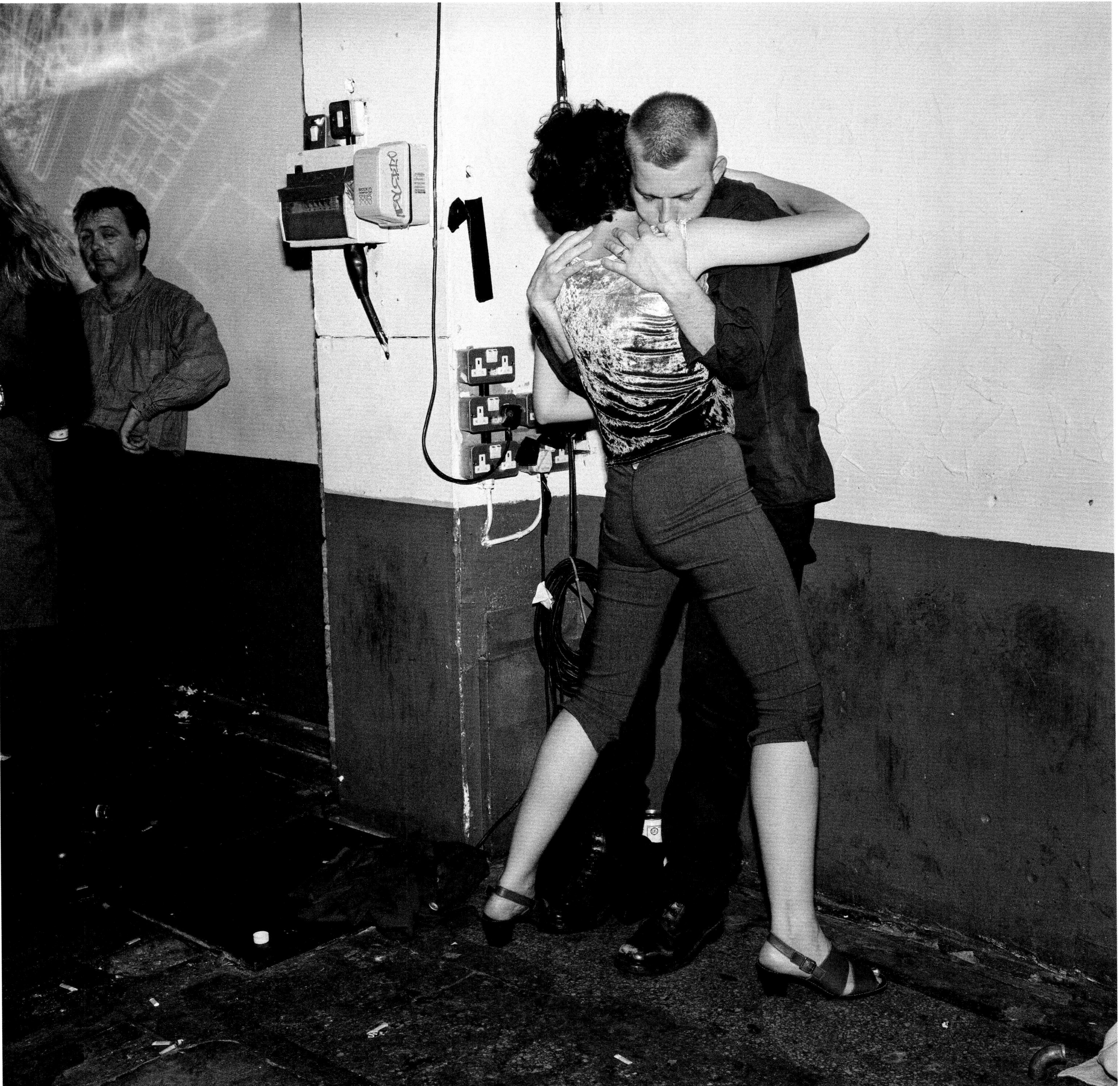

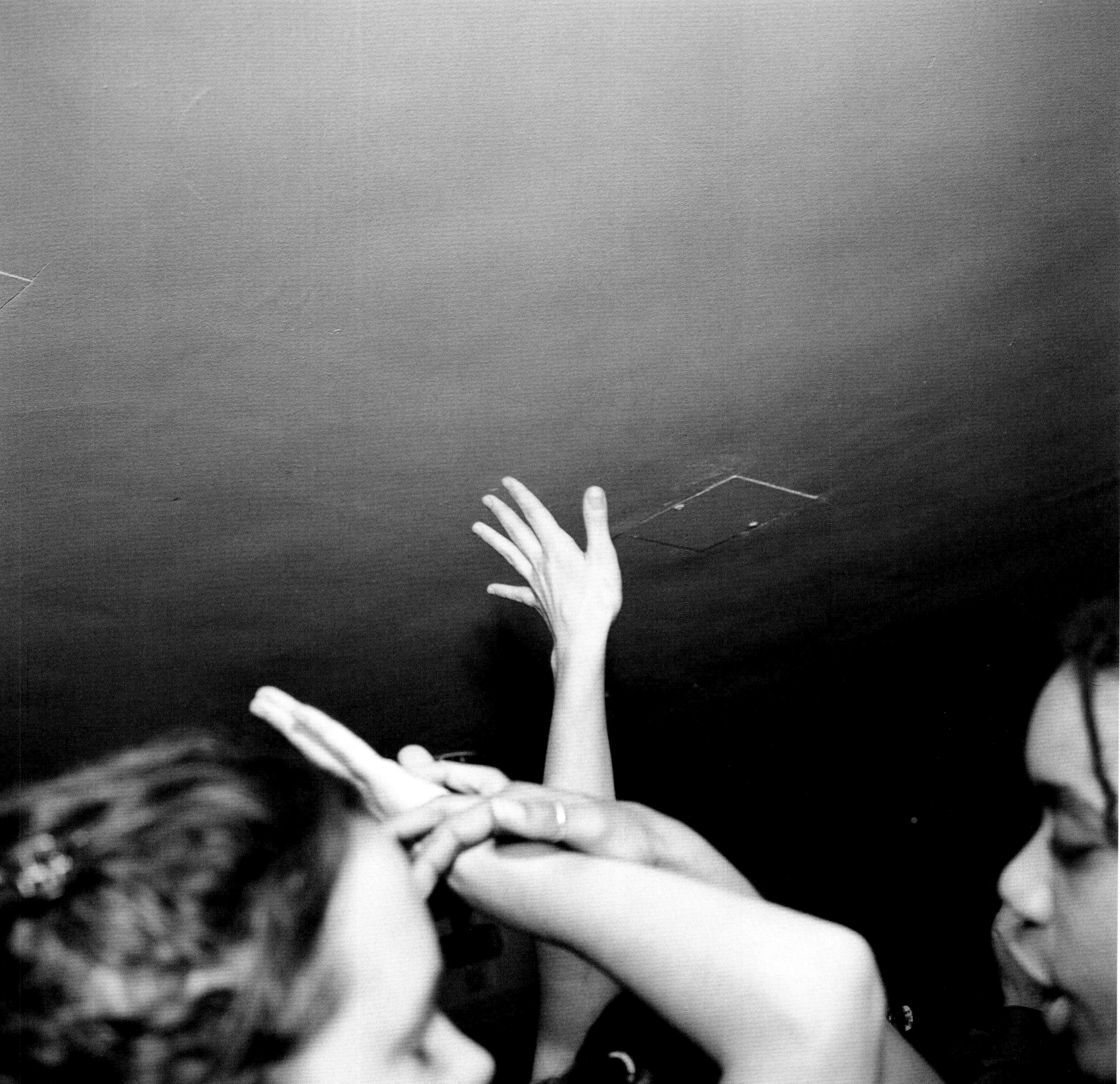

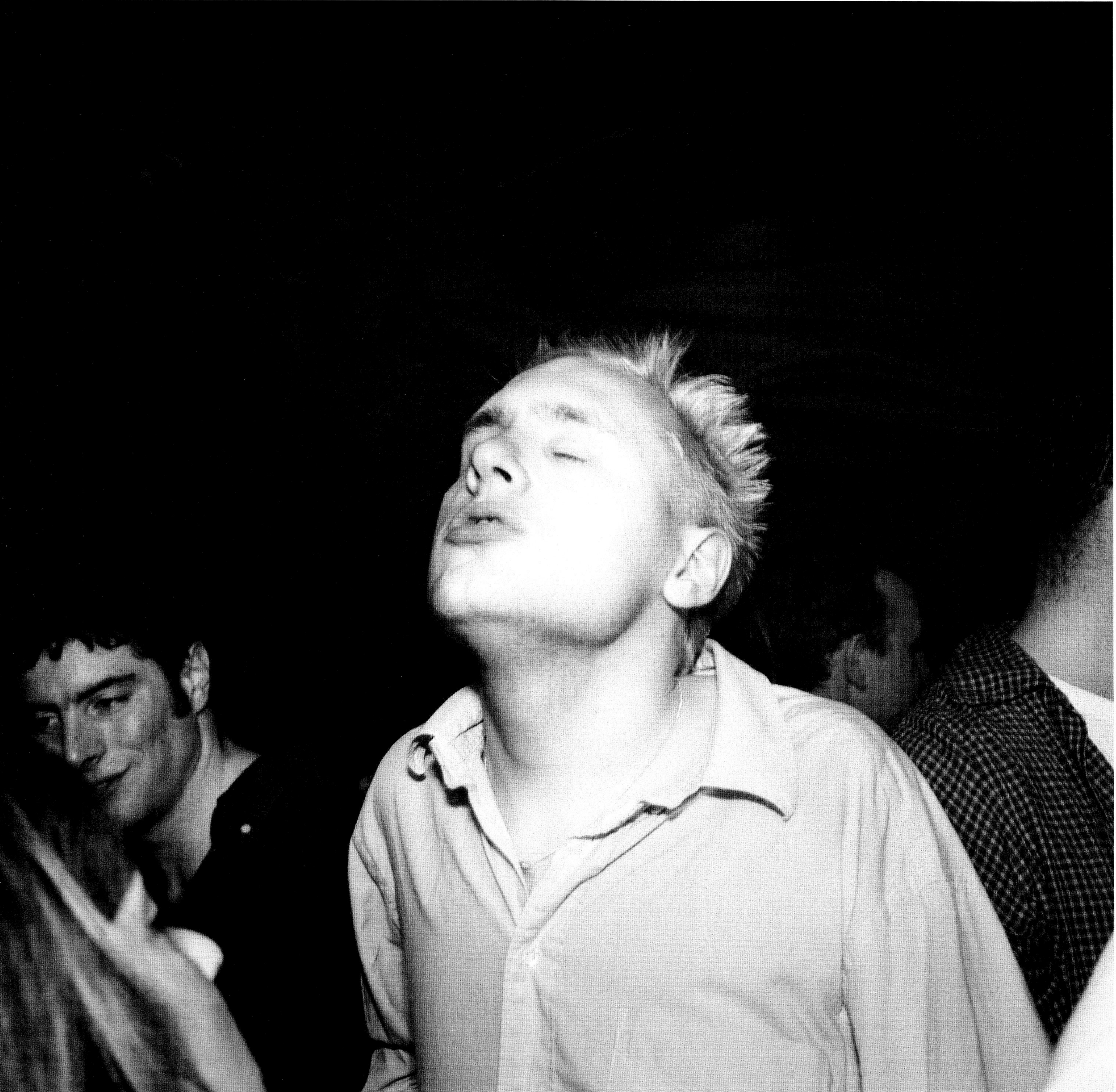

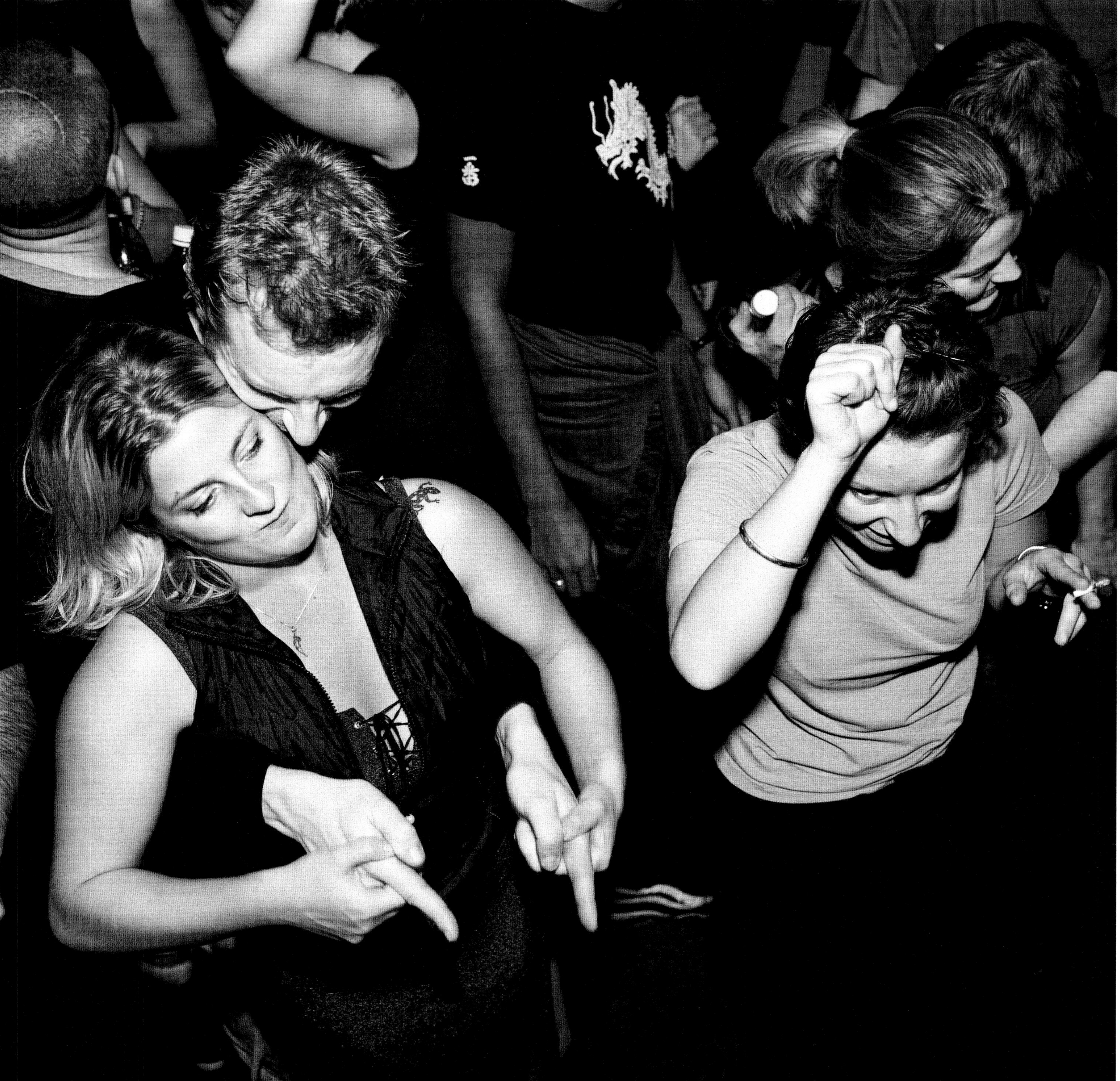

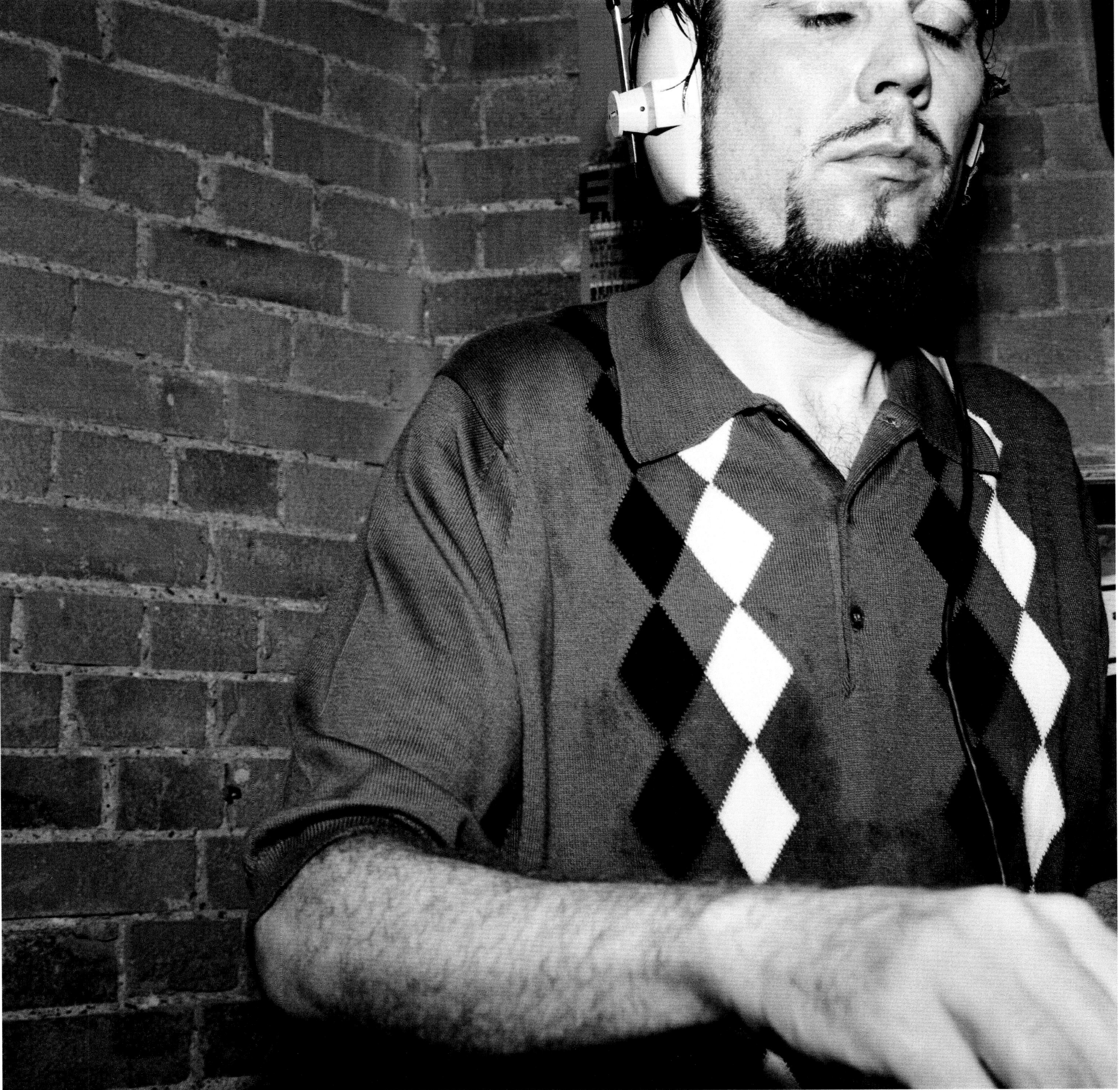

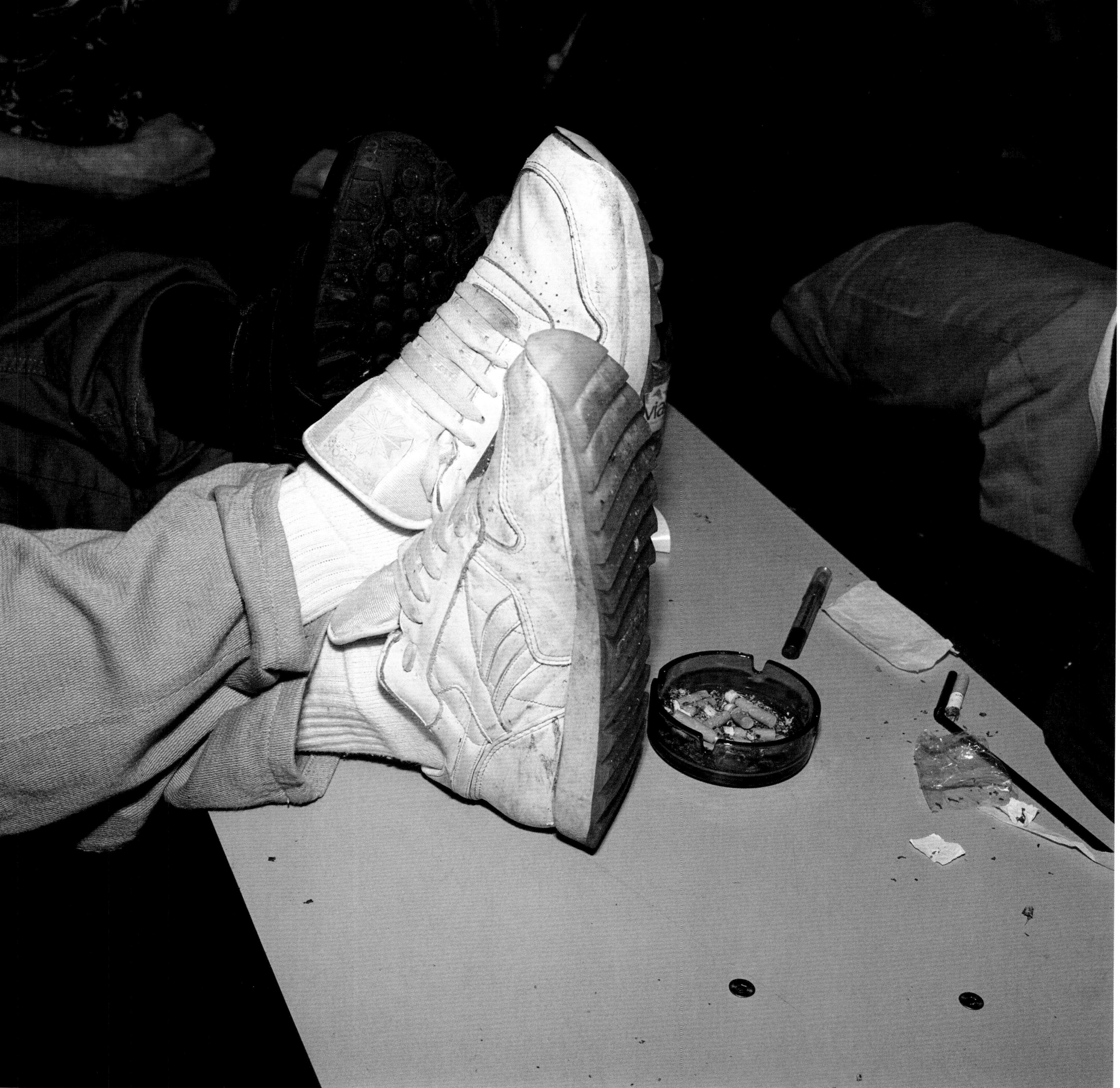

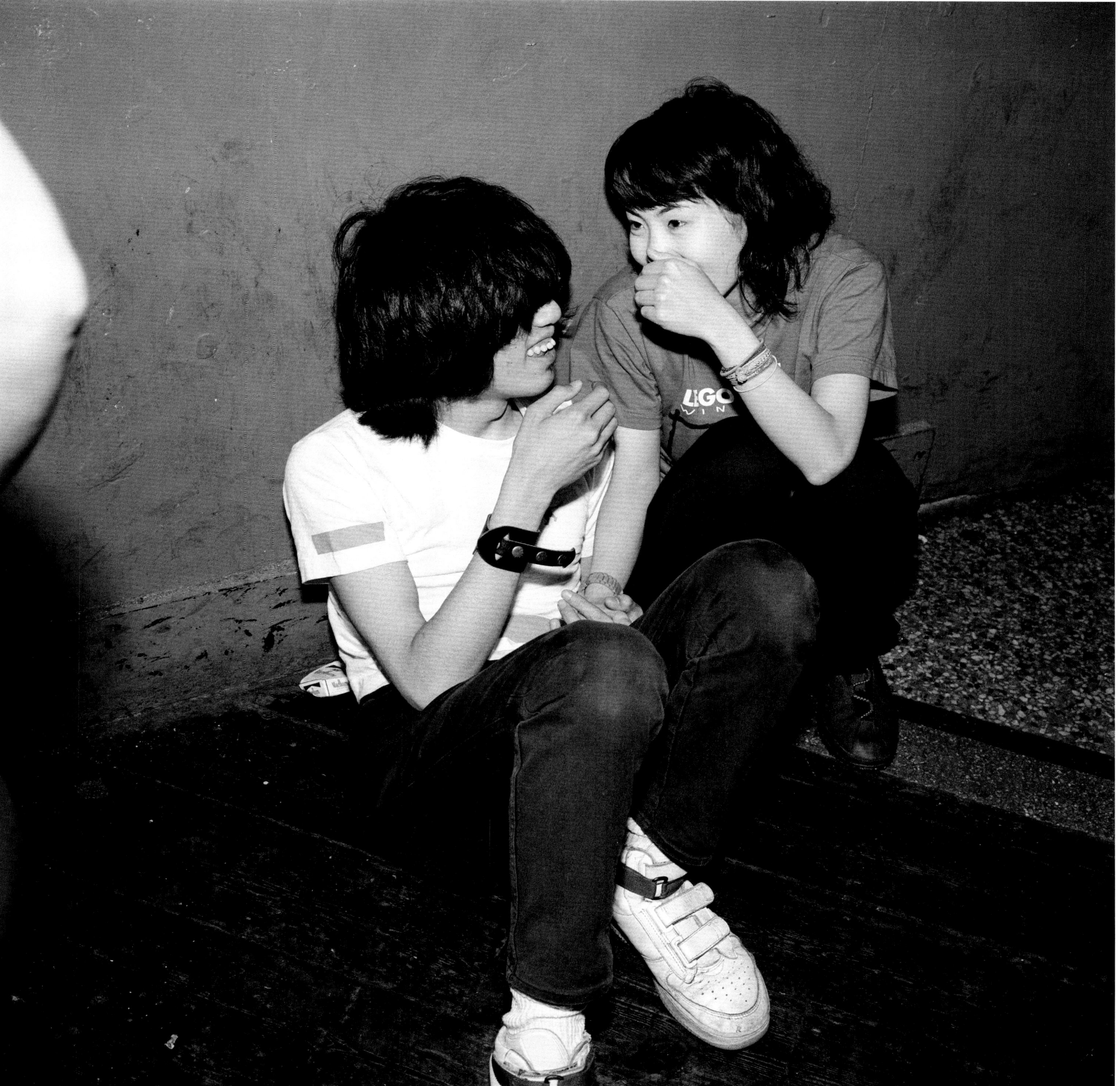

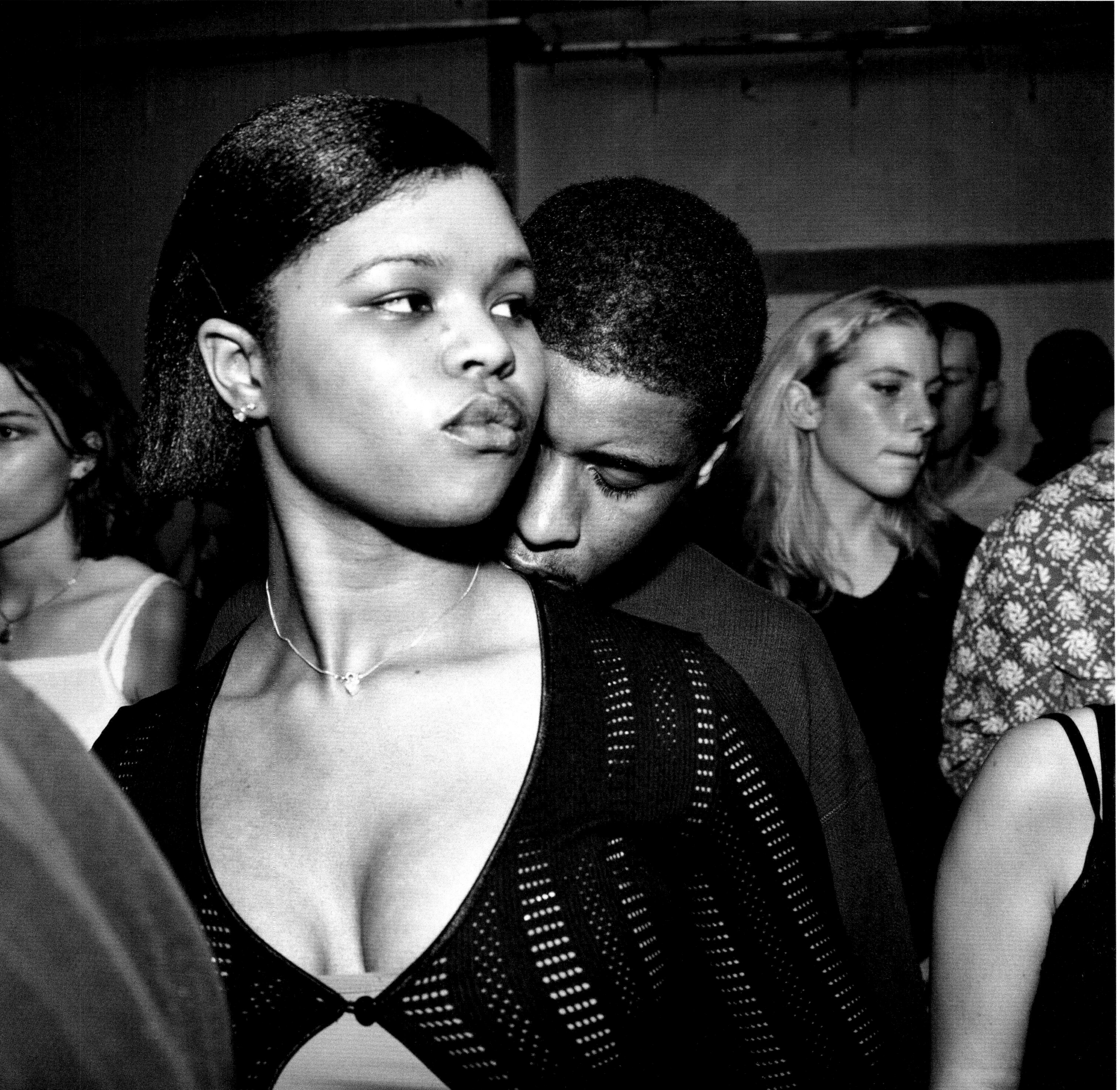

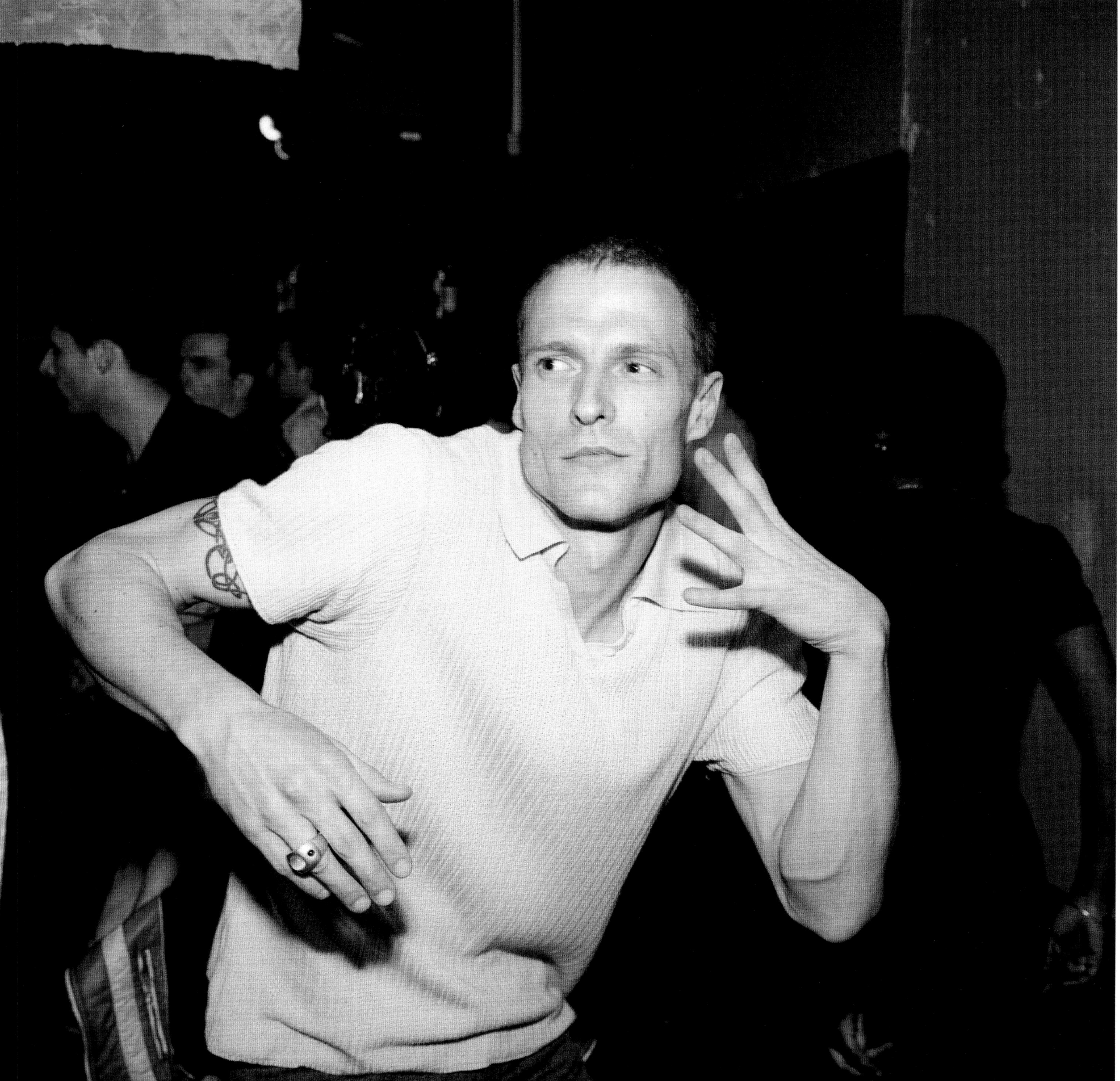

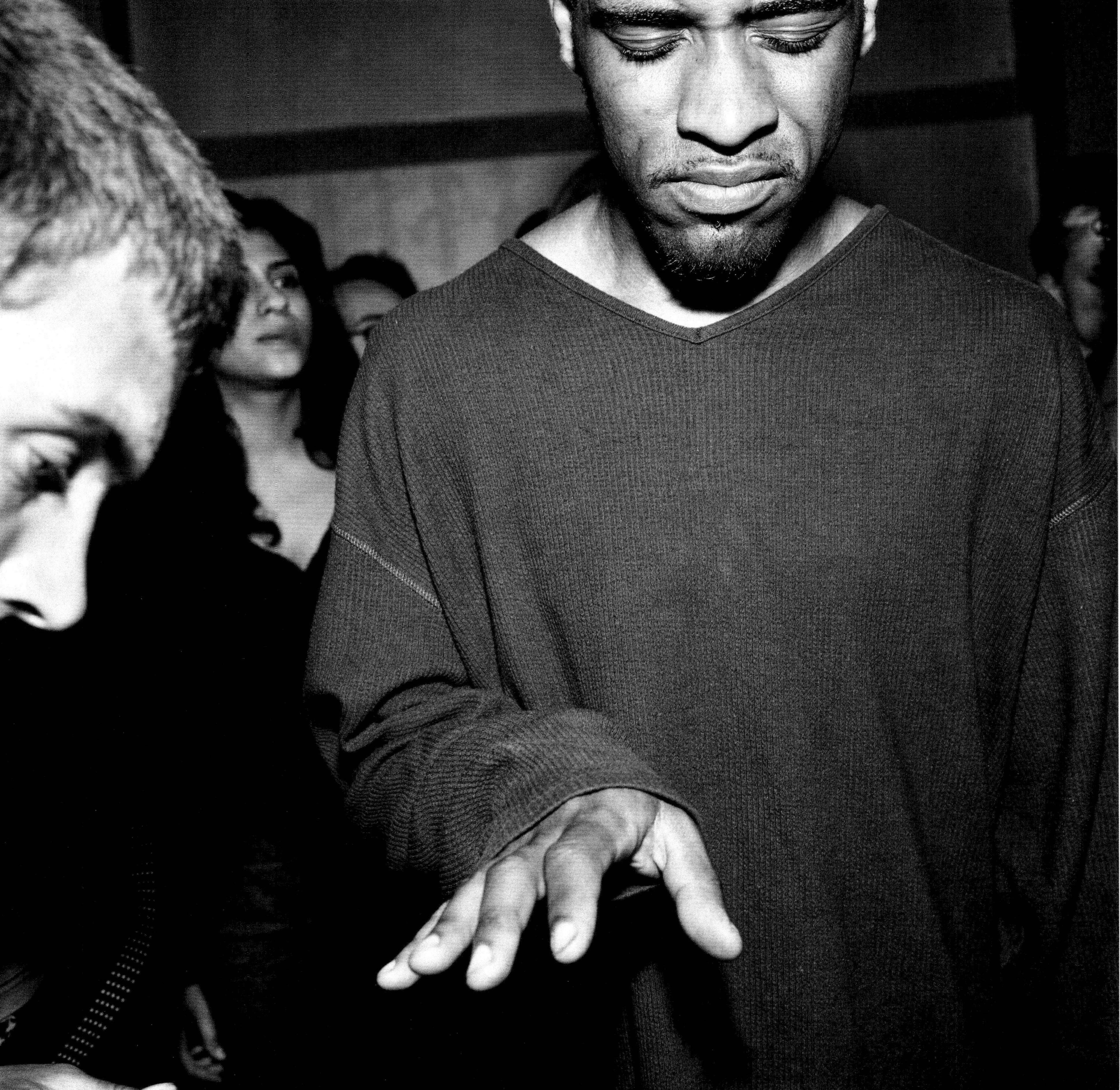

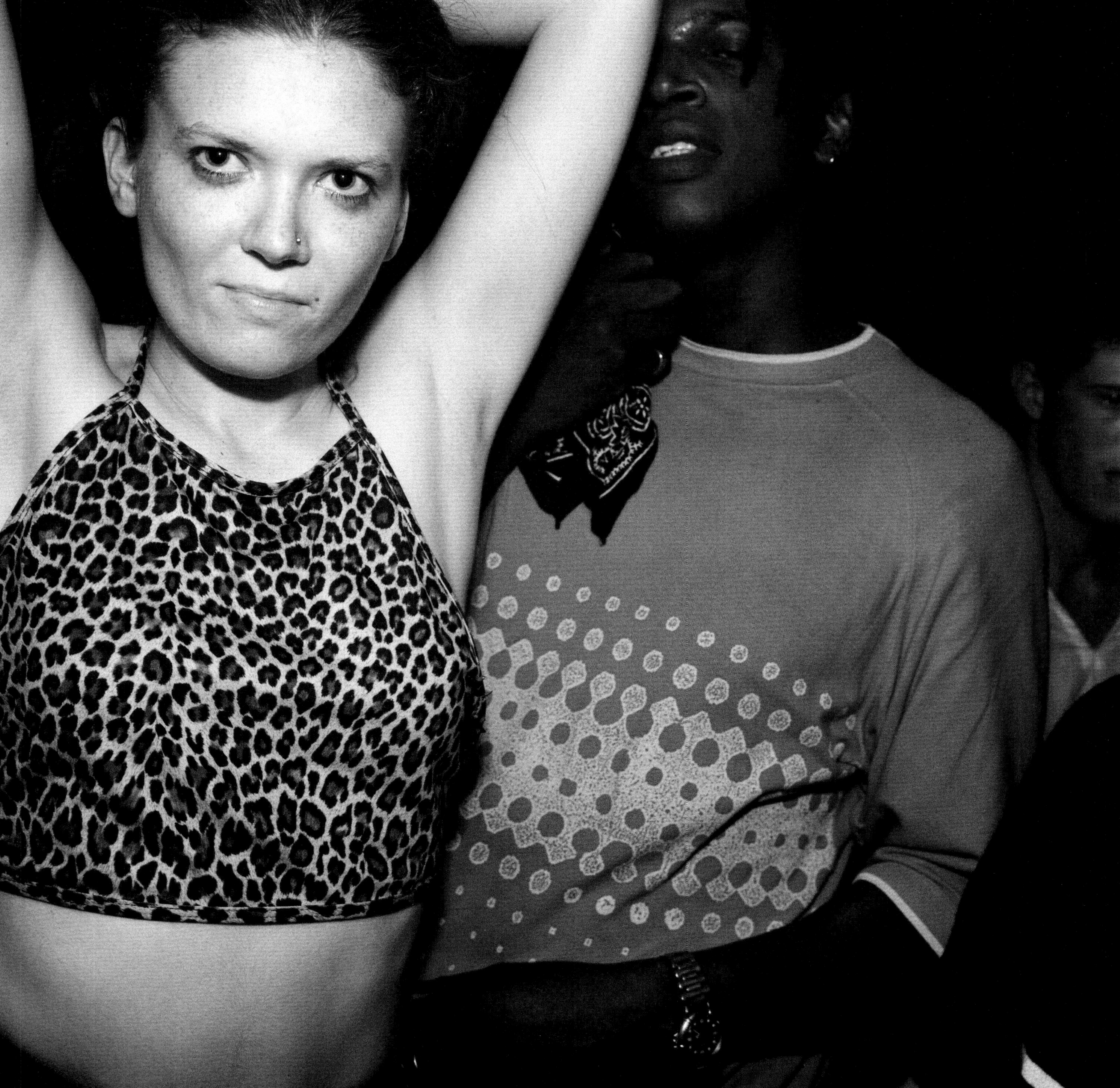

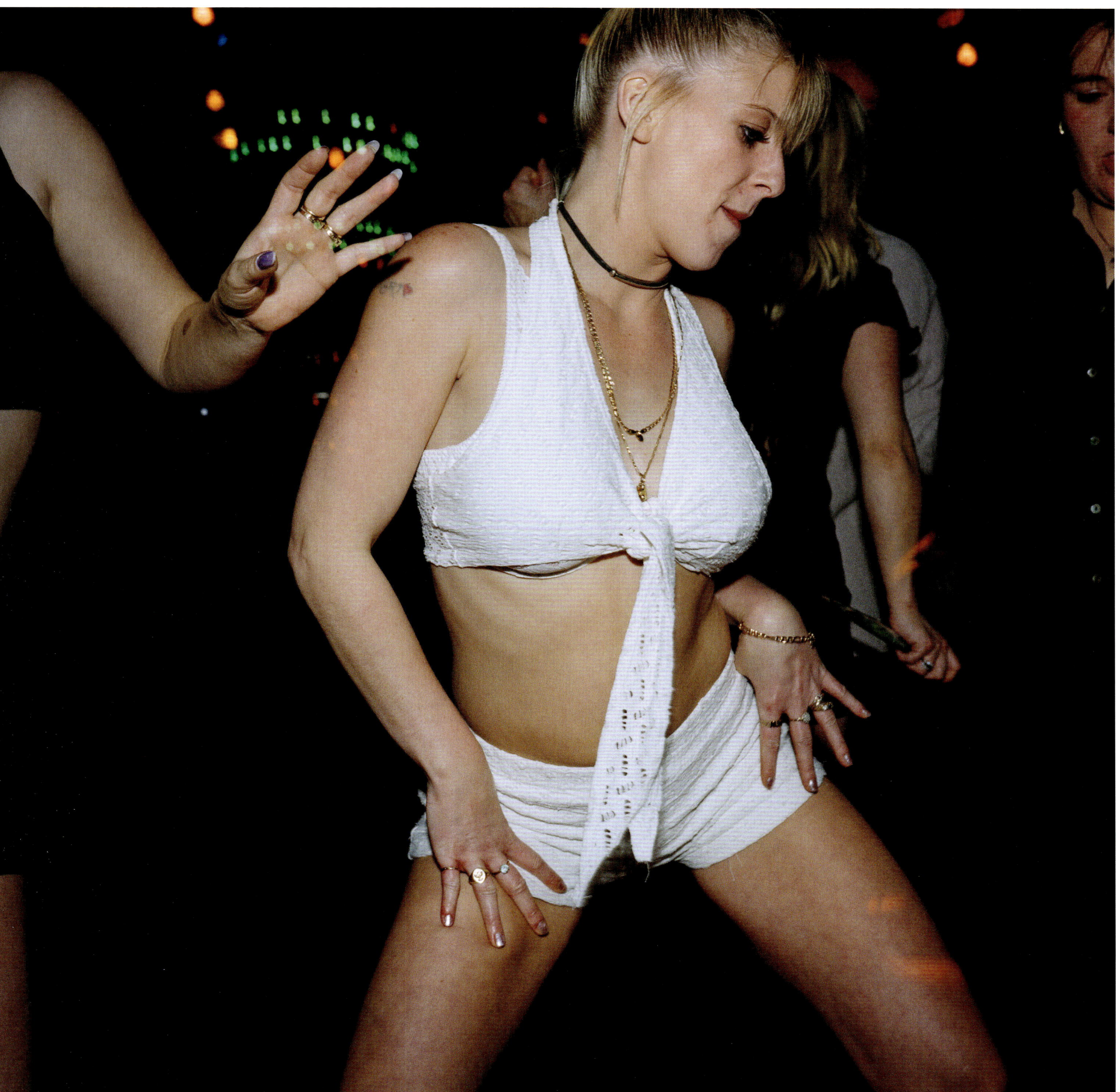

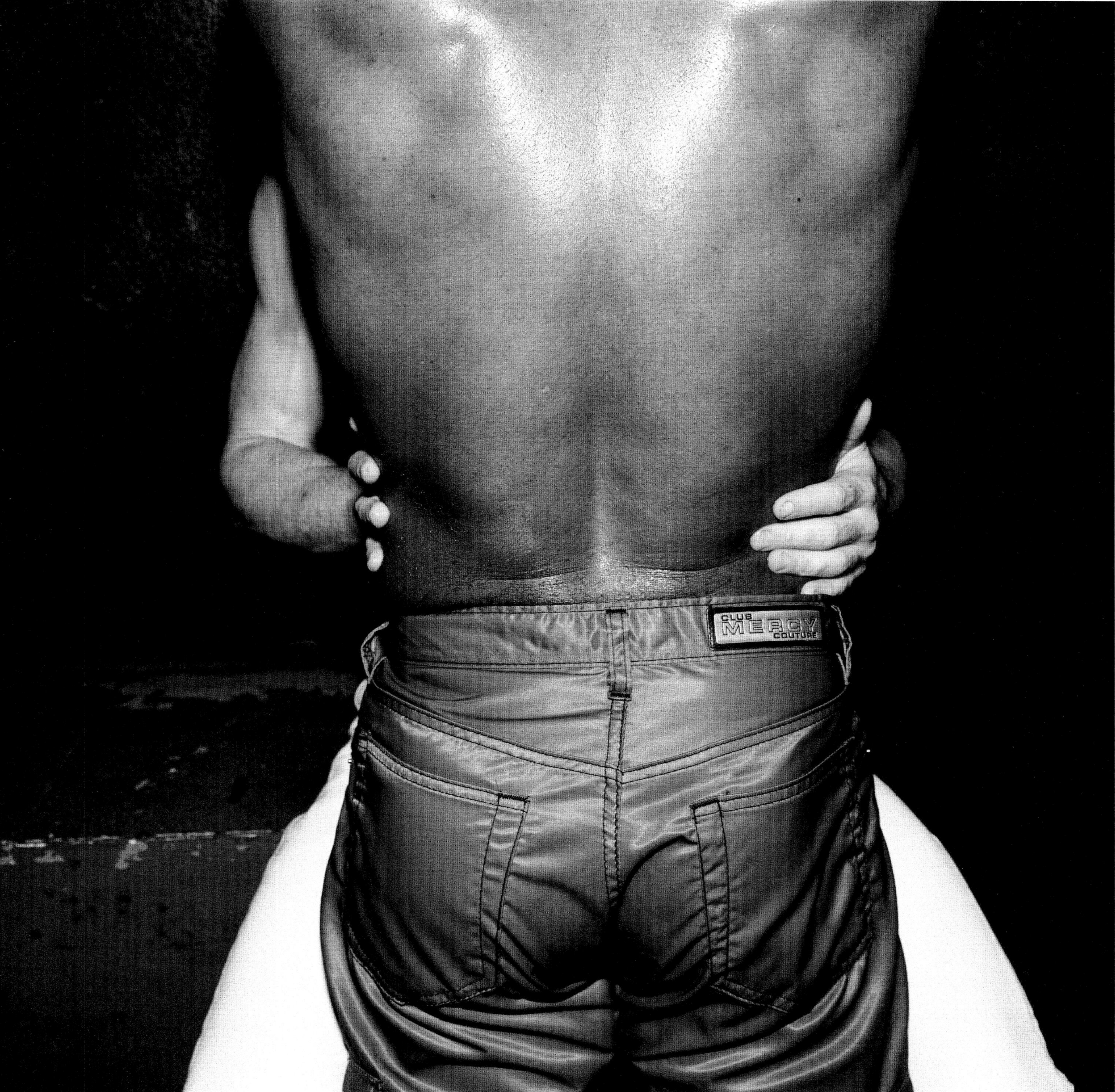
CLUB
MERCY
COUTURE

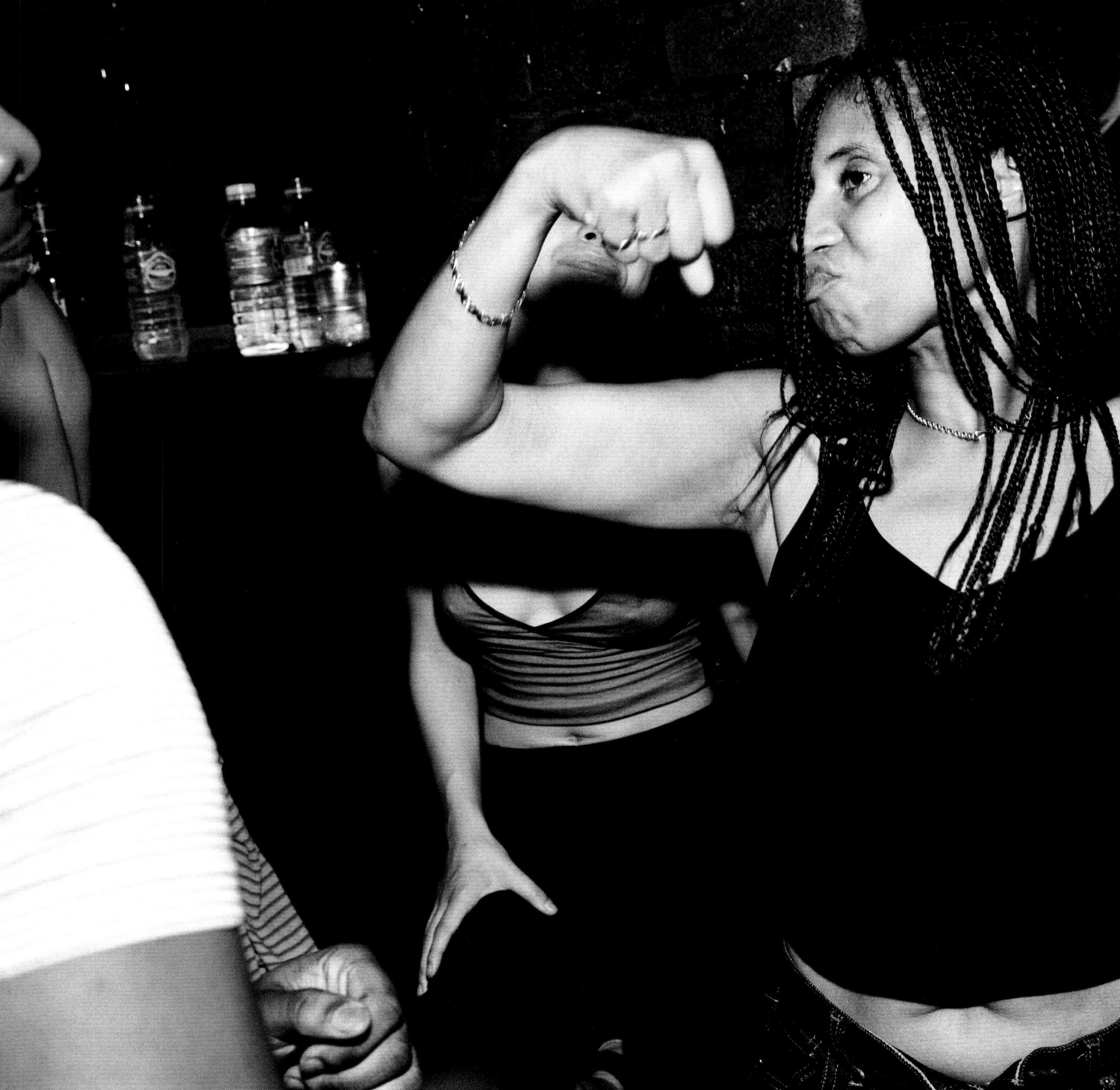

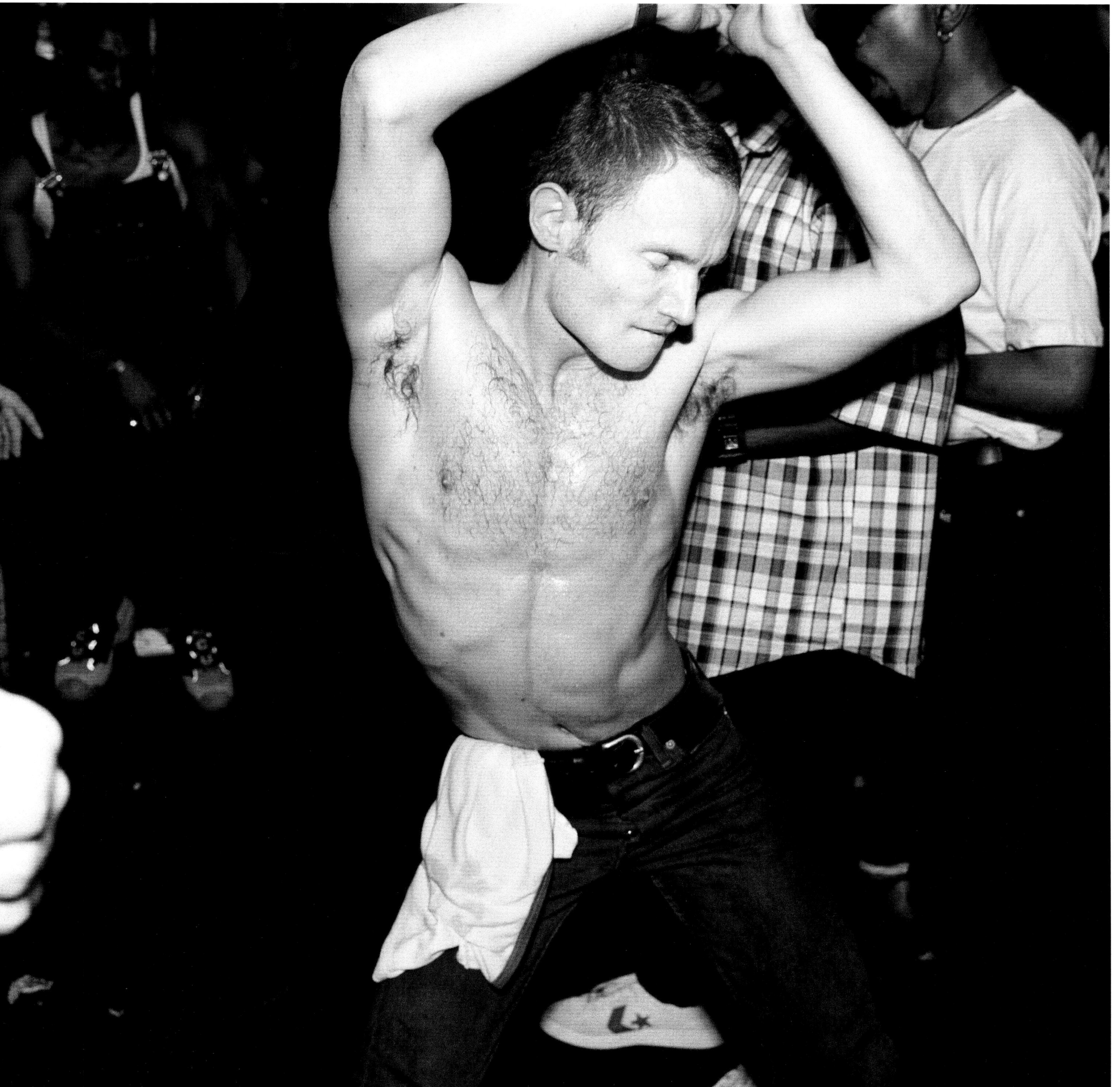

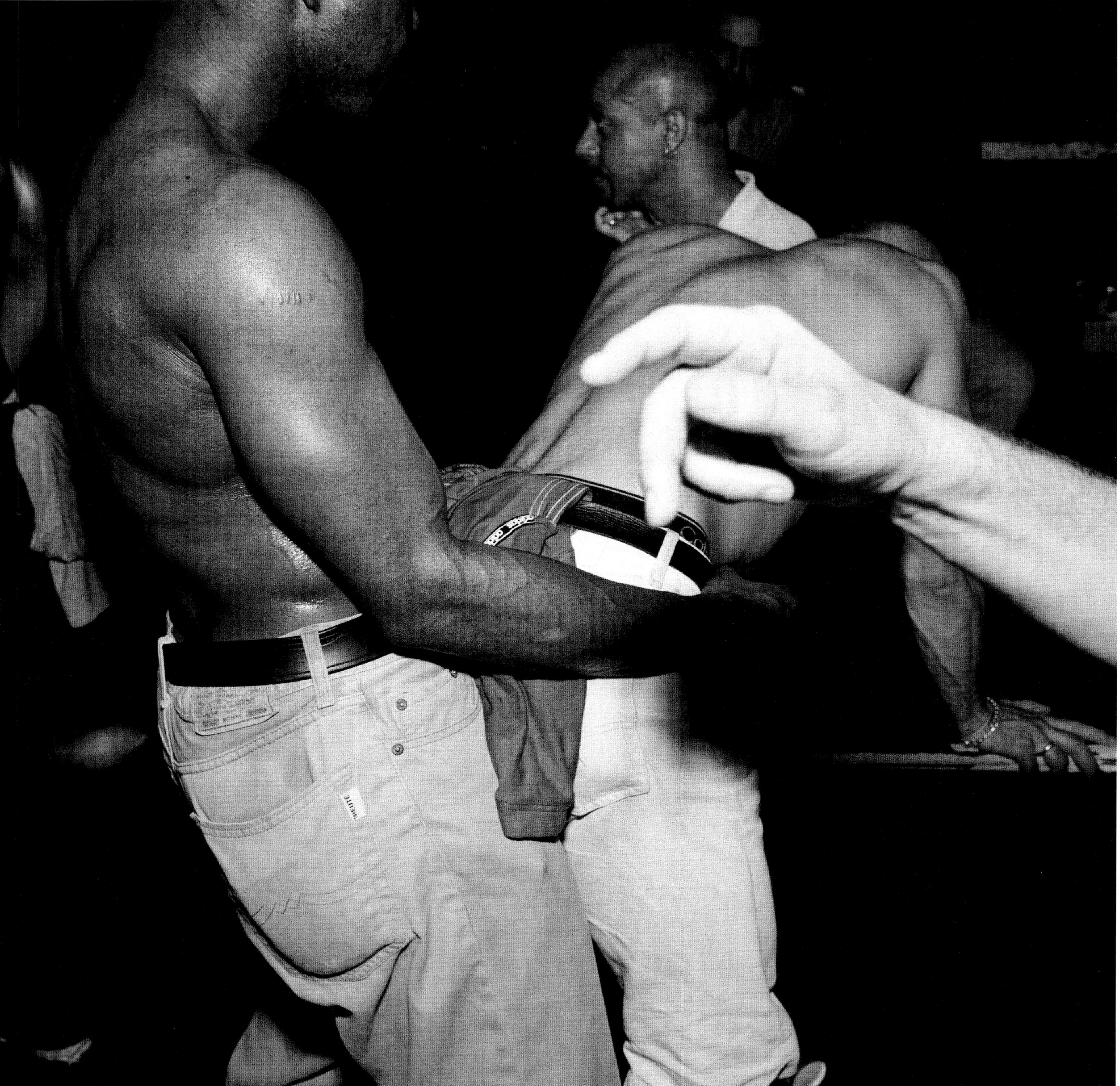

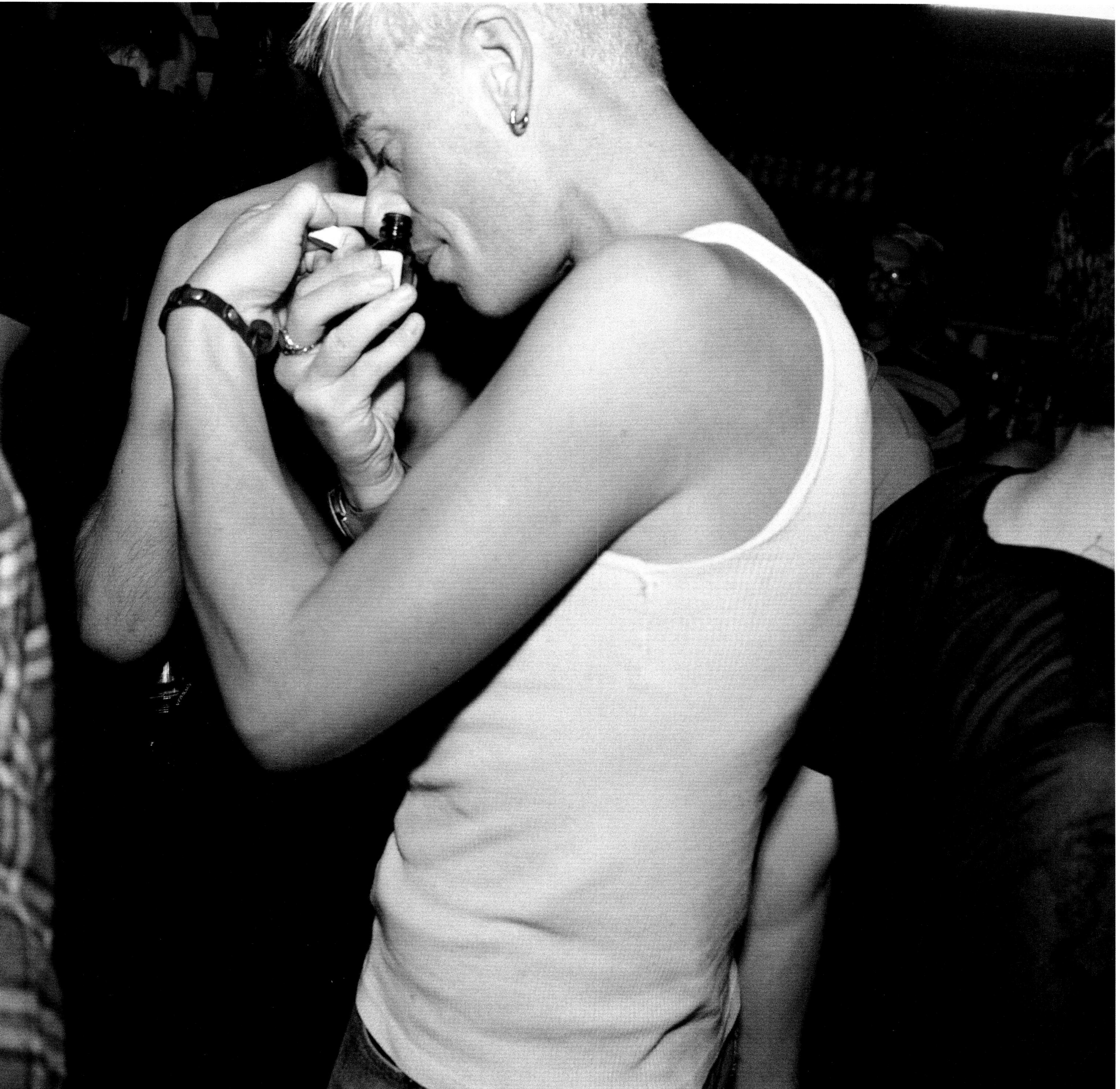

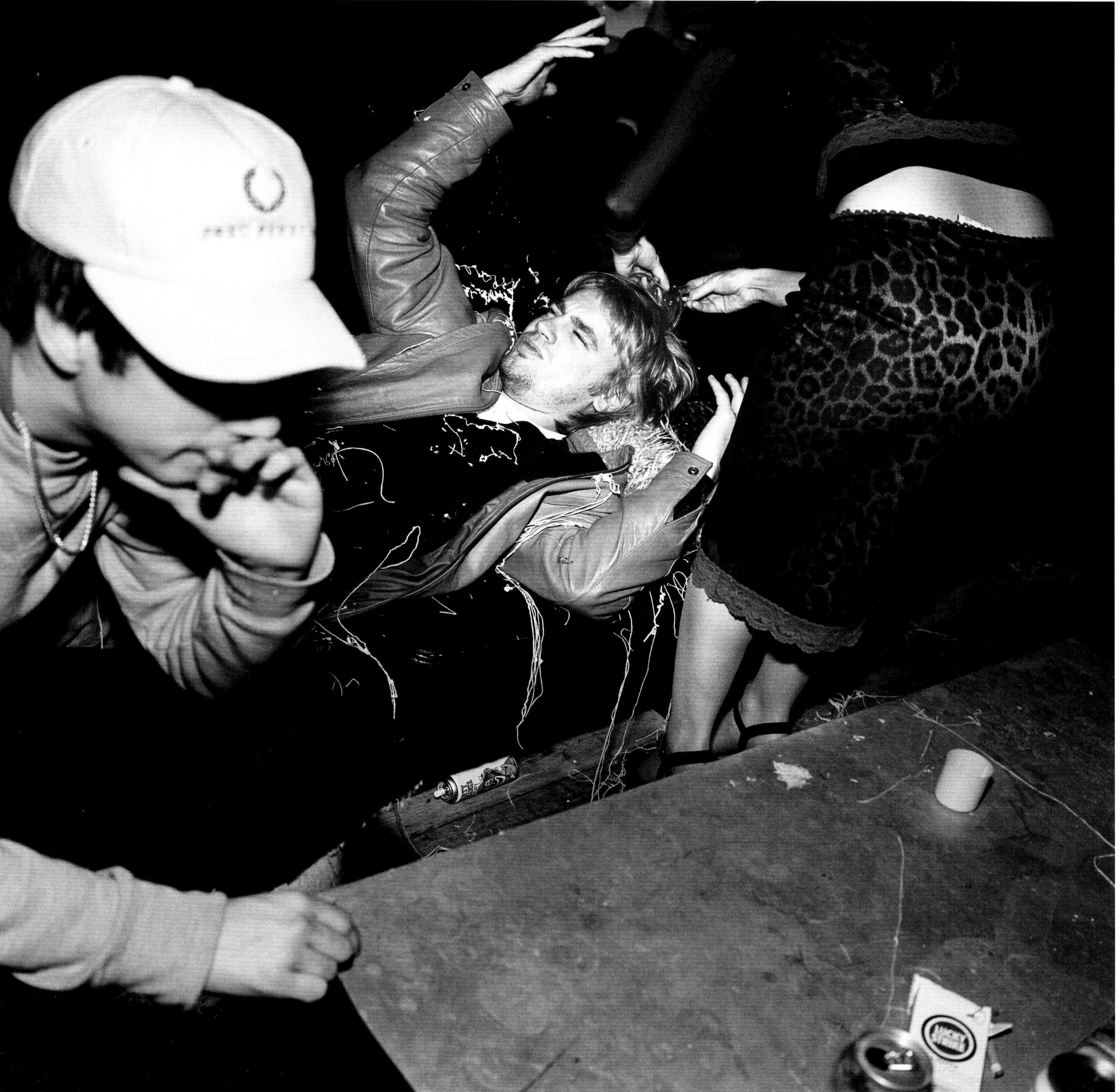

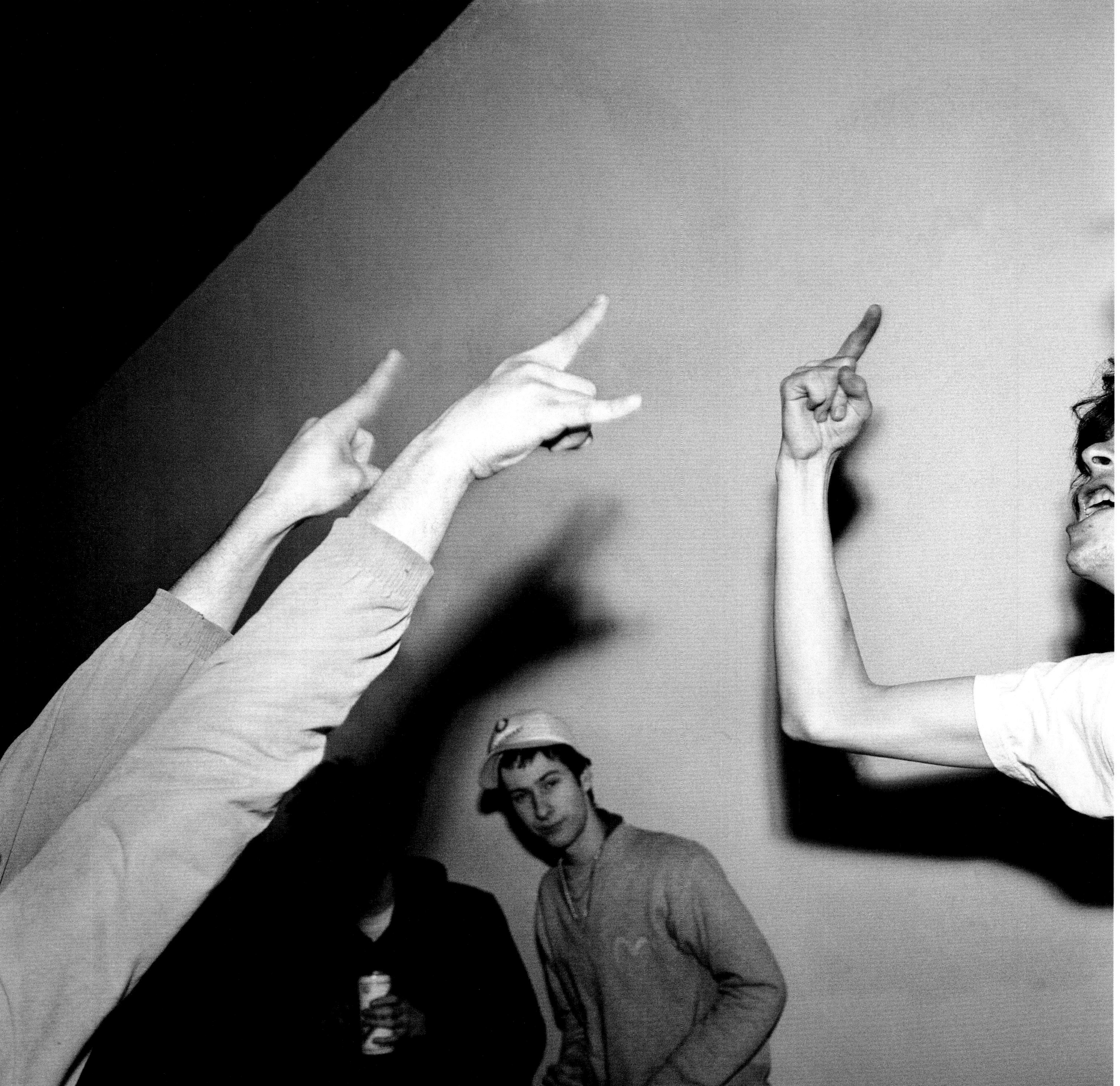

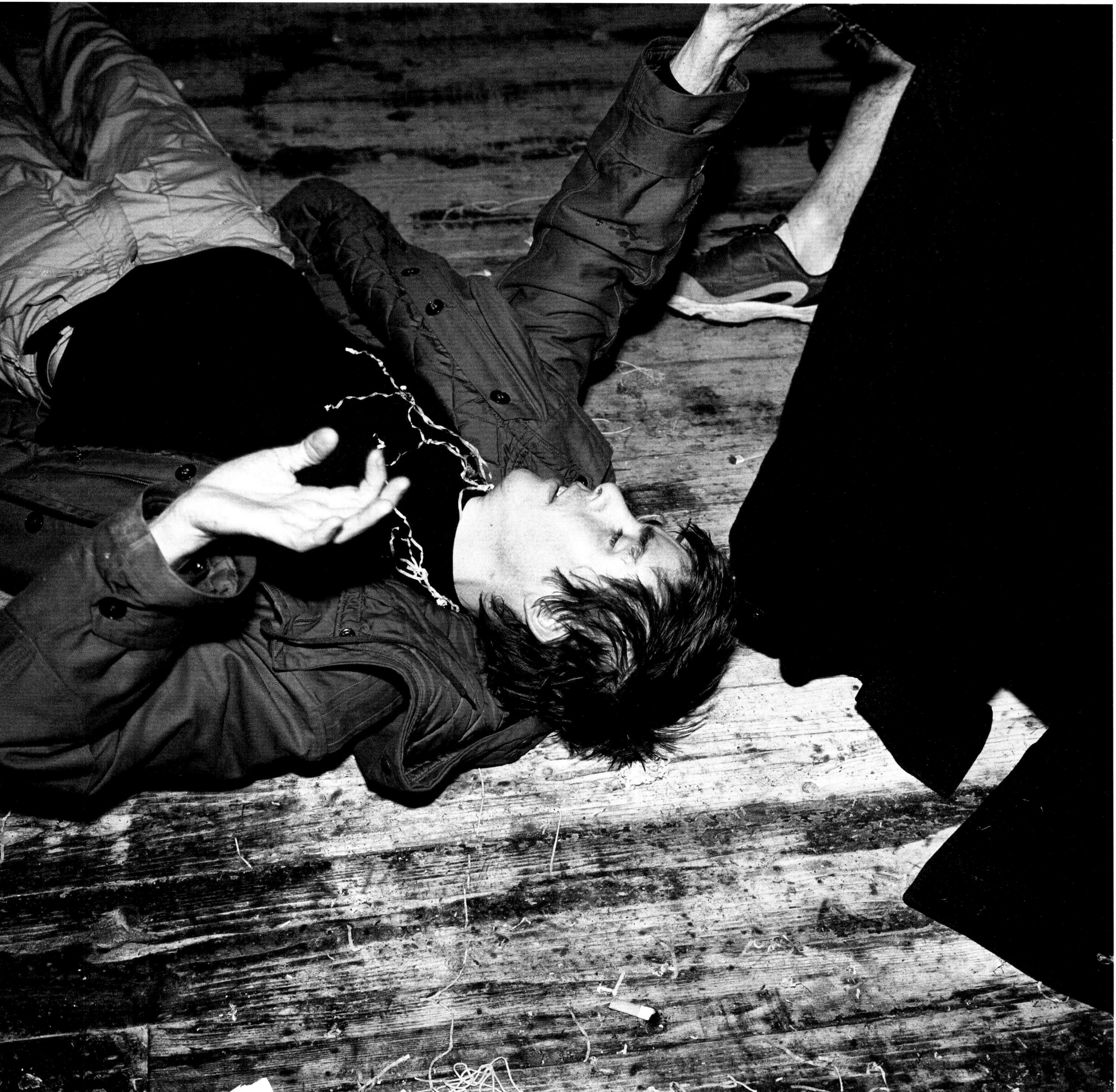

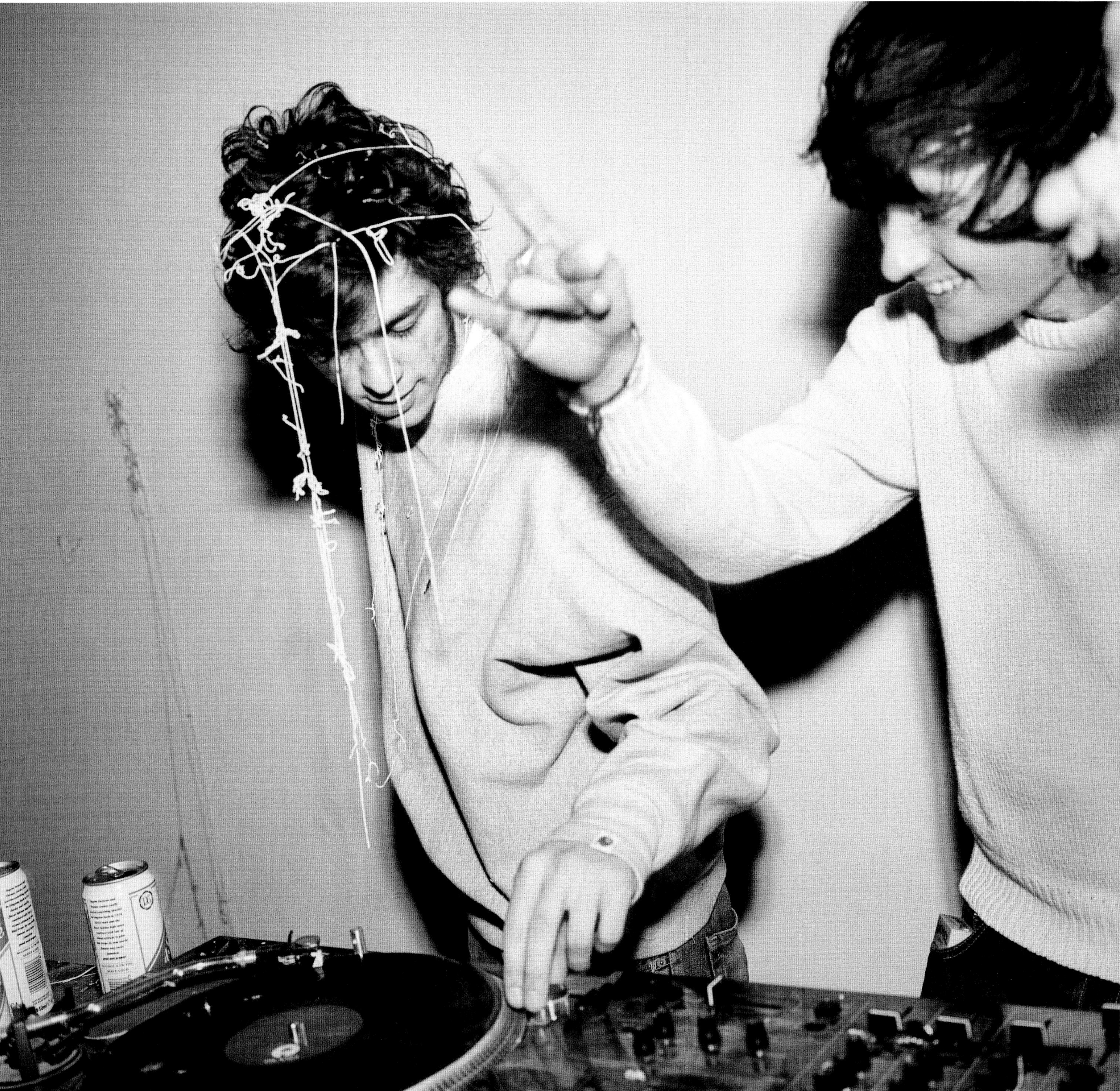

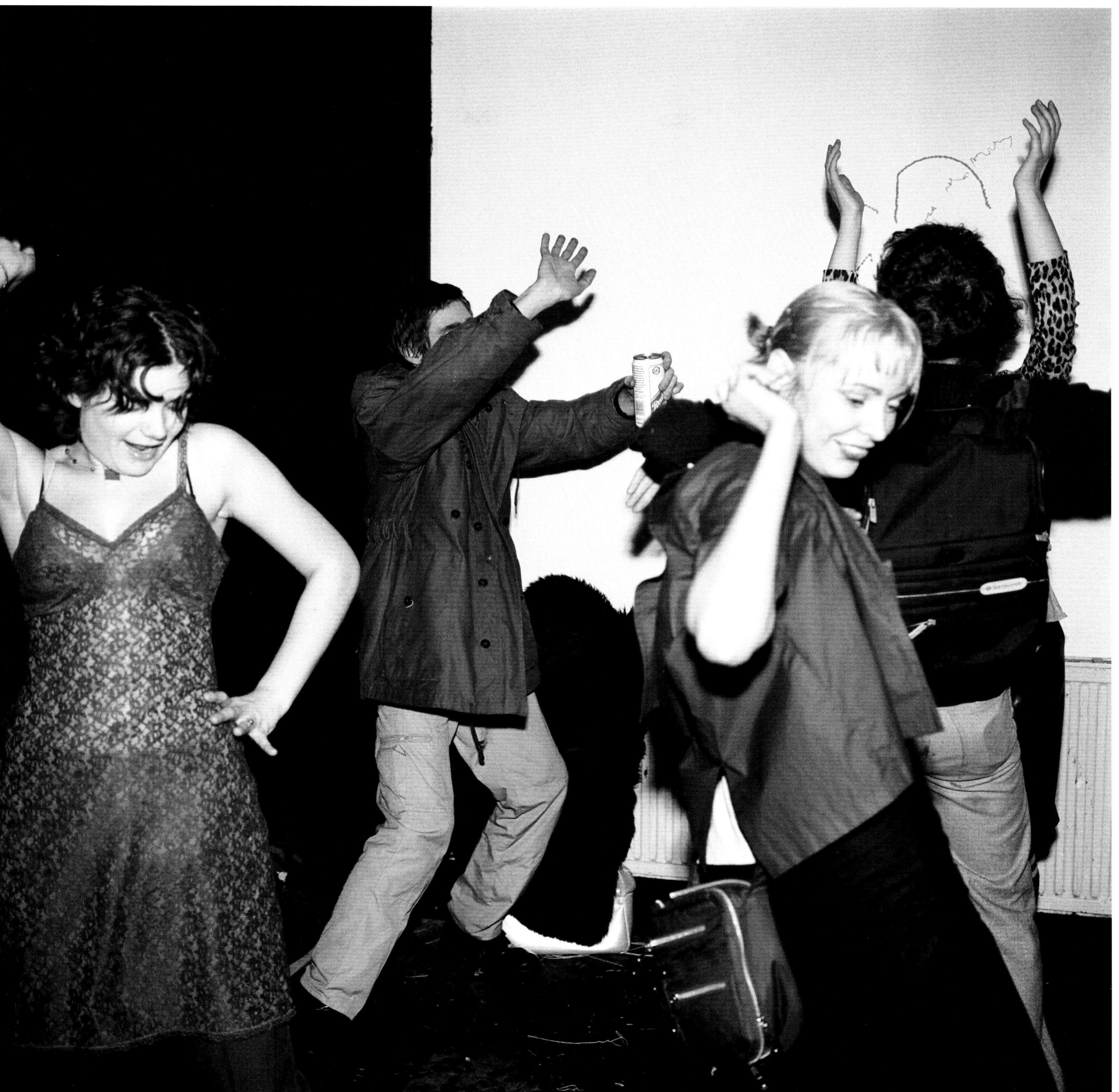

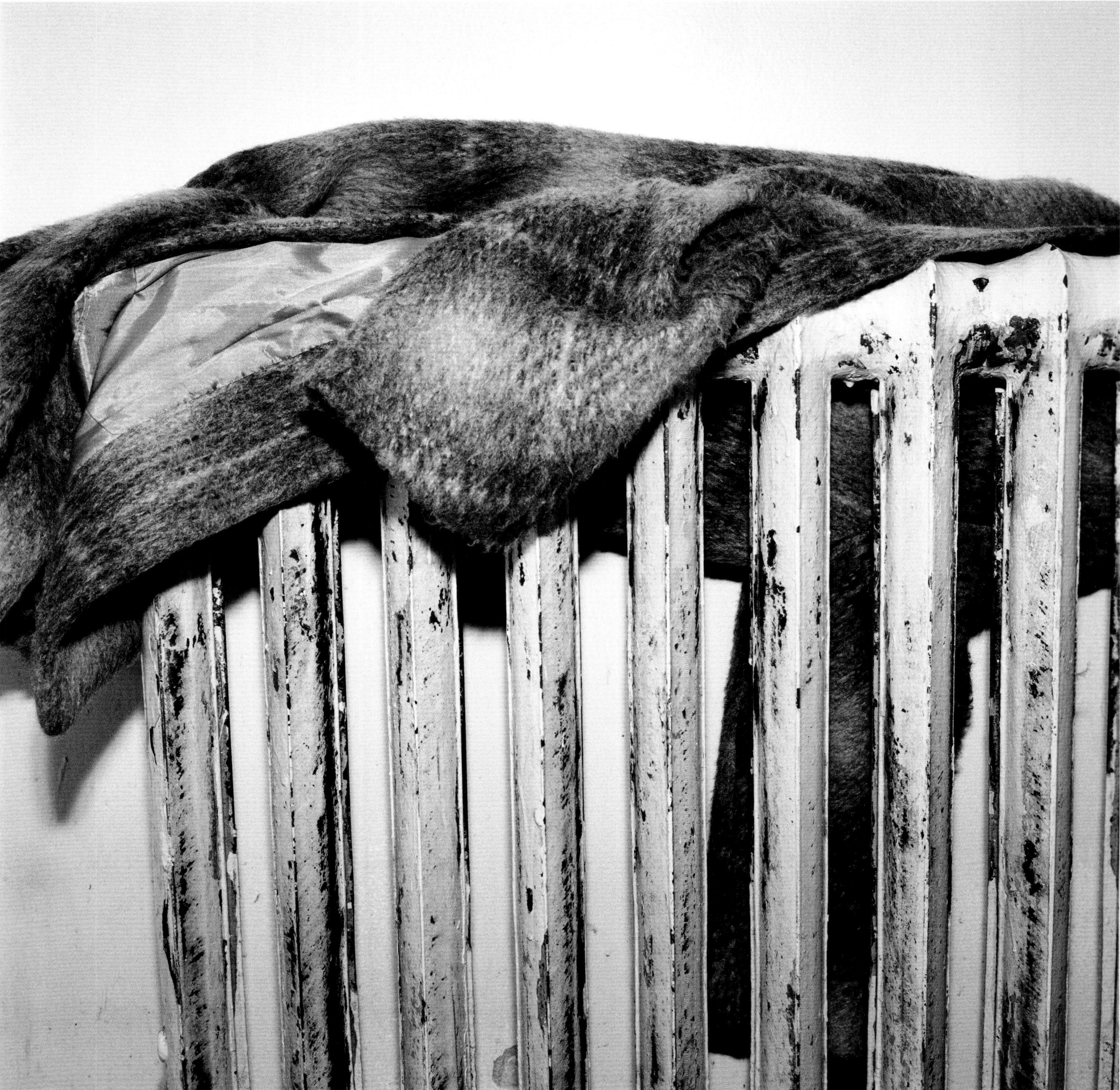

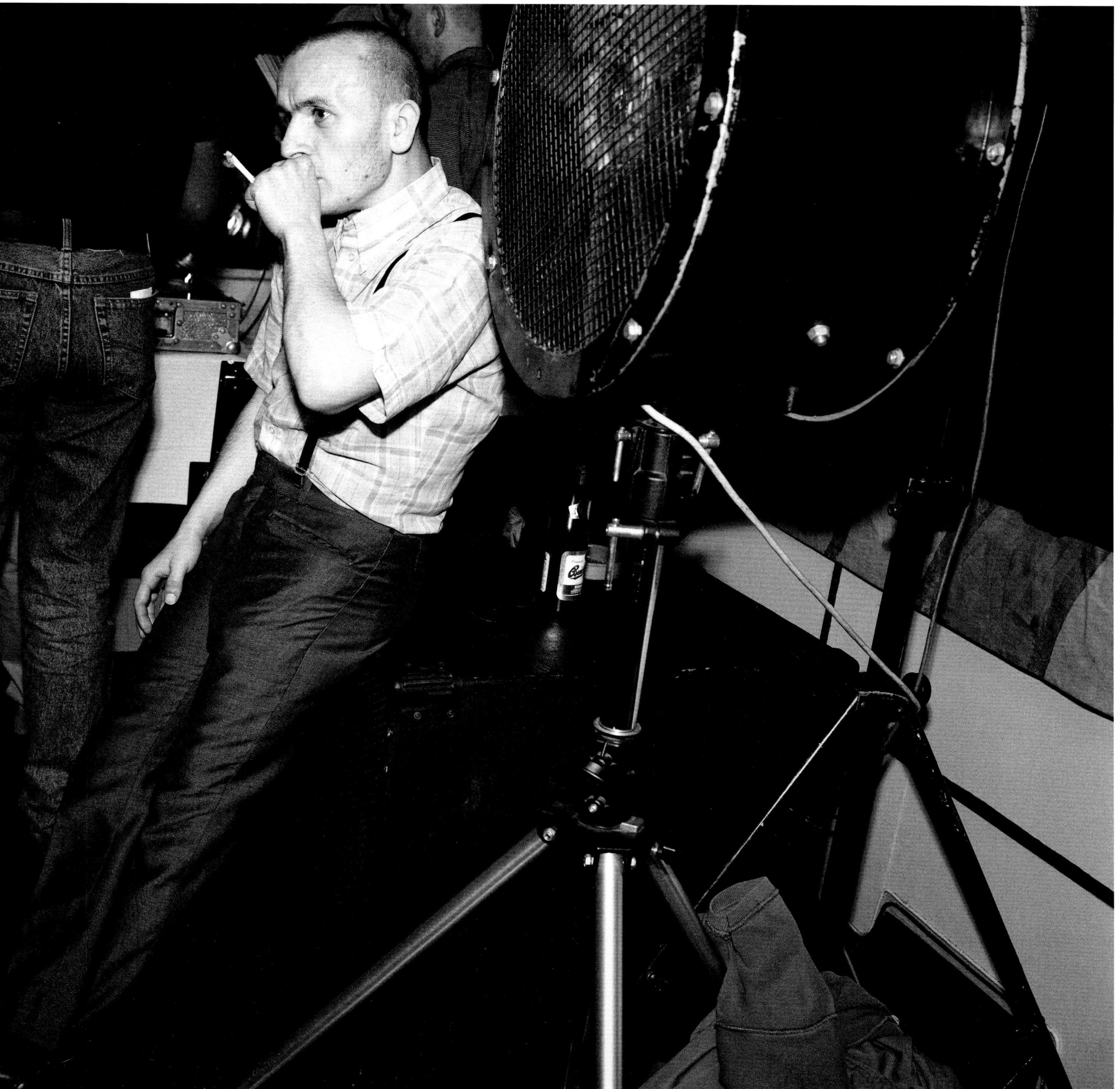

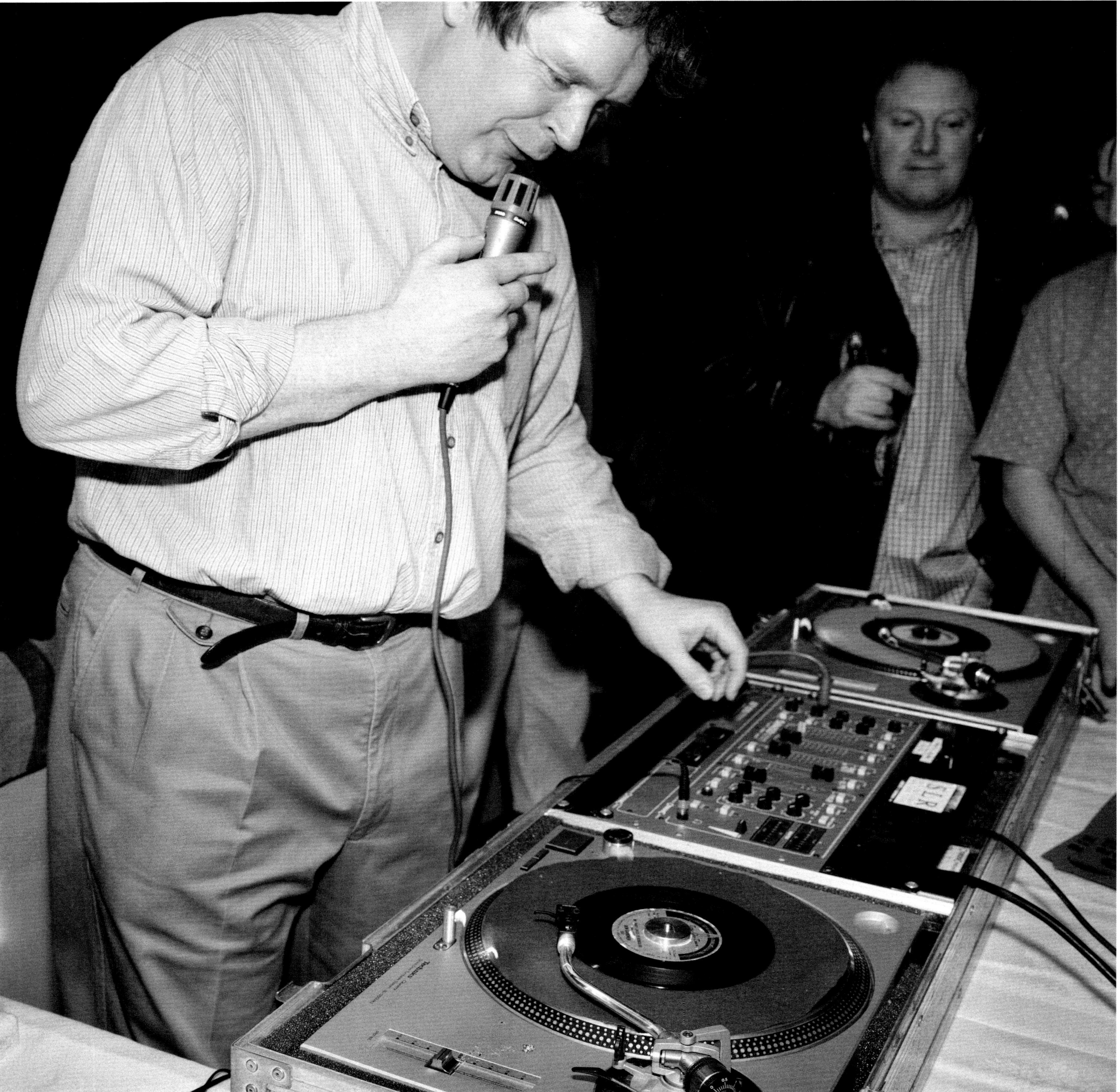

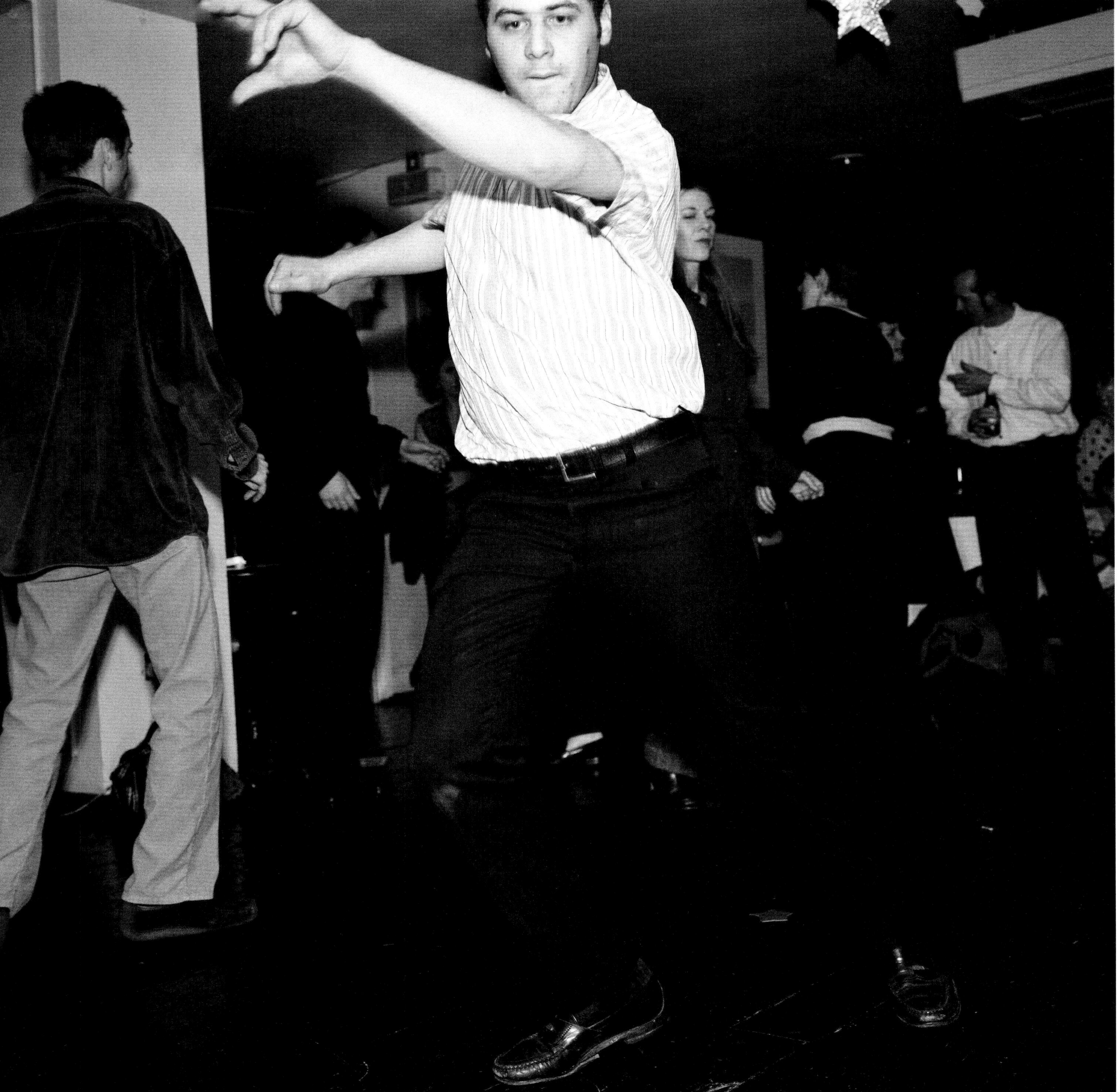

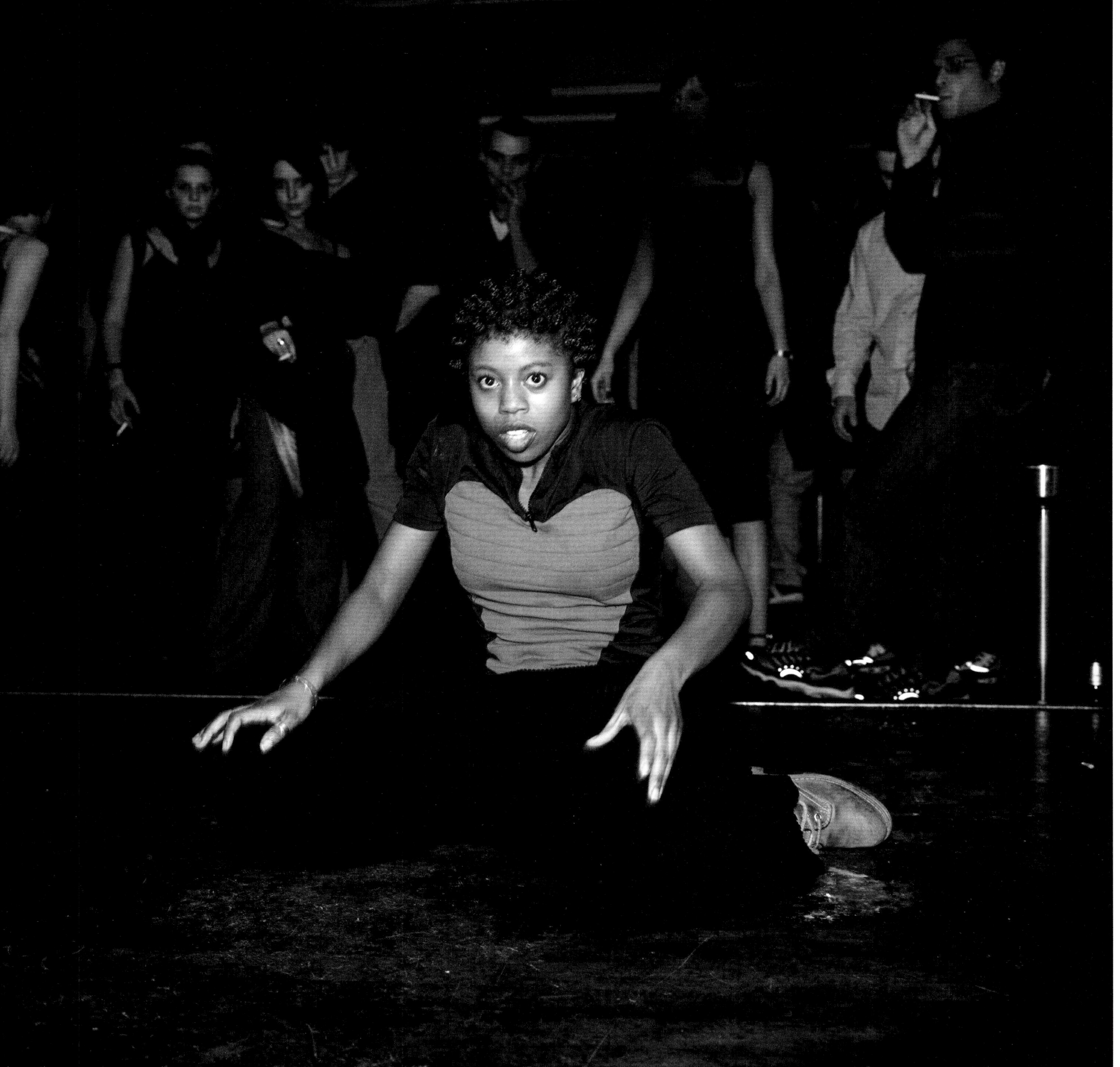

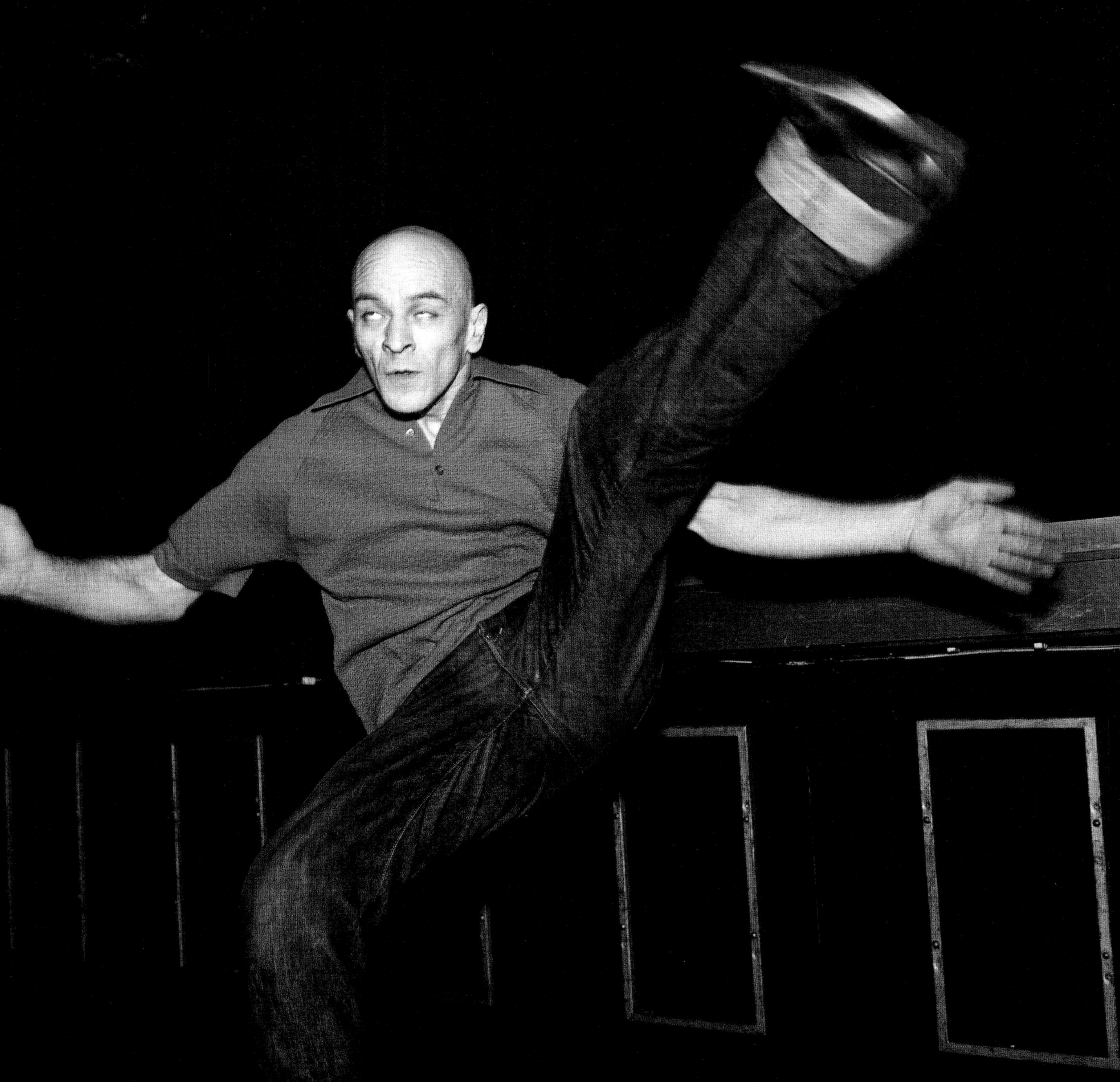

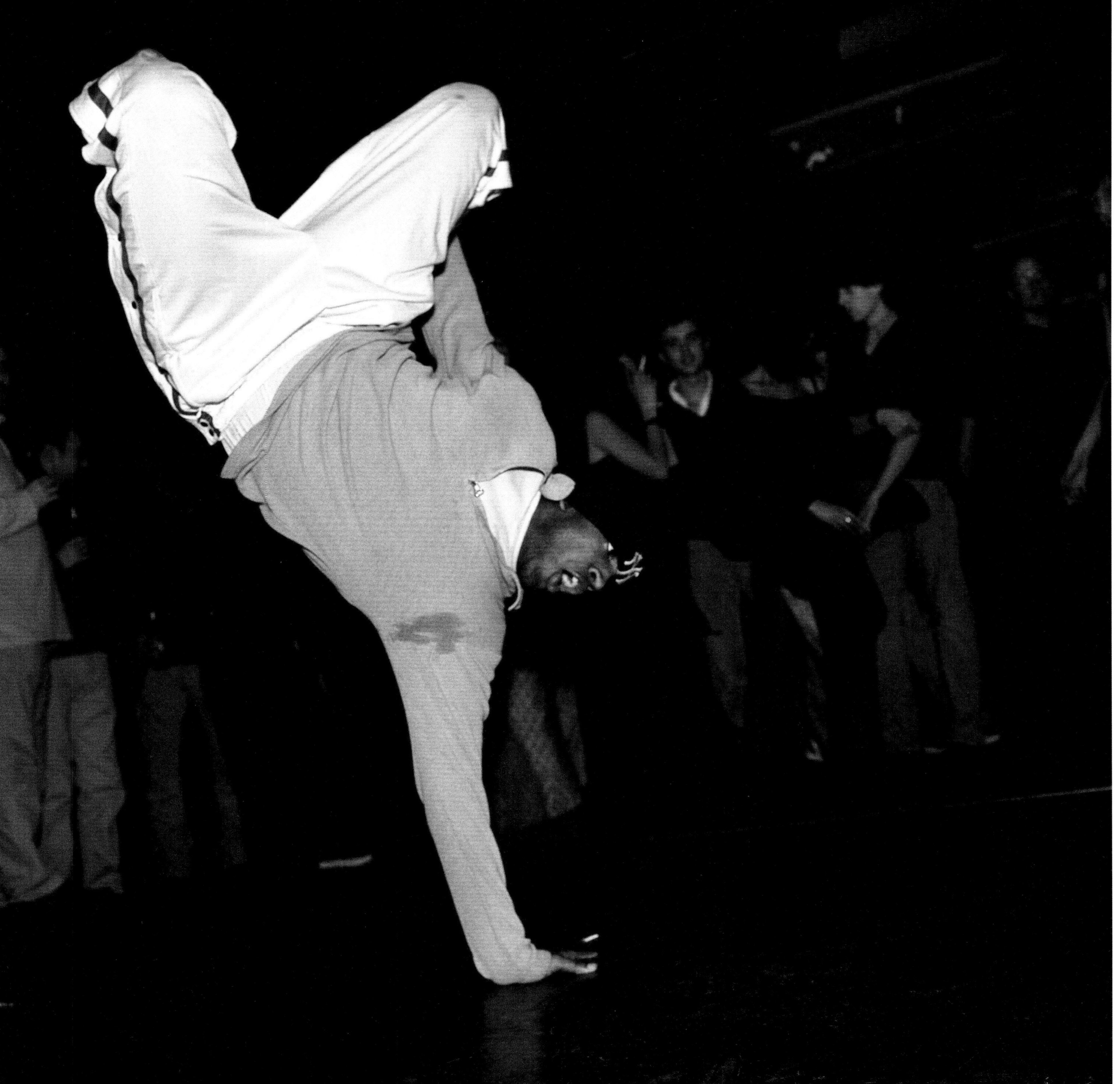

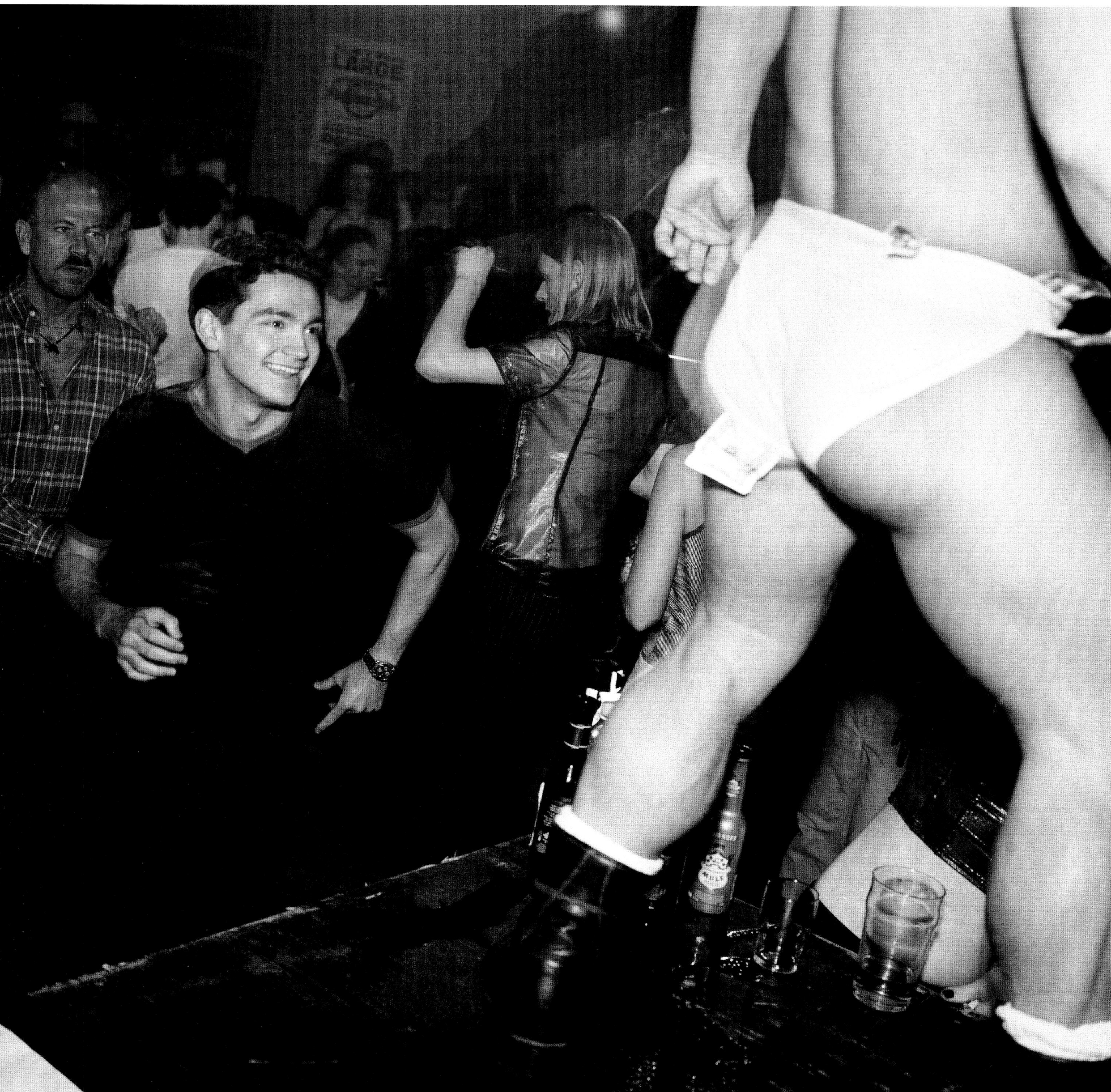
LARGE
MULE

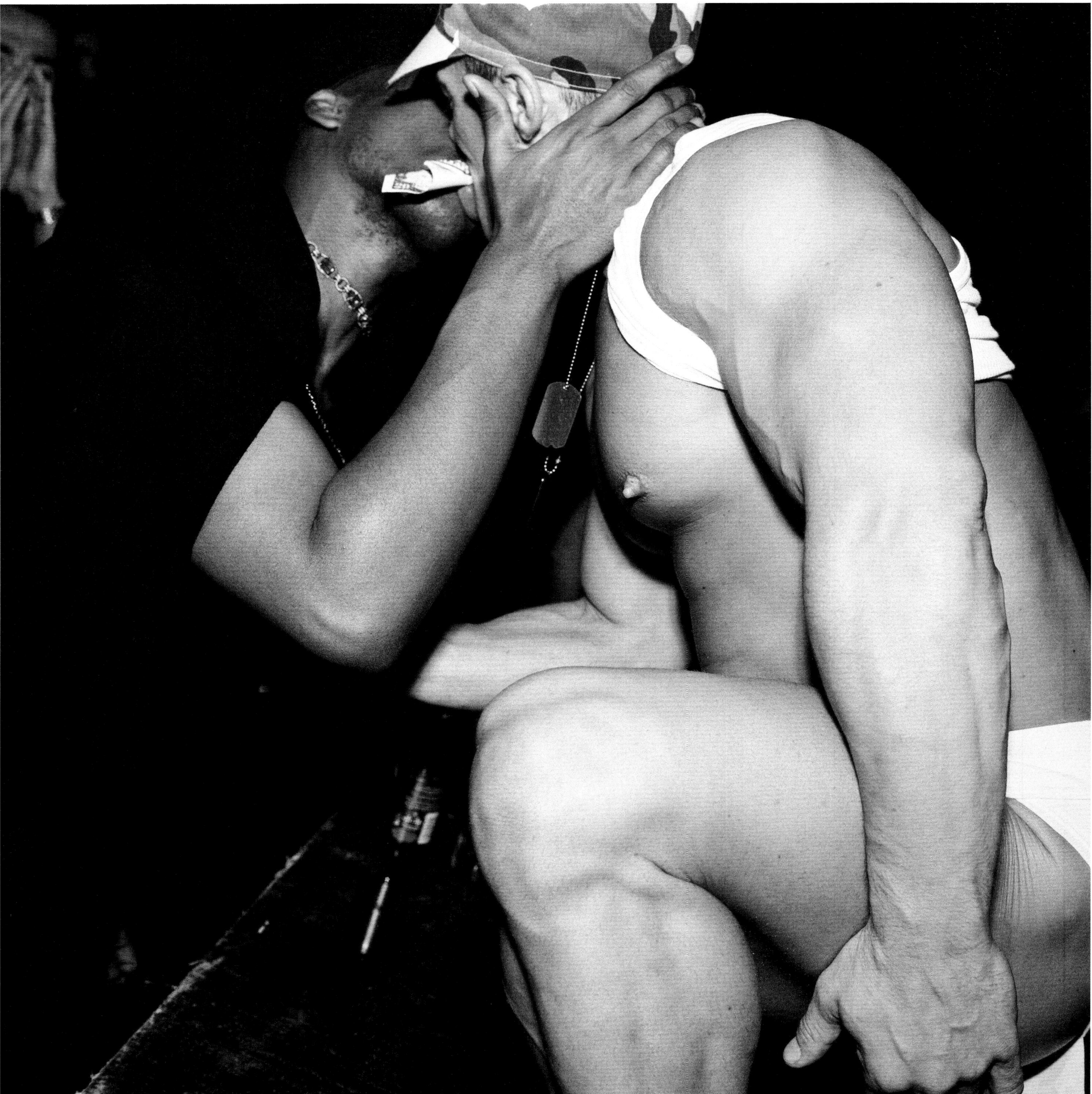

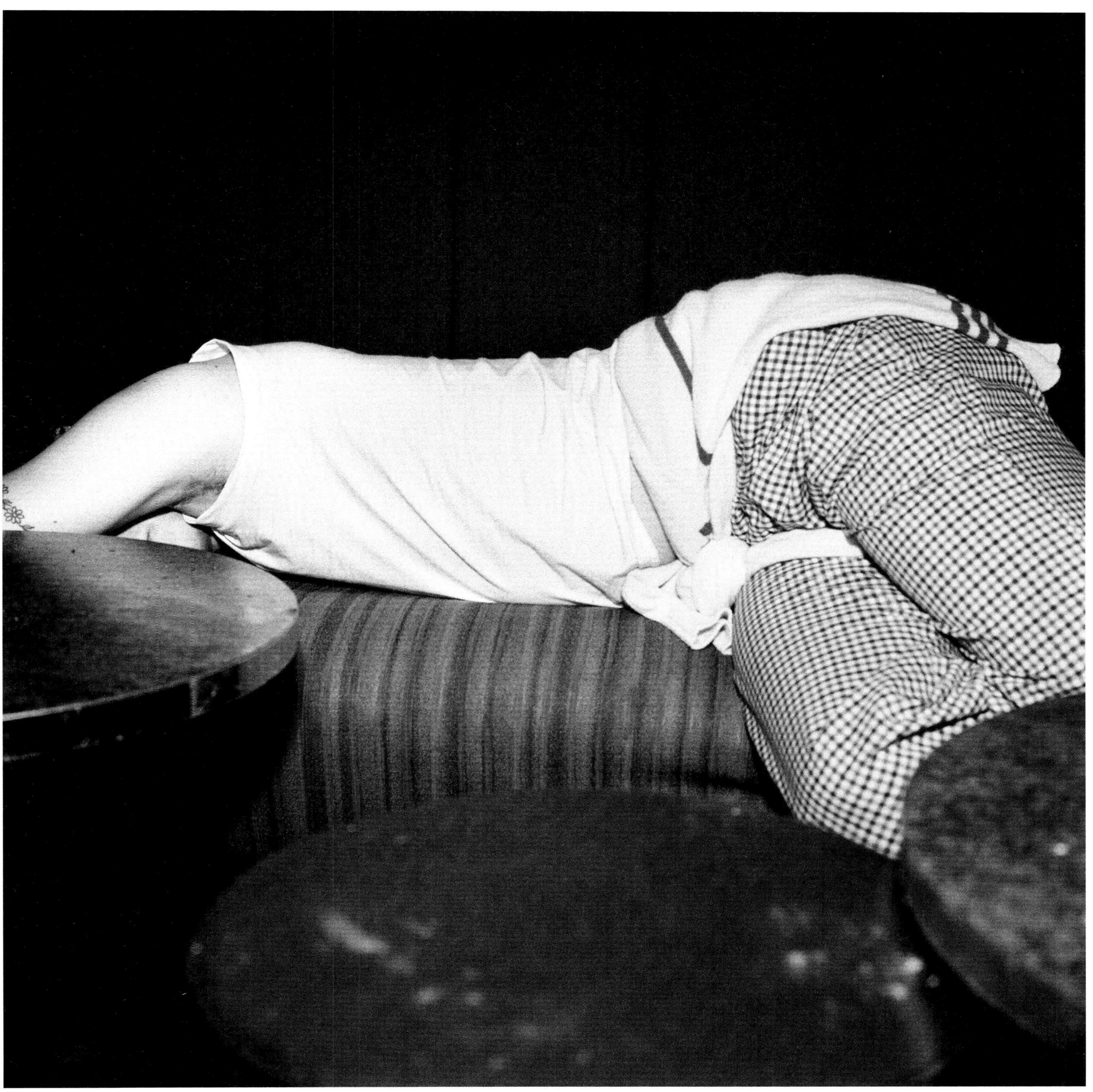

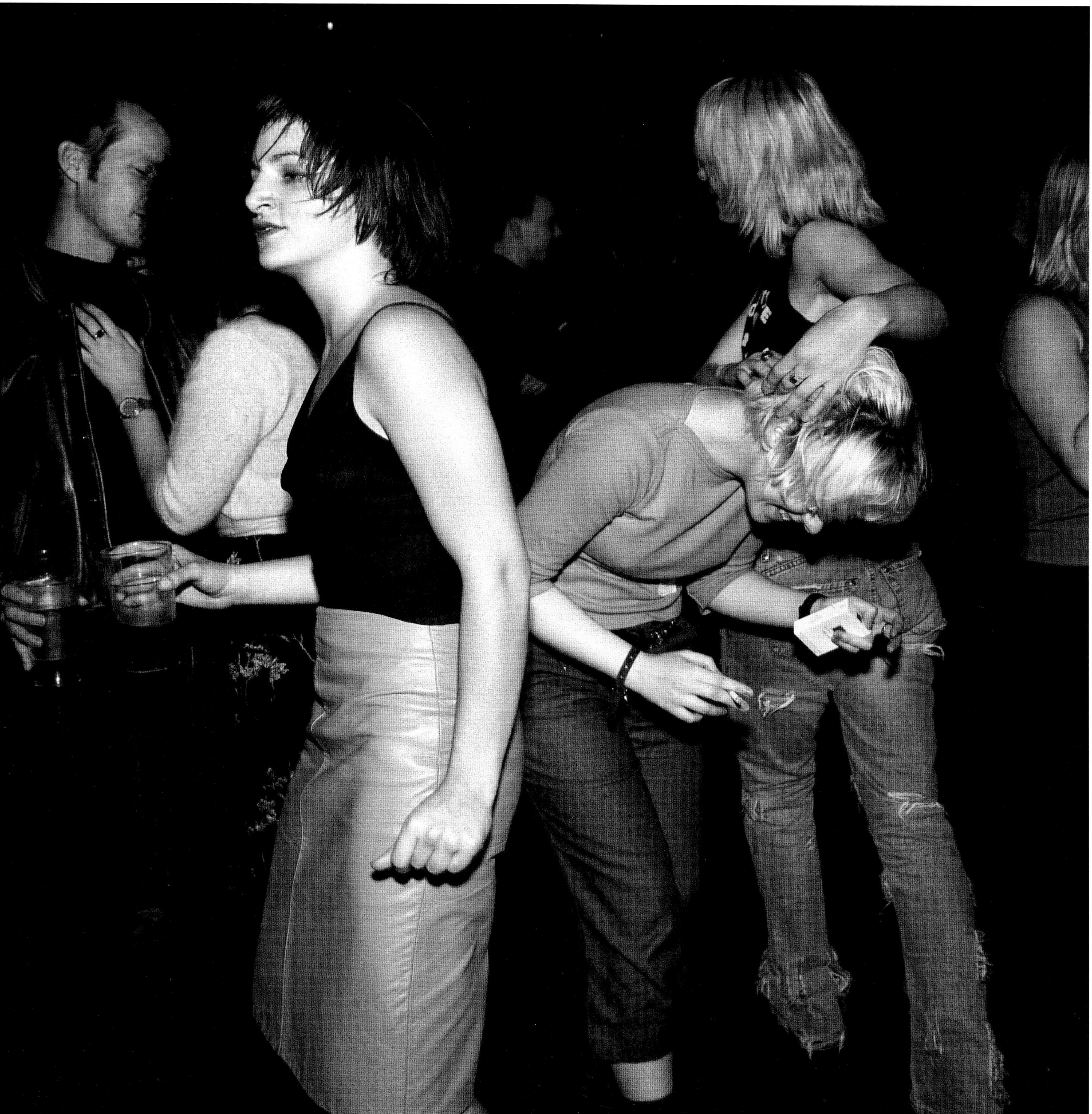

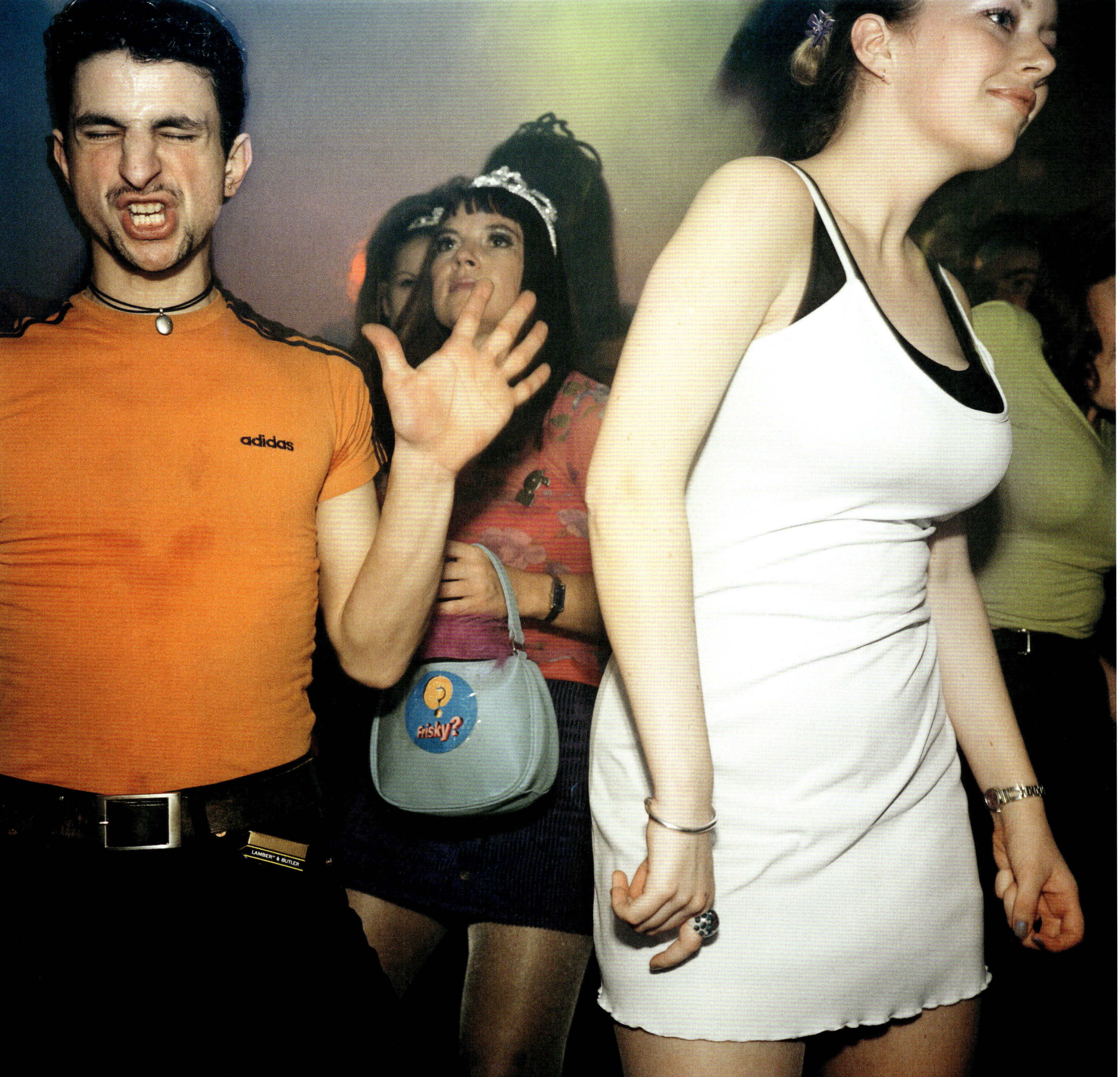
adidas
Frisky?
LAMBERT & BUTLER

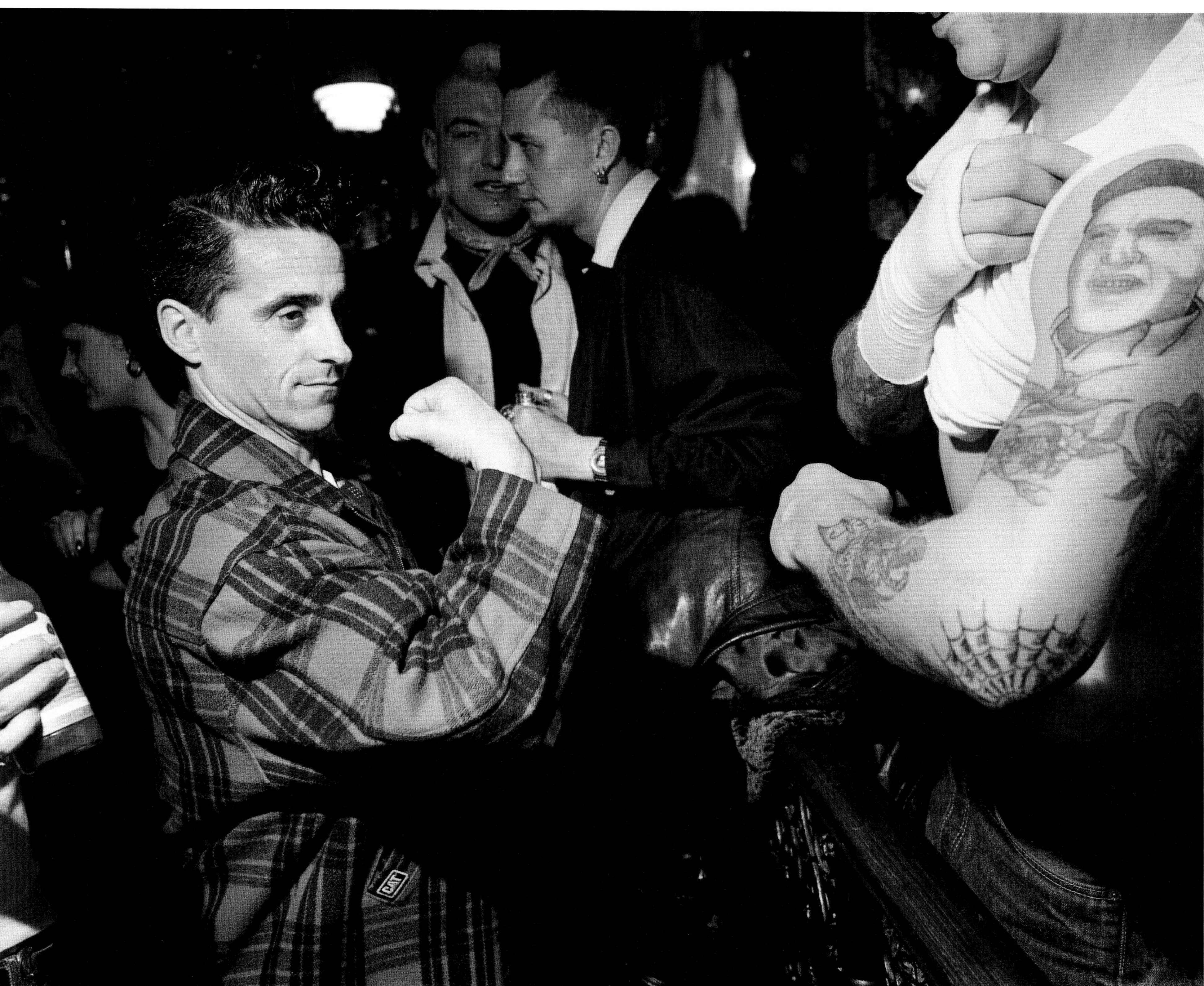
CAT

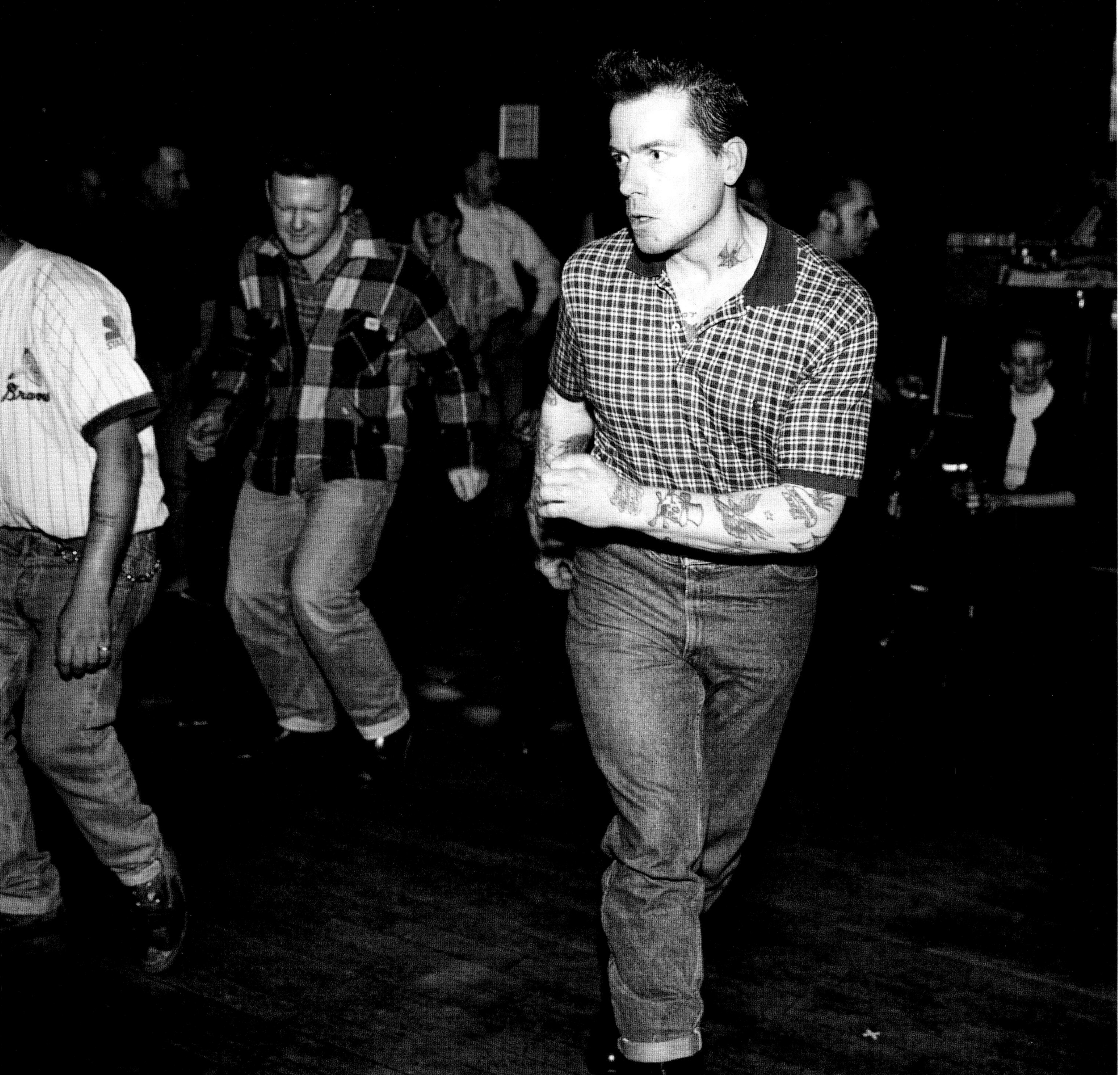

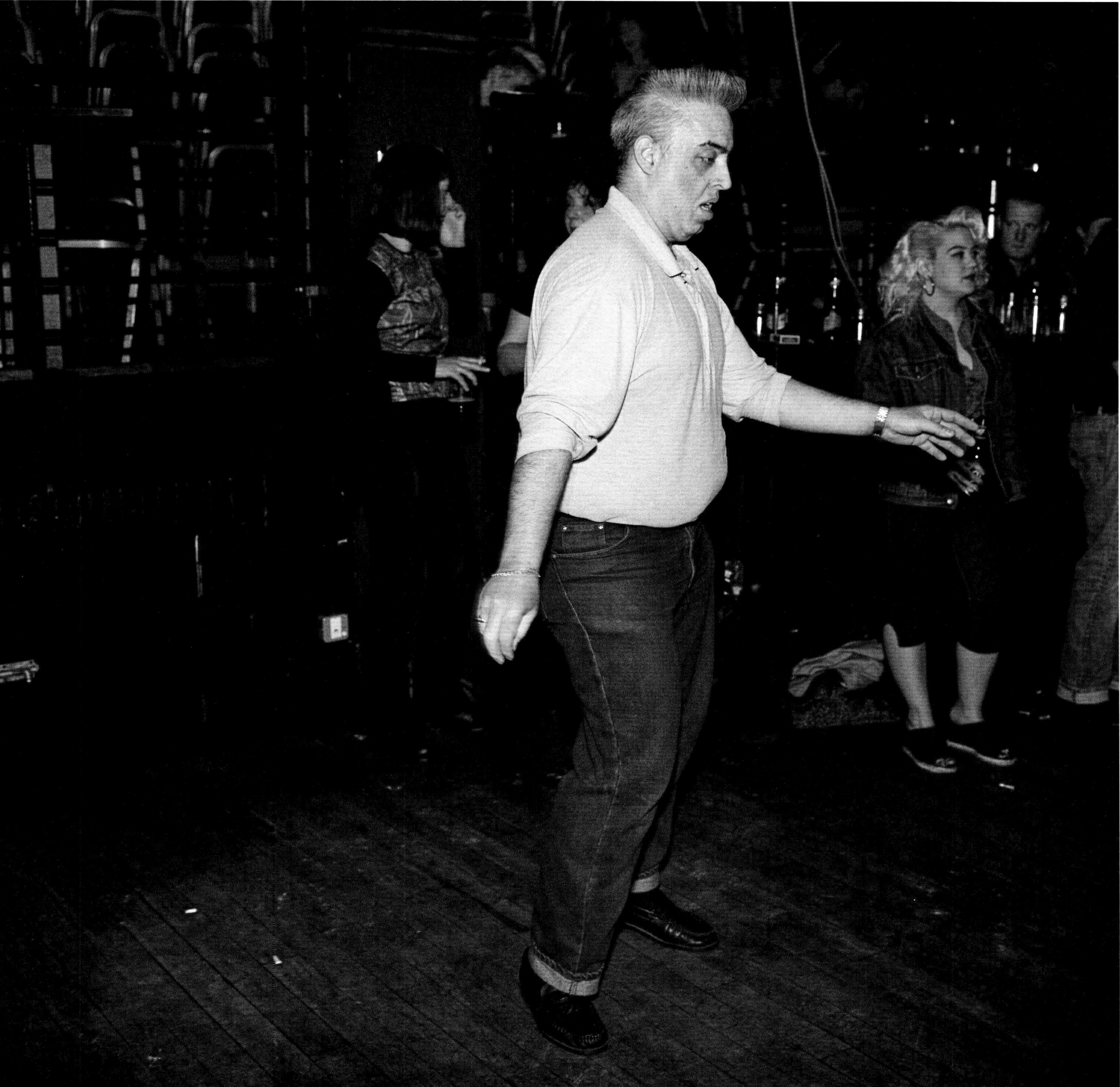

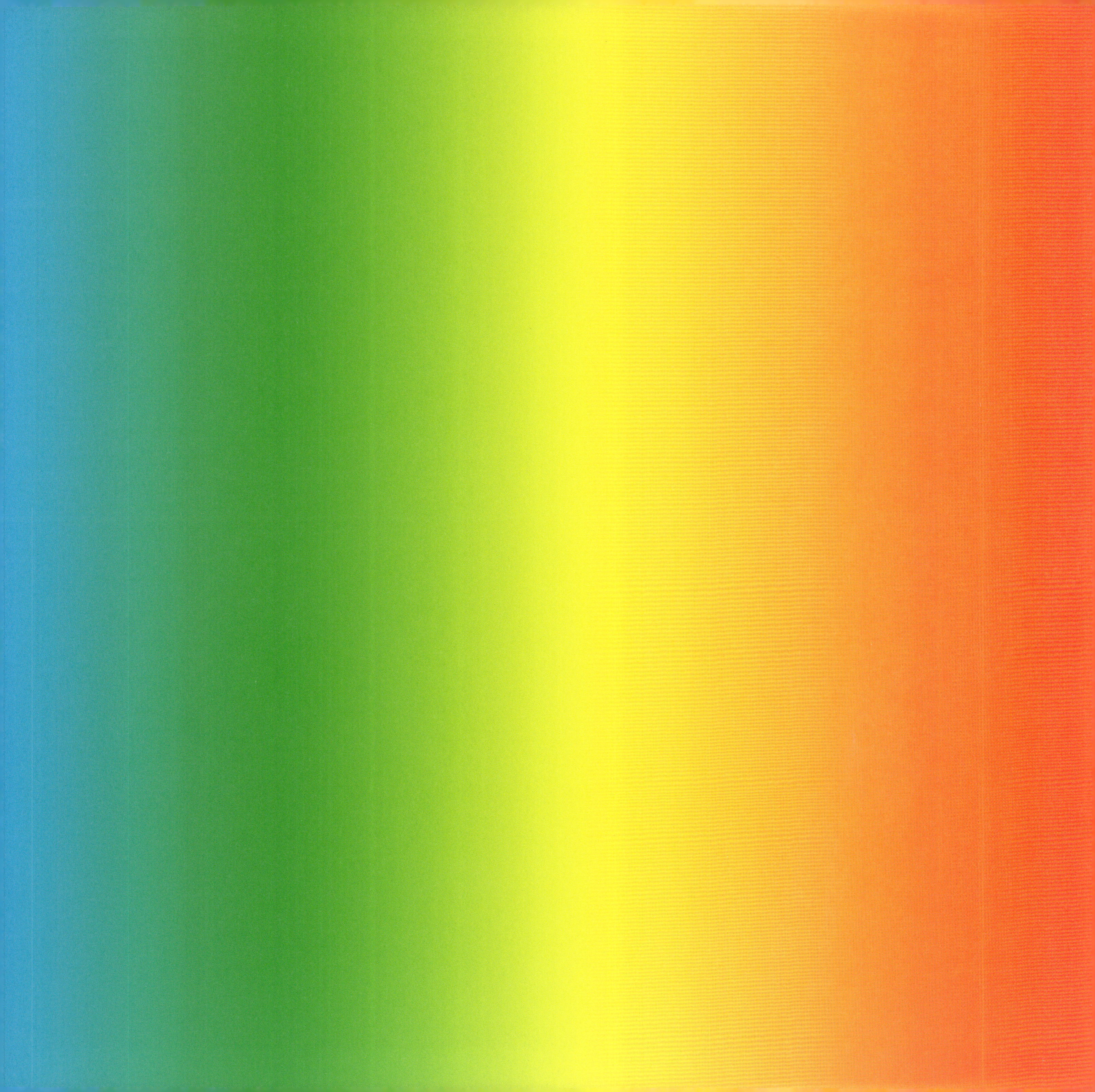

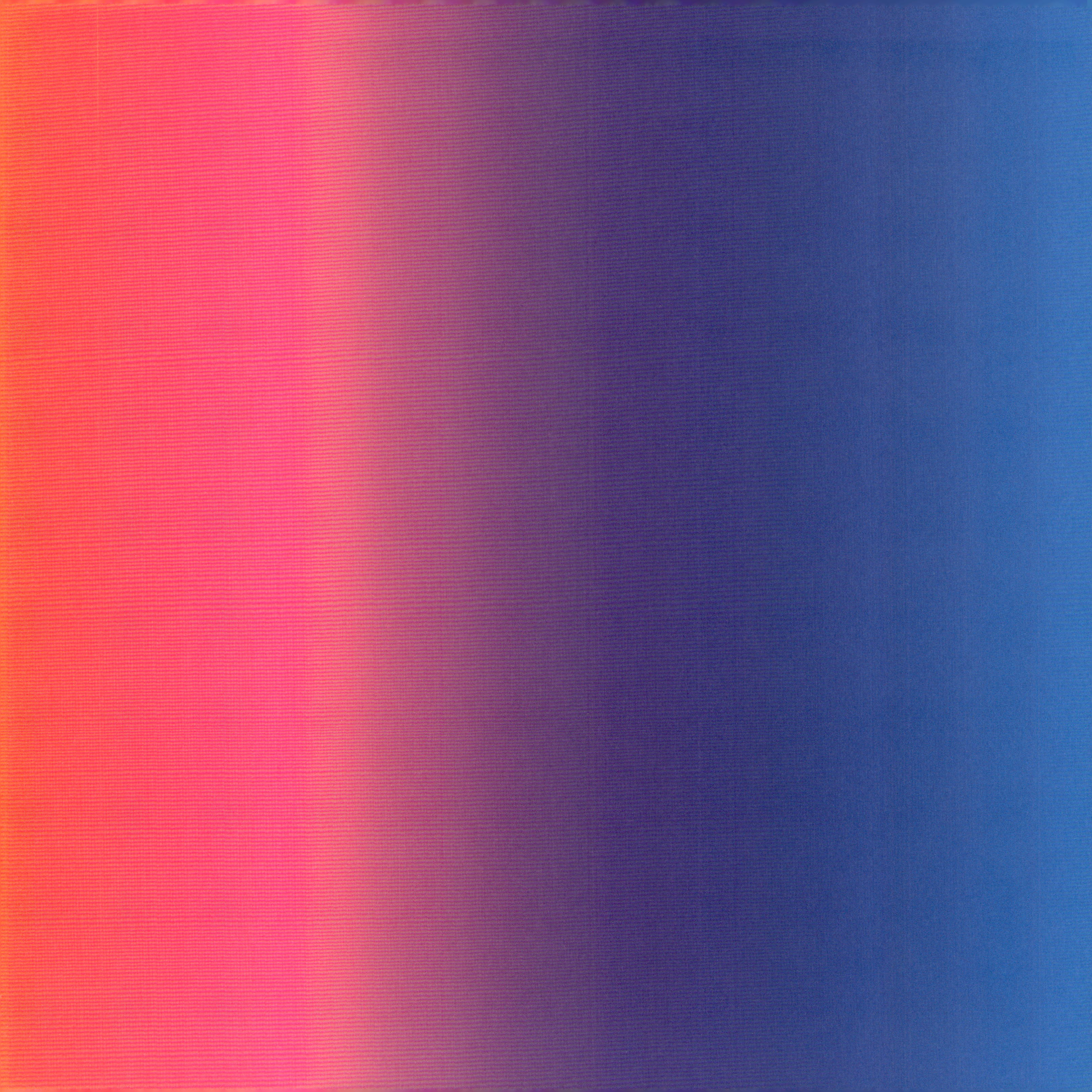

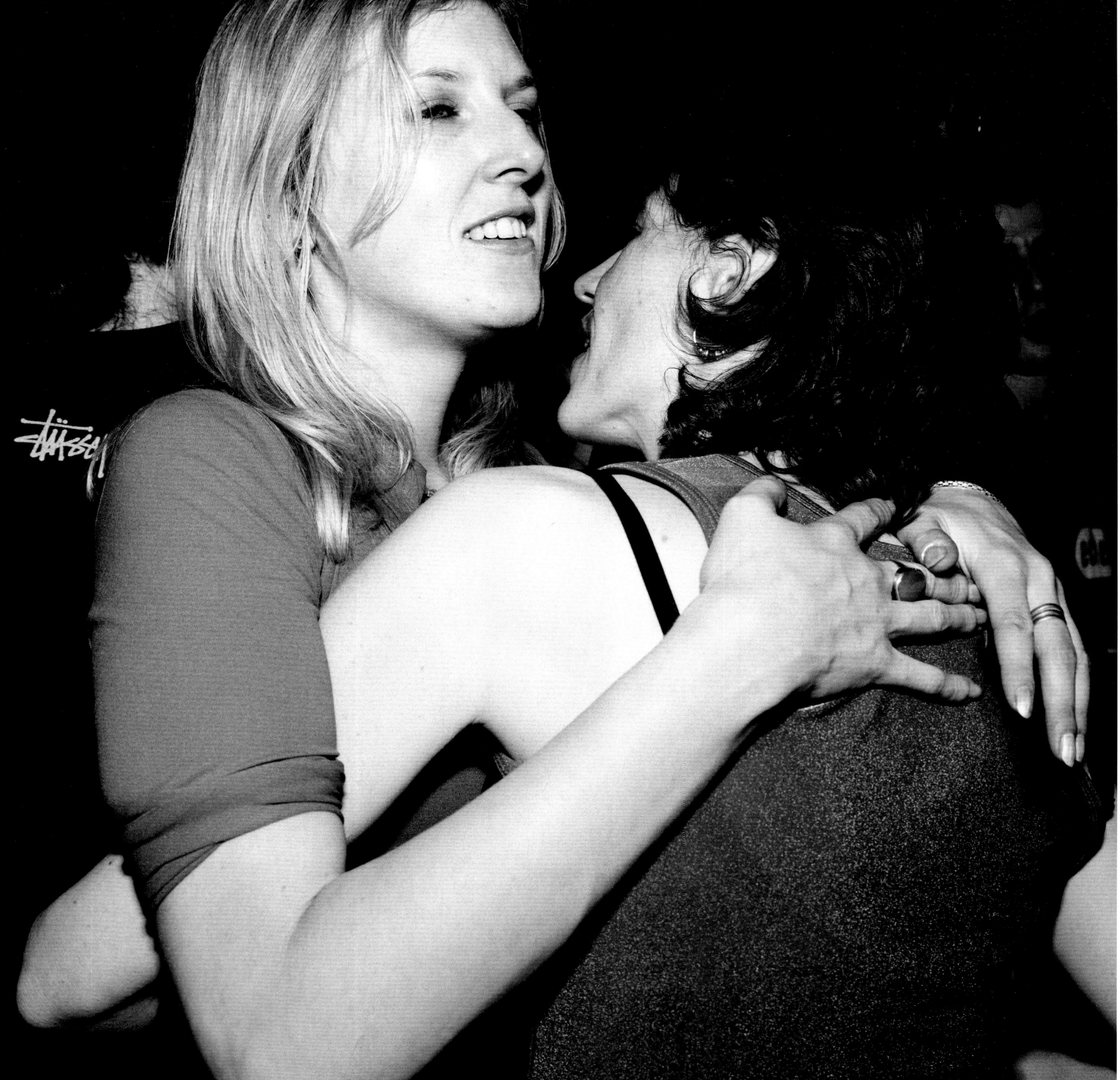

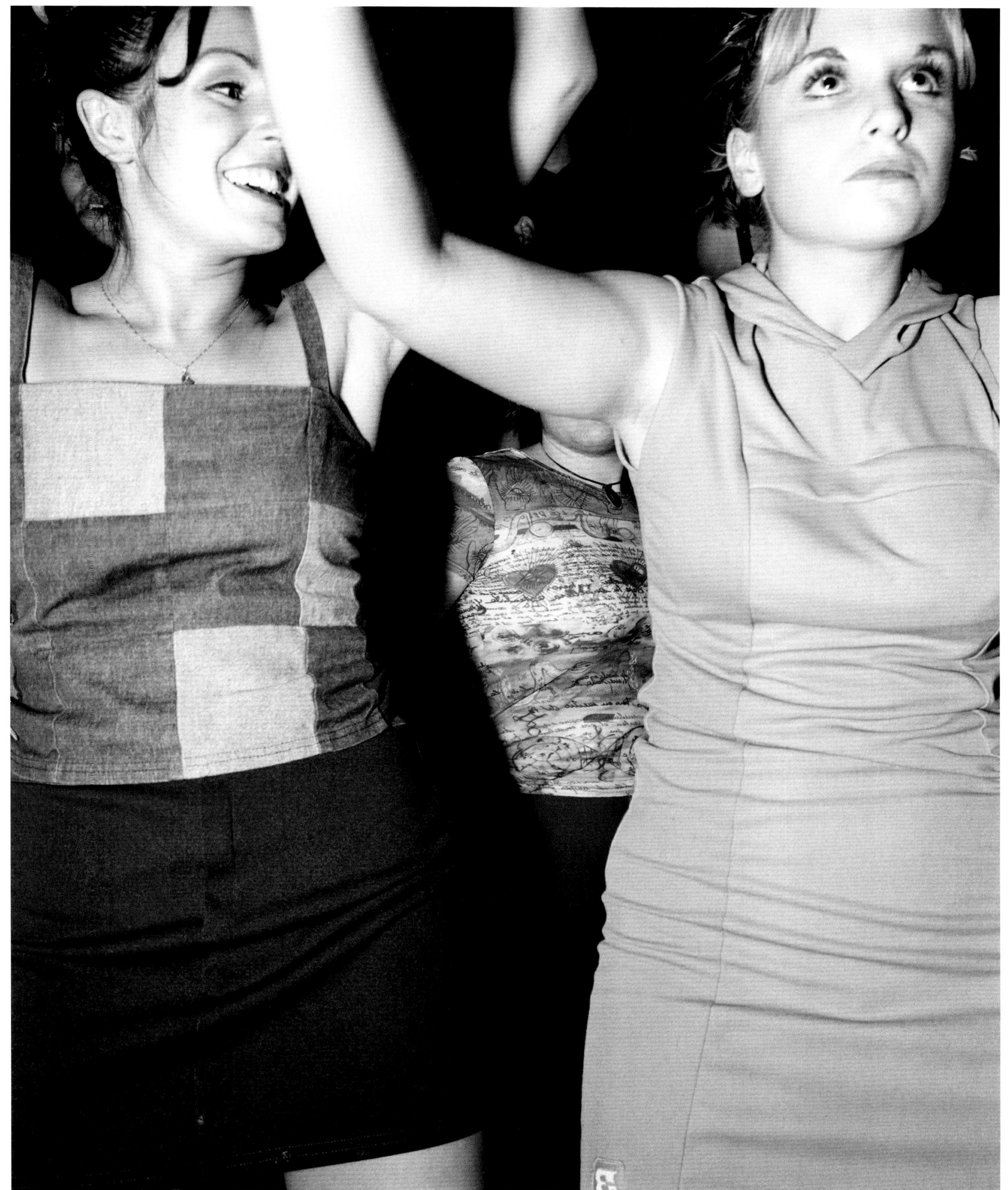

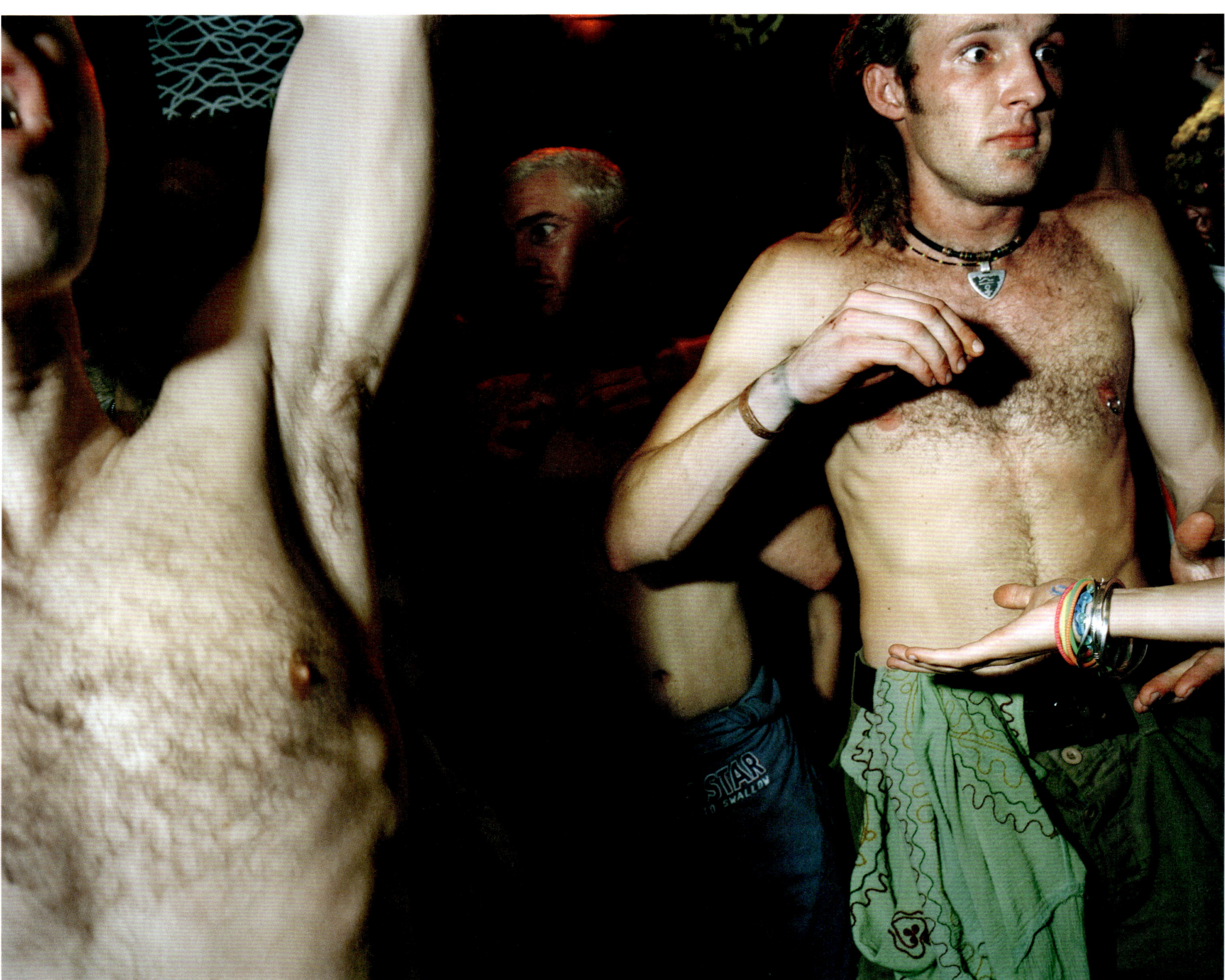
STAR
SWALLOW

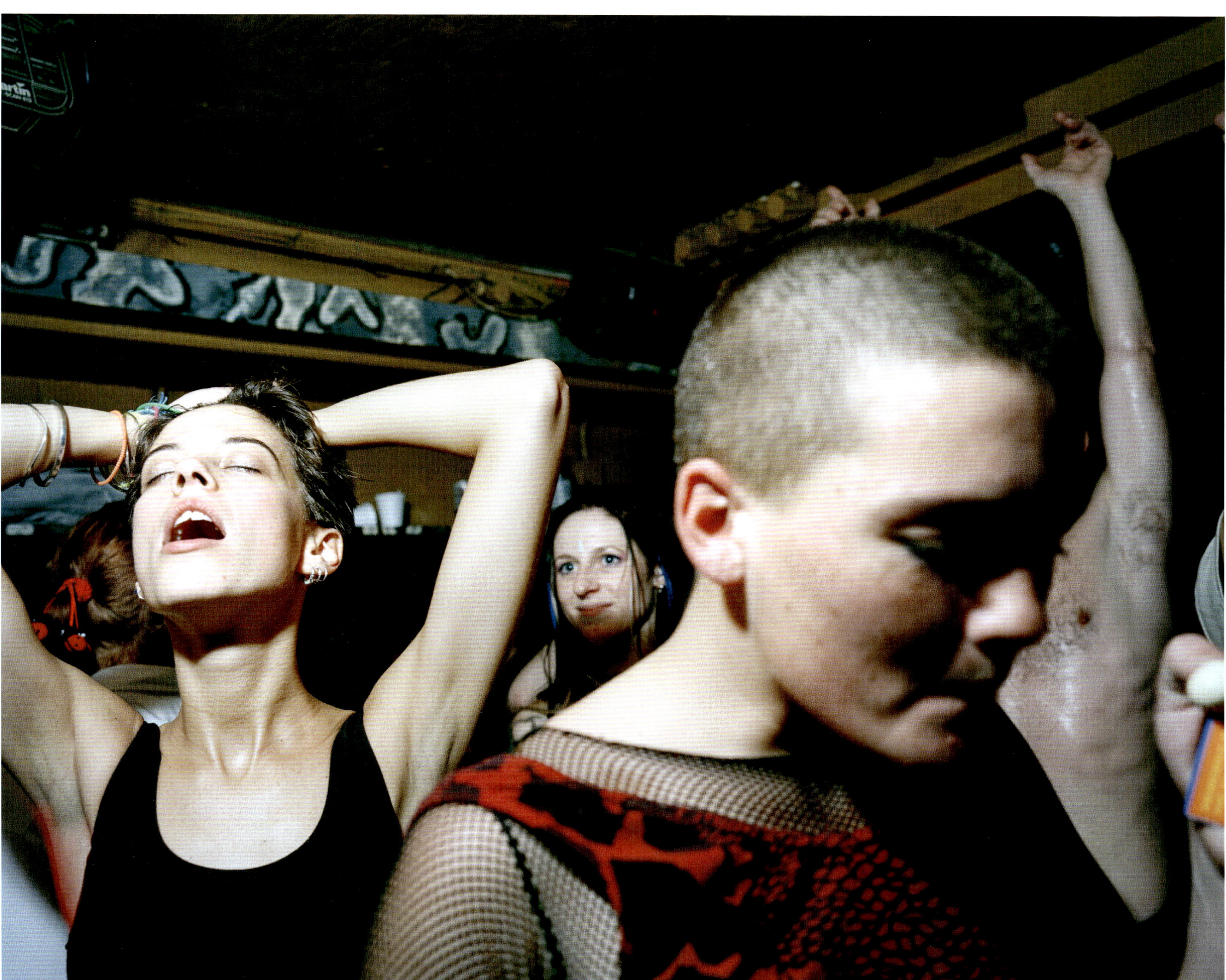

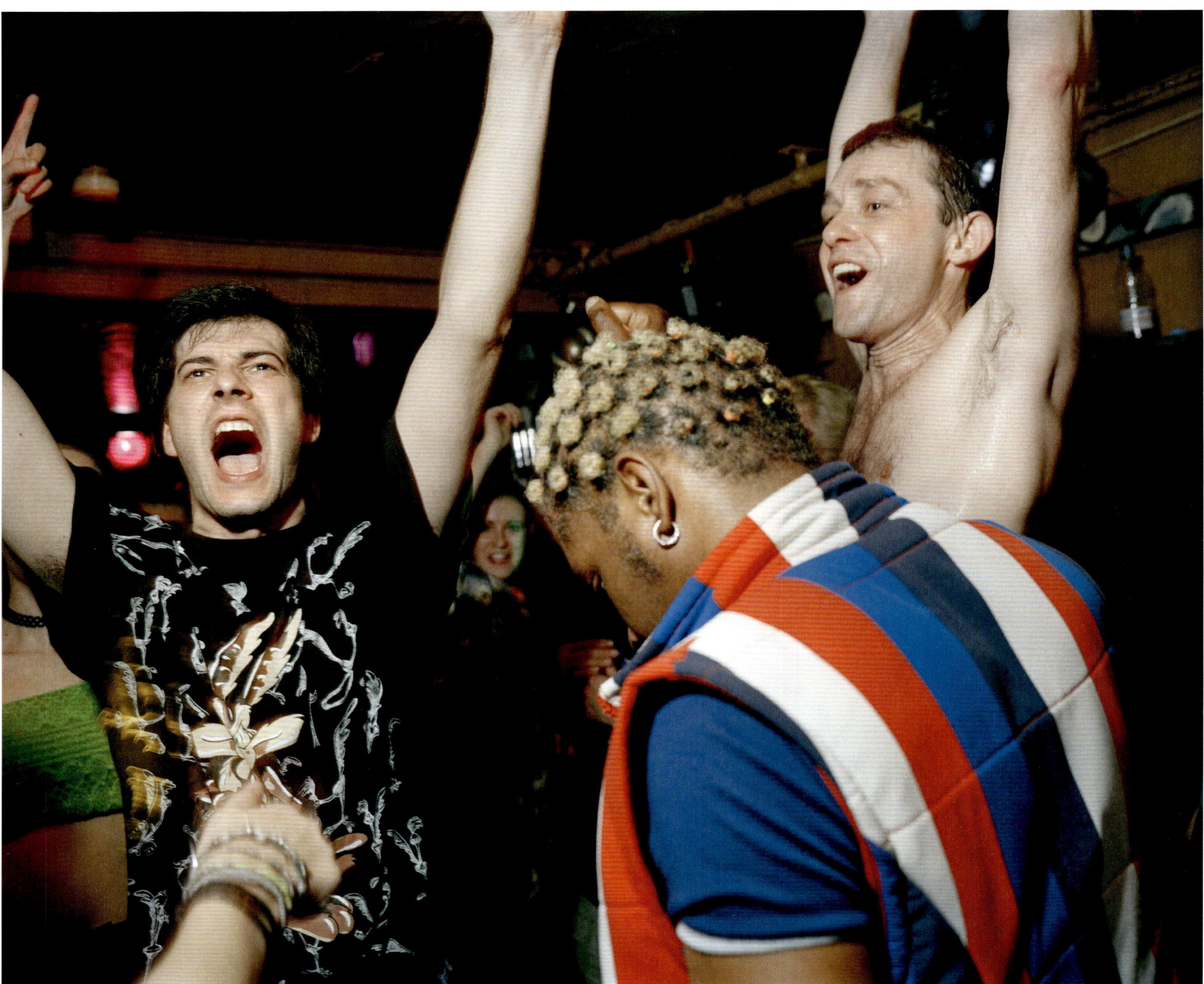

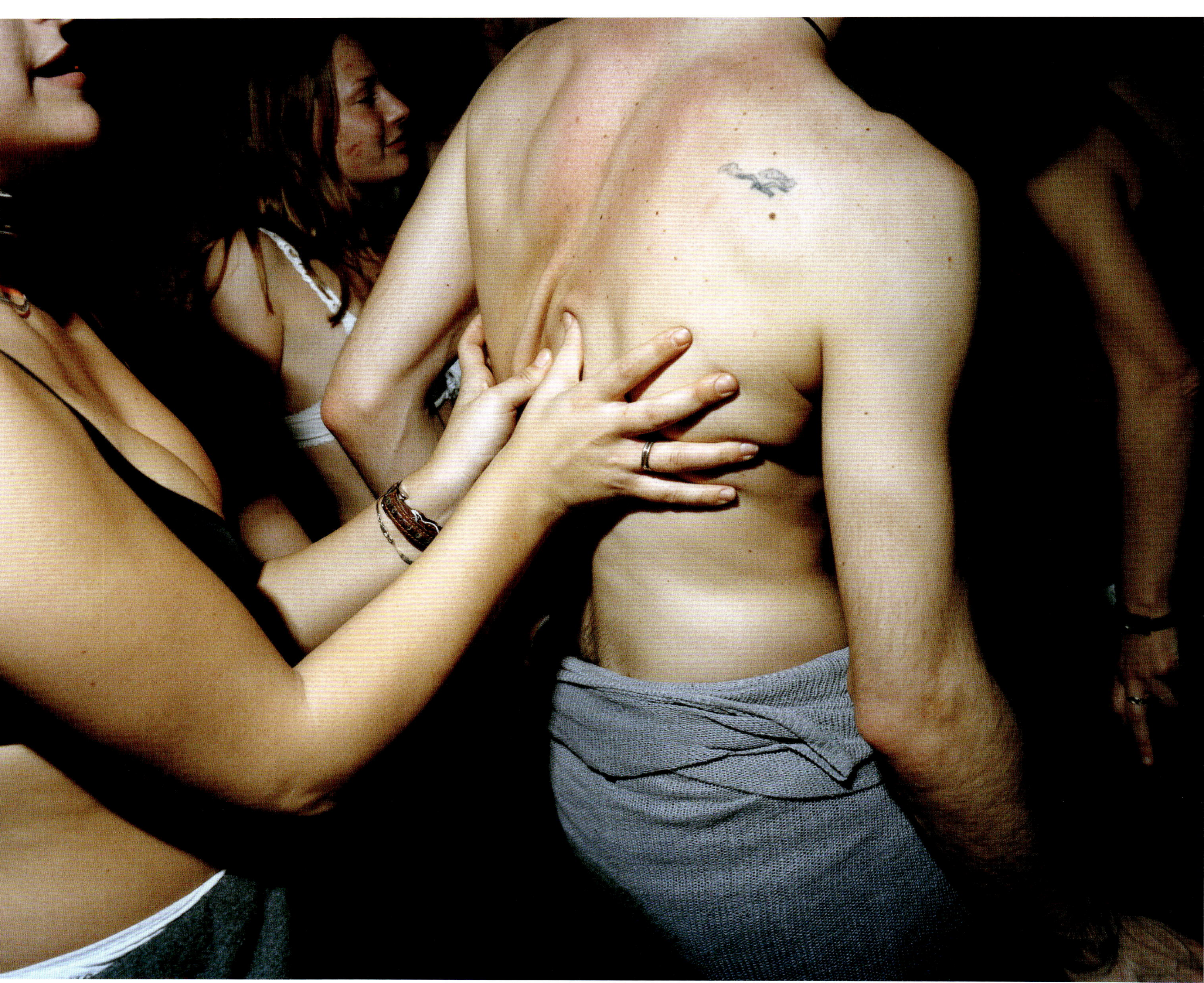

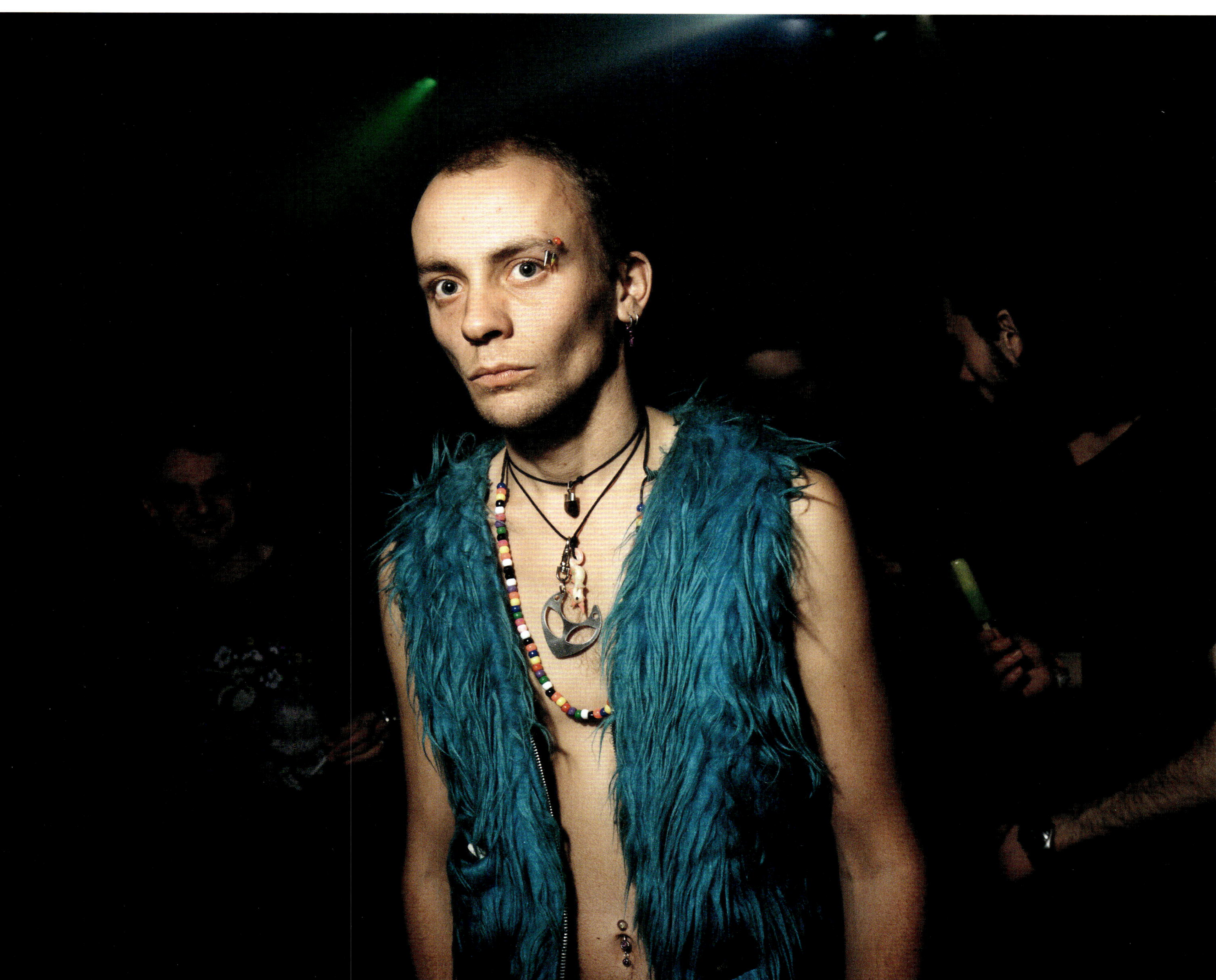

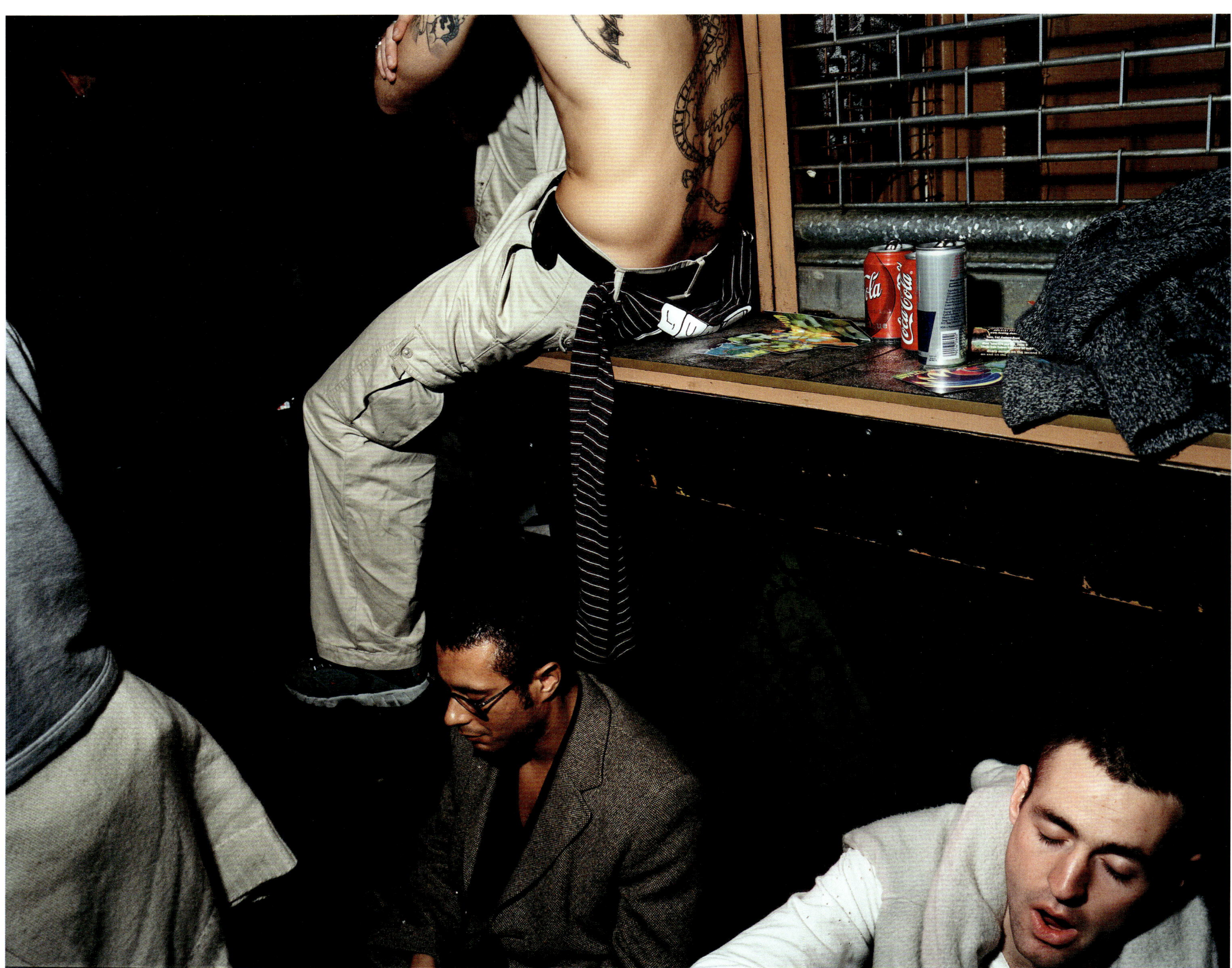
Coca-Cola

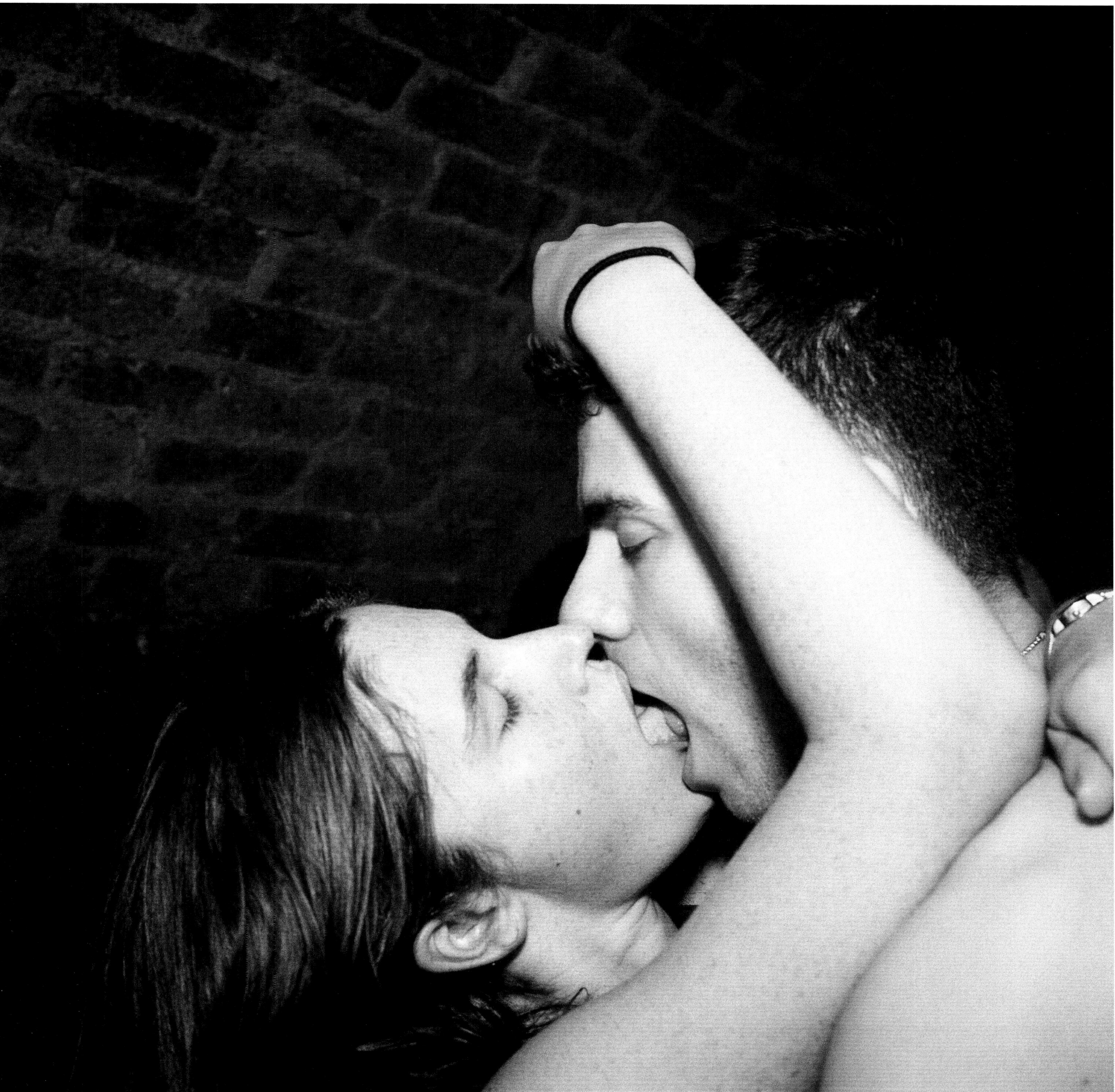

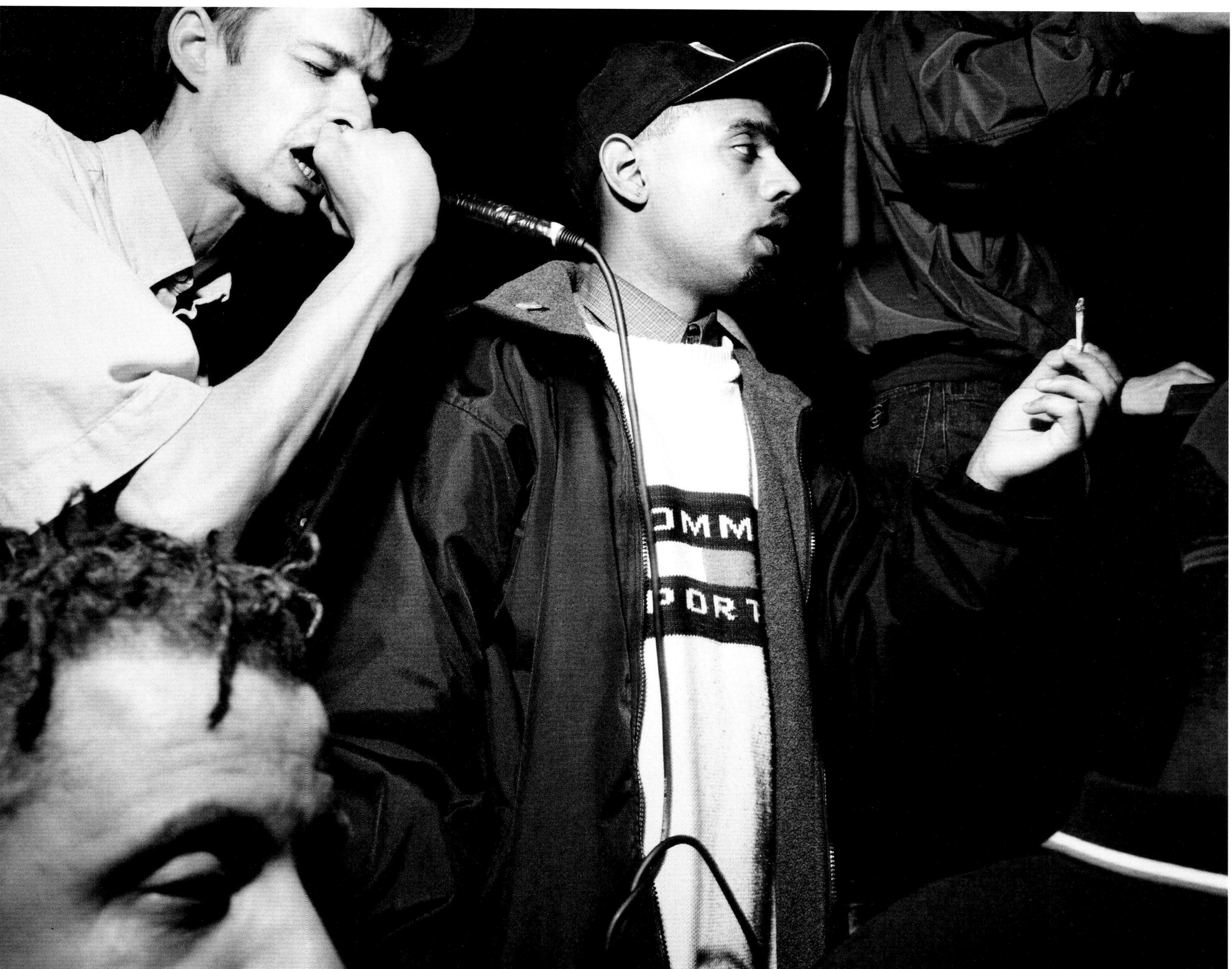
OMM
PORT

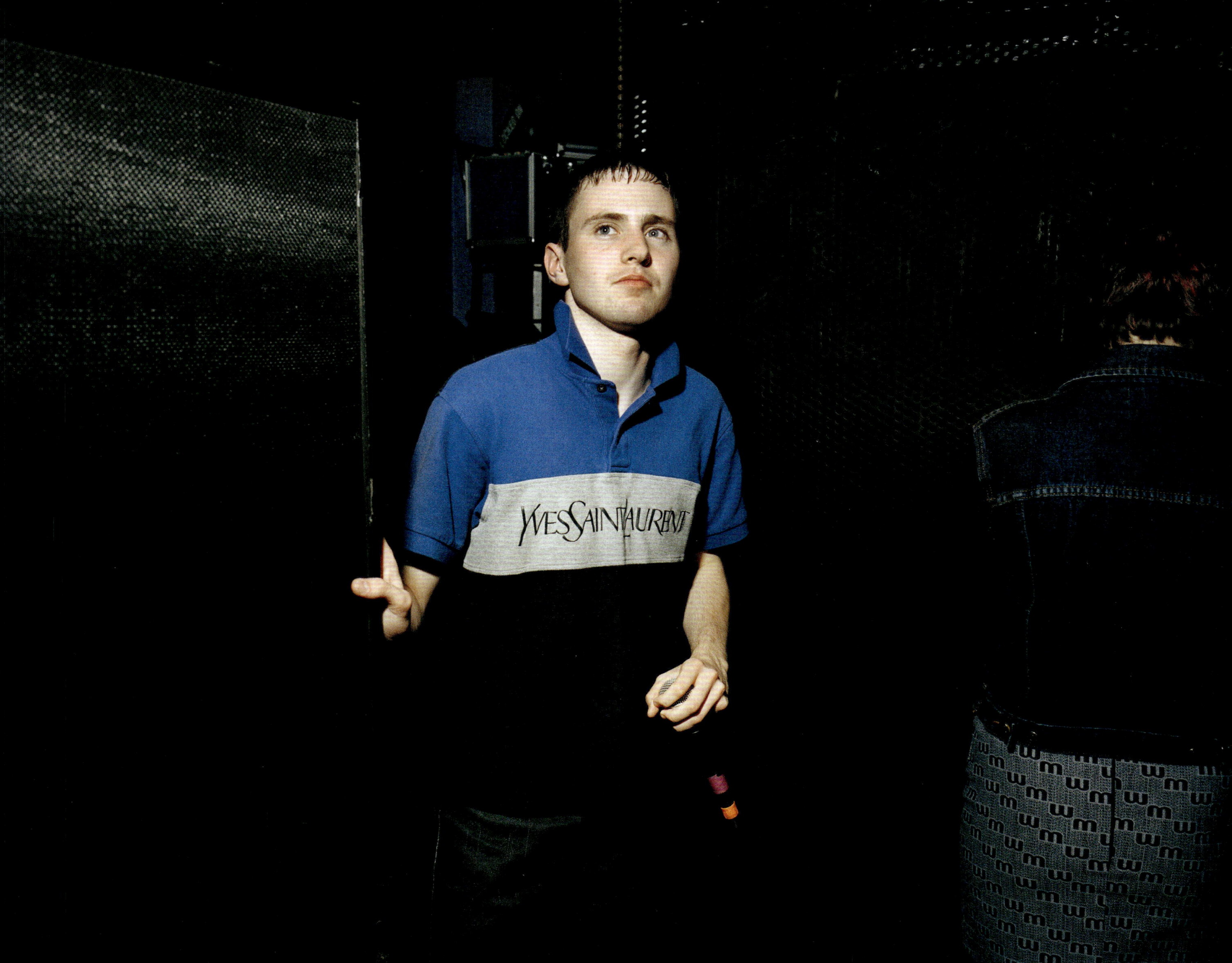
YVESSAINTLAURENT

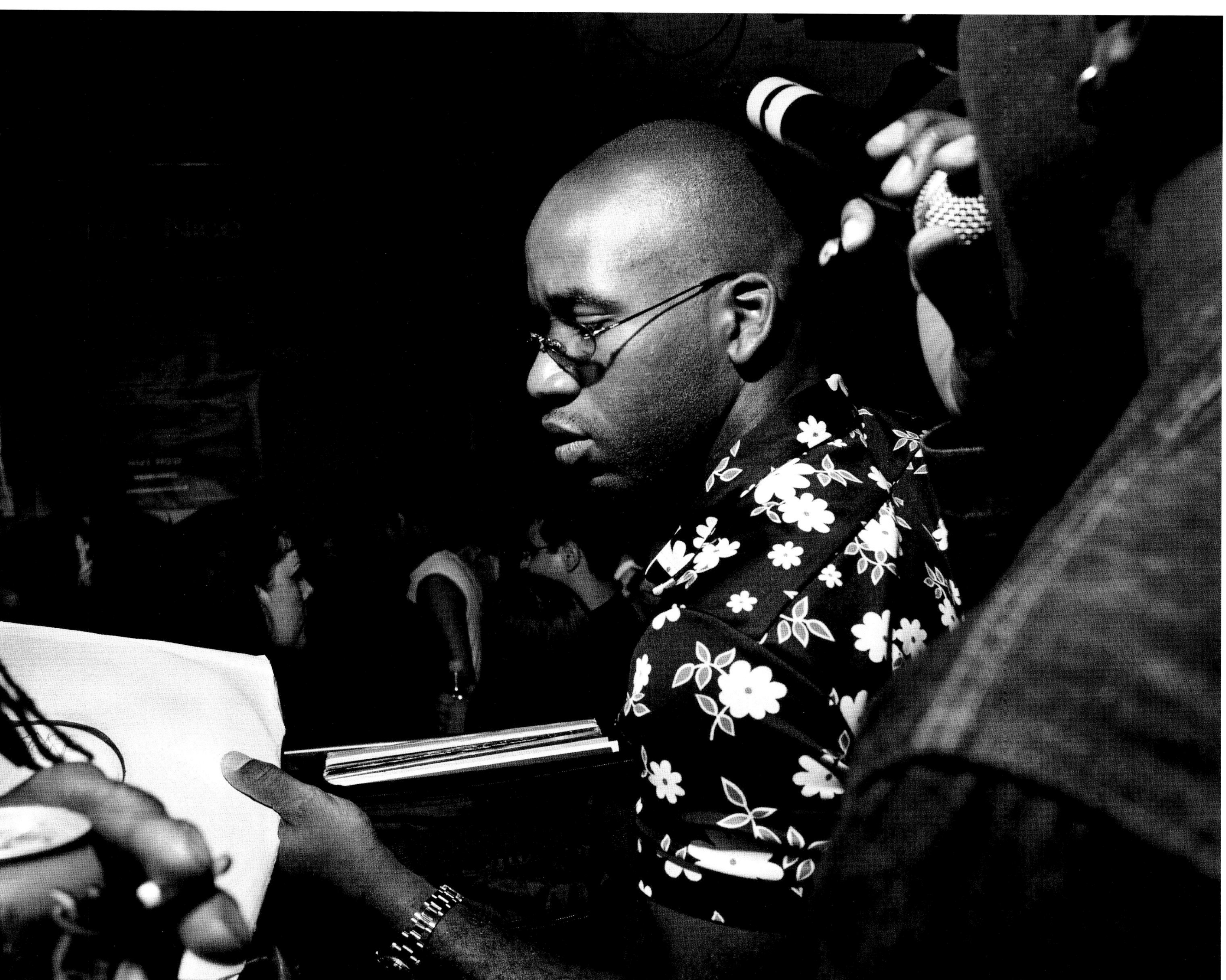

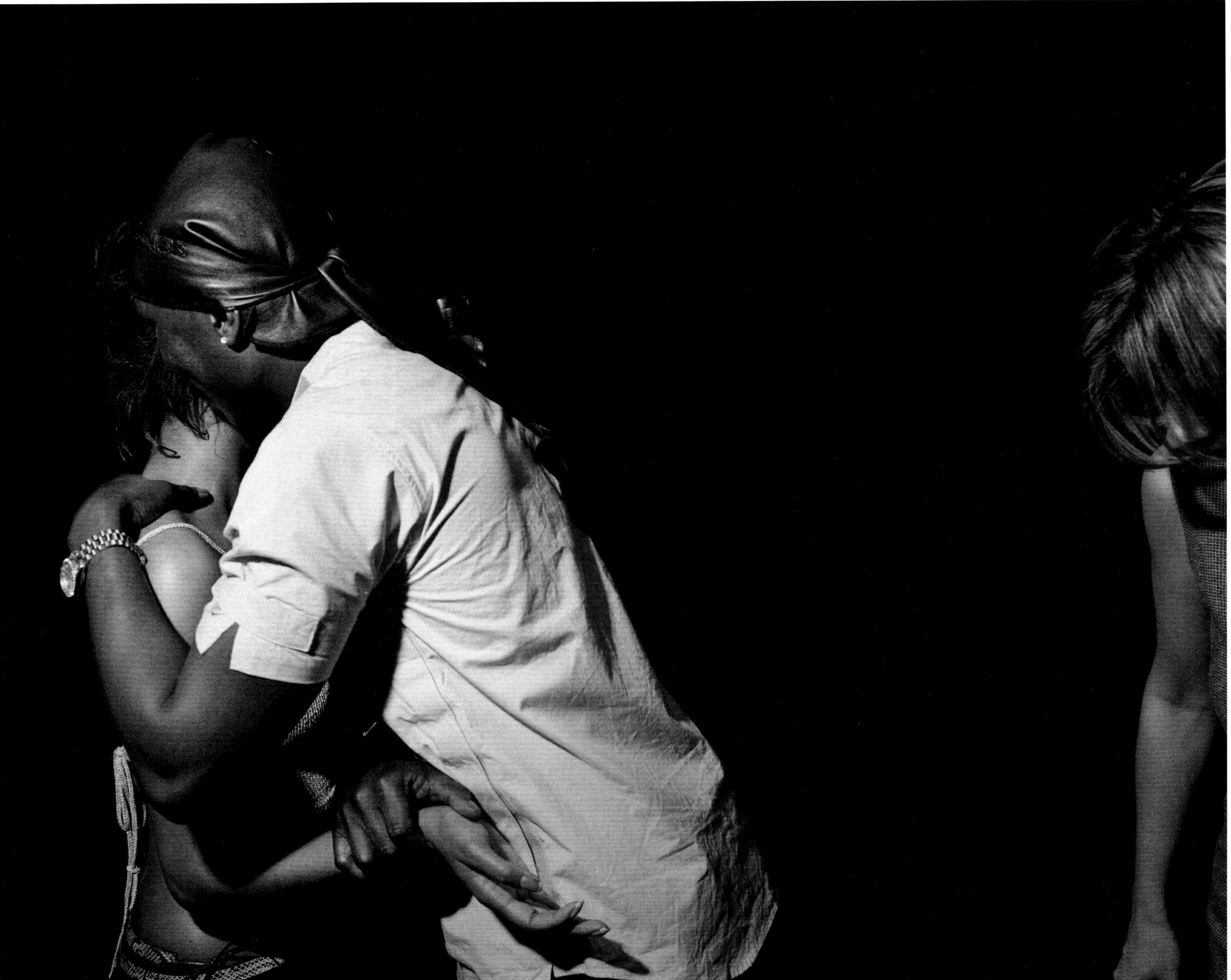

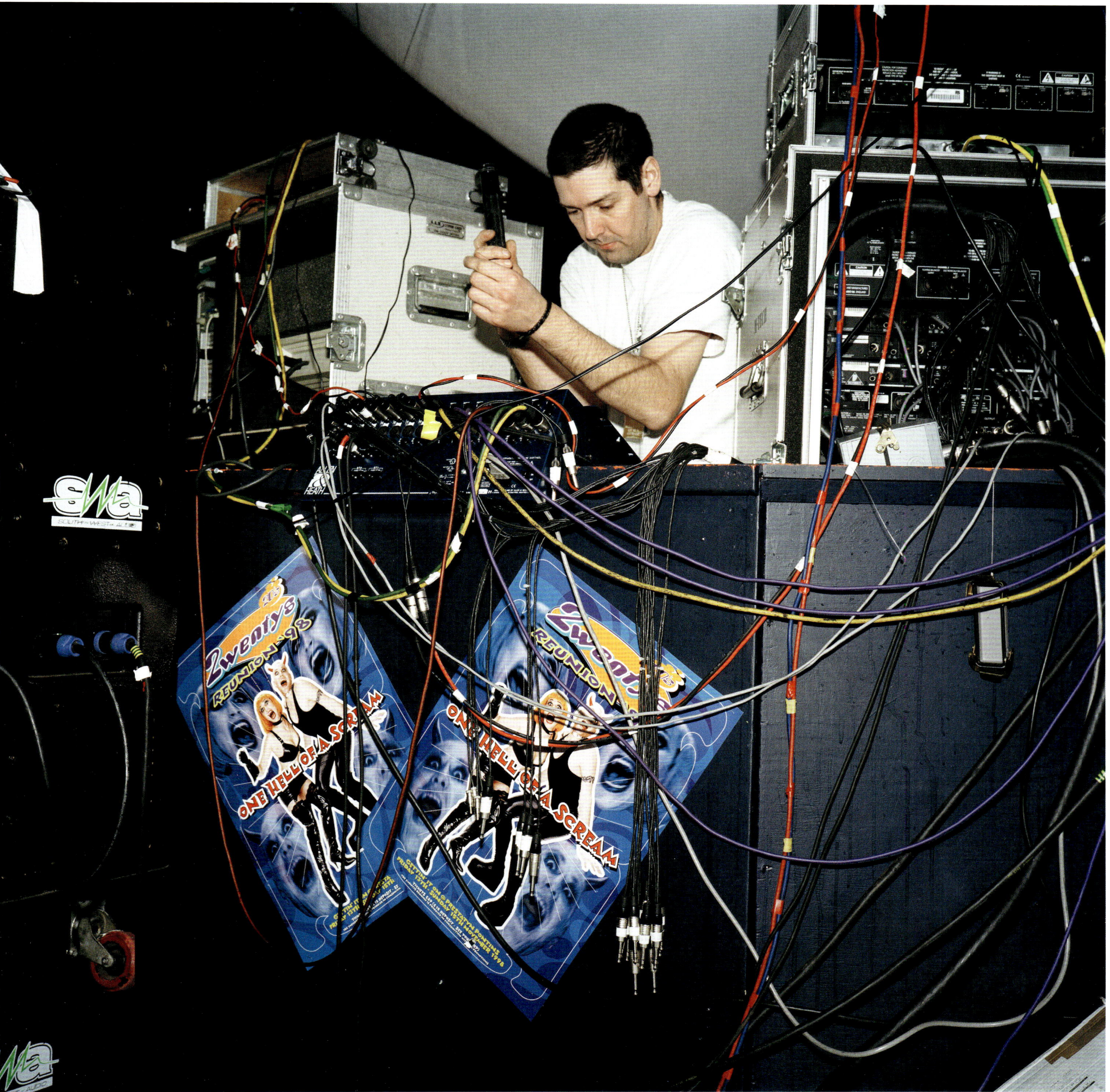

swa
2wentys
REUNION '98
ONE HELL OF A SCREAM
2wentys
REUNION '98
ONE HELL OF A SCREAM

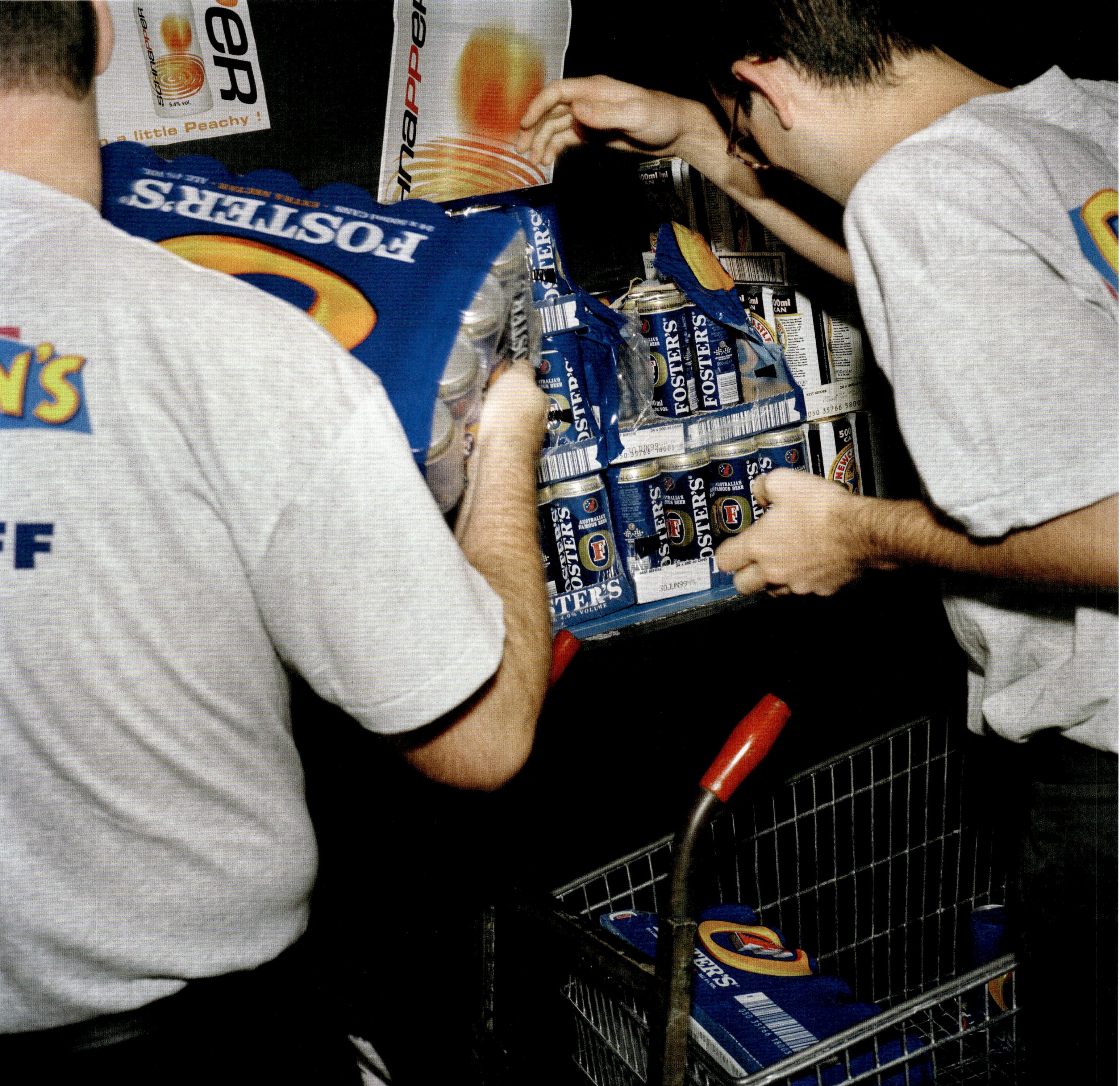
a little Peachy !
FOSTER'S
FOSTER'S
AUSTRALIA'S FAMOUS BEER
30JUN99

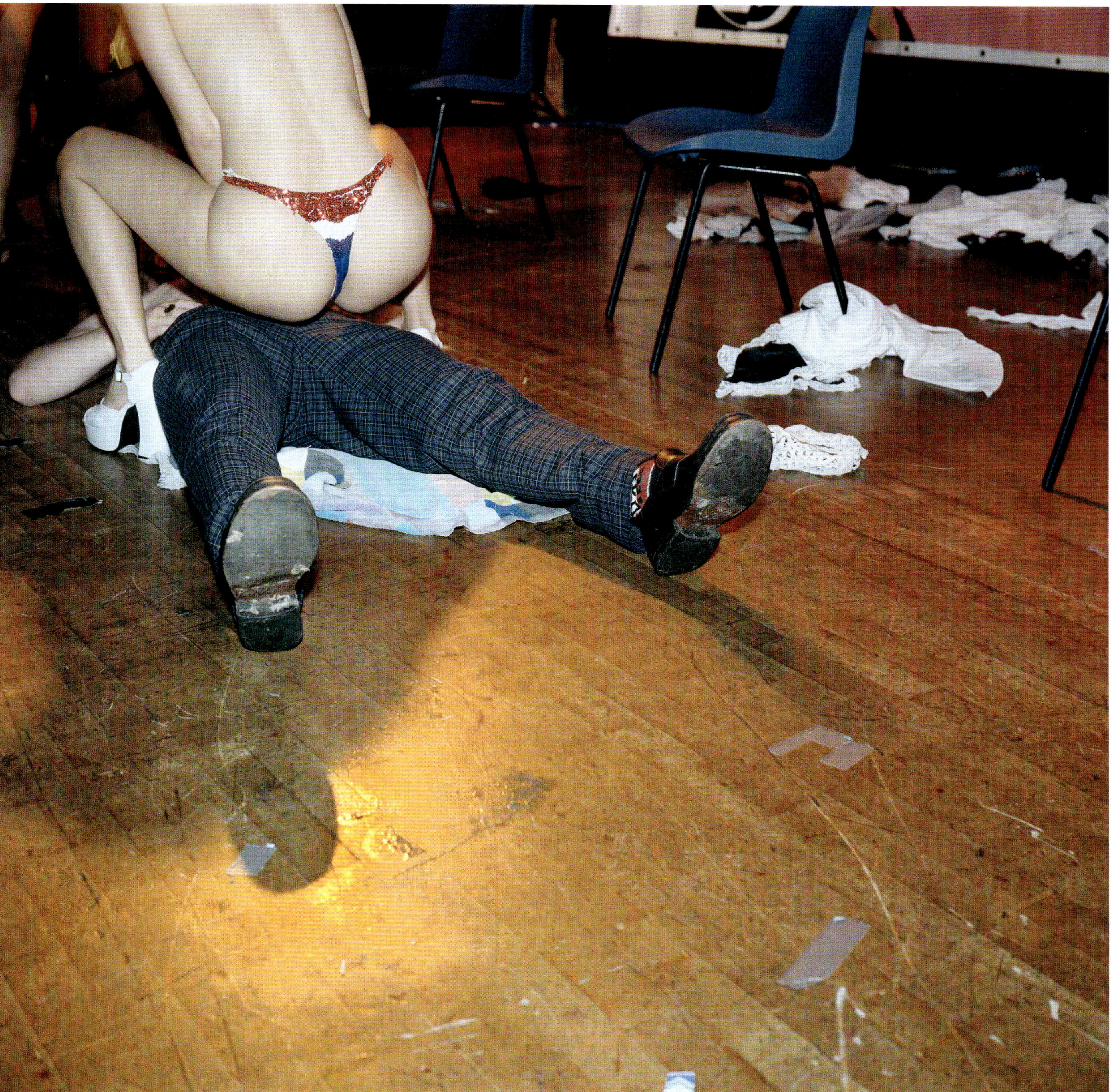

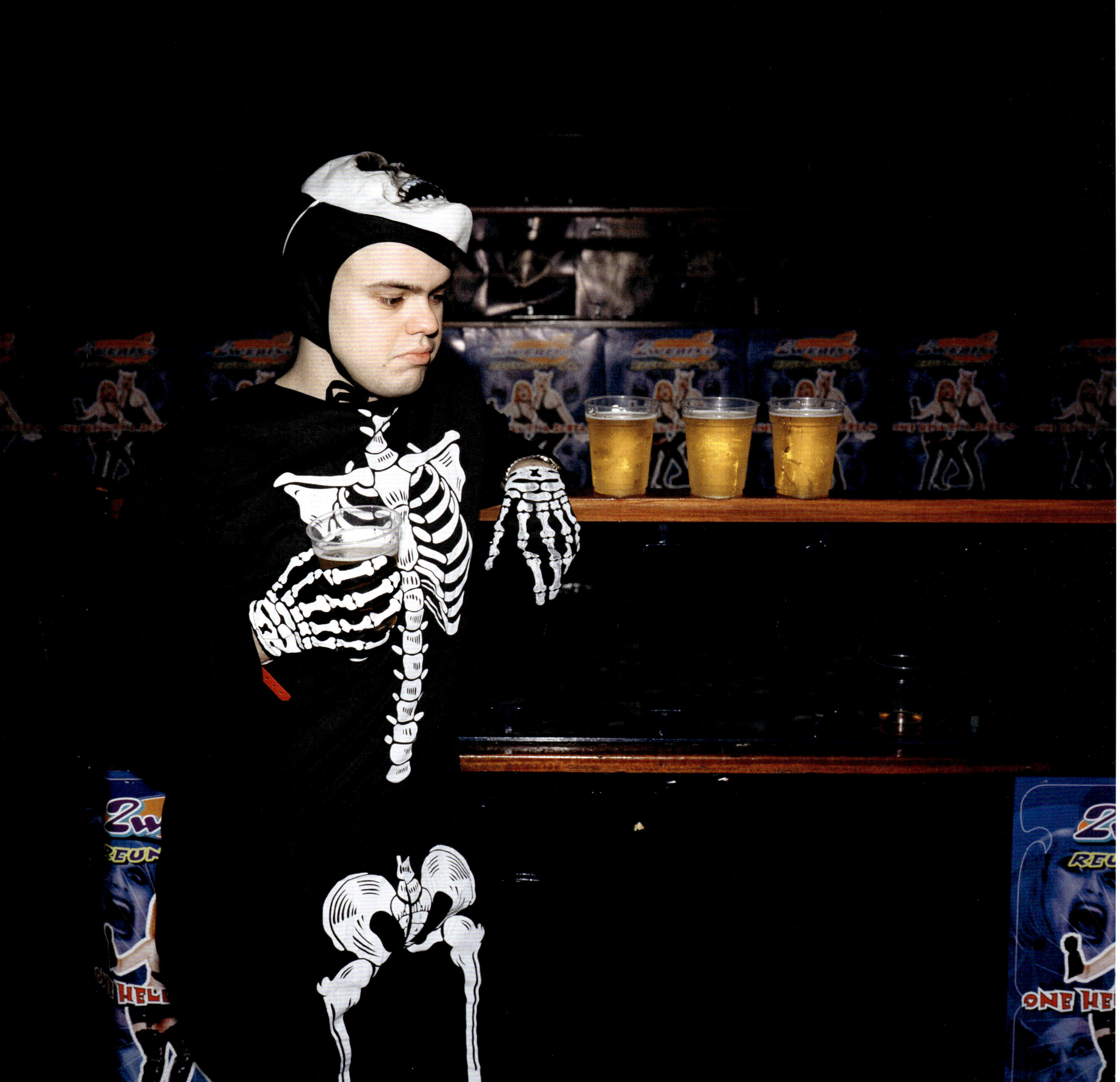

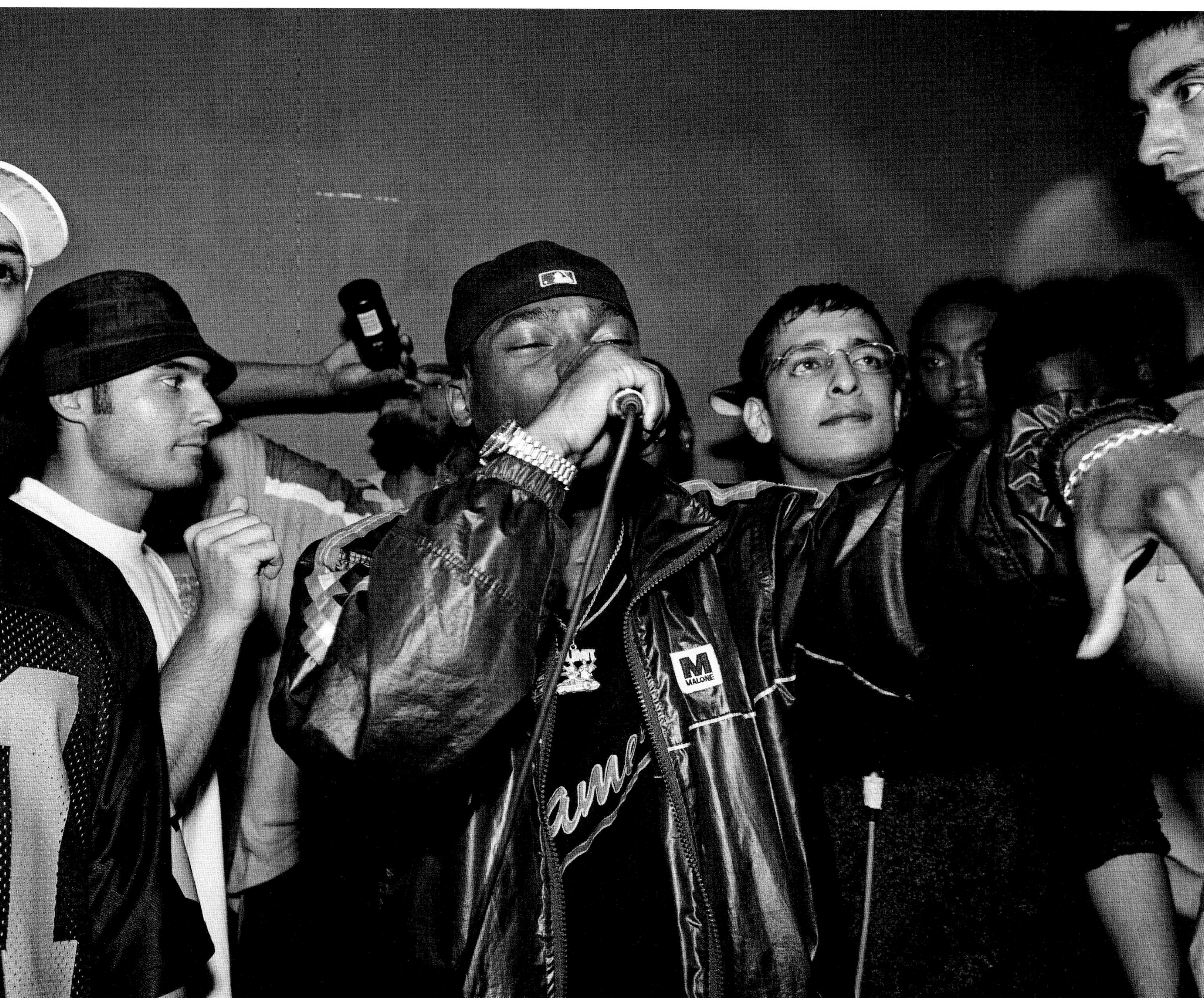
M
MALONE

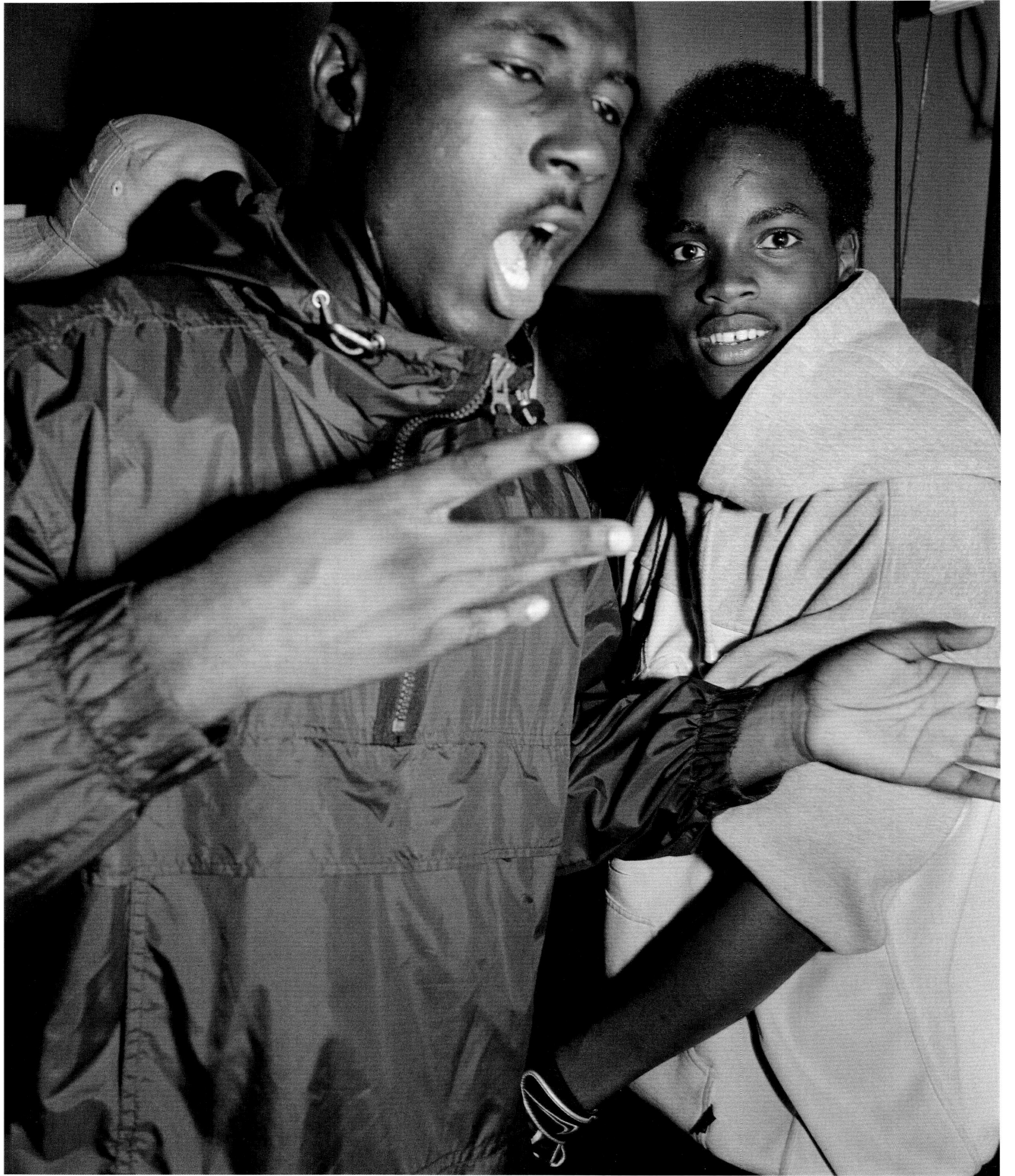

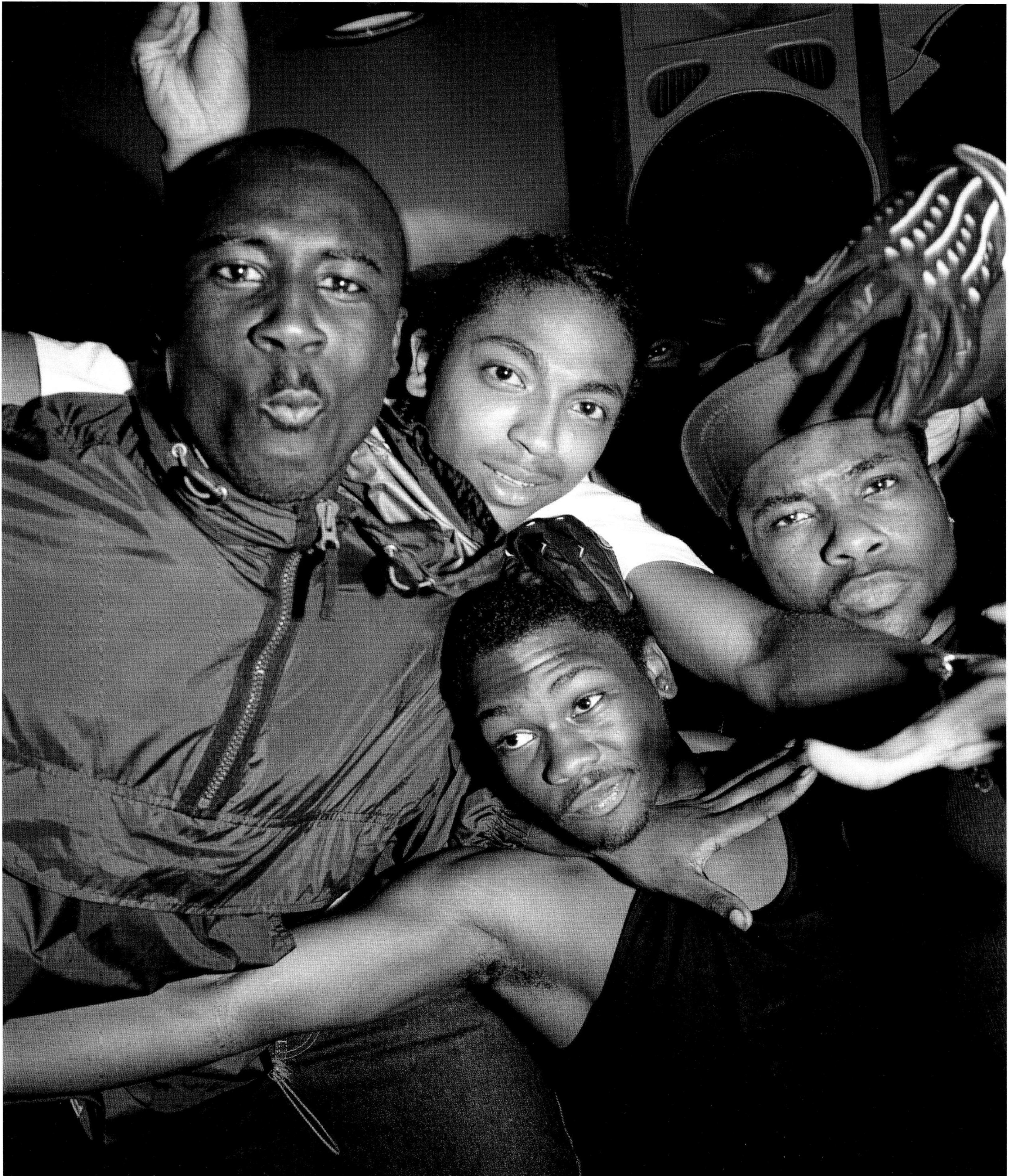

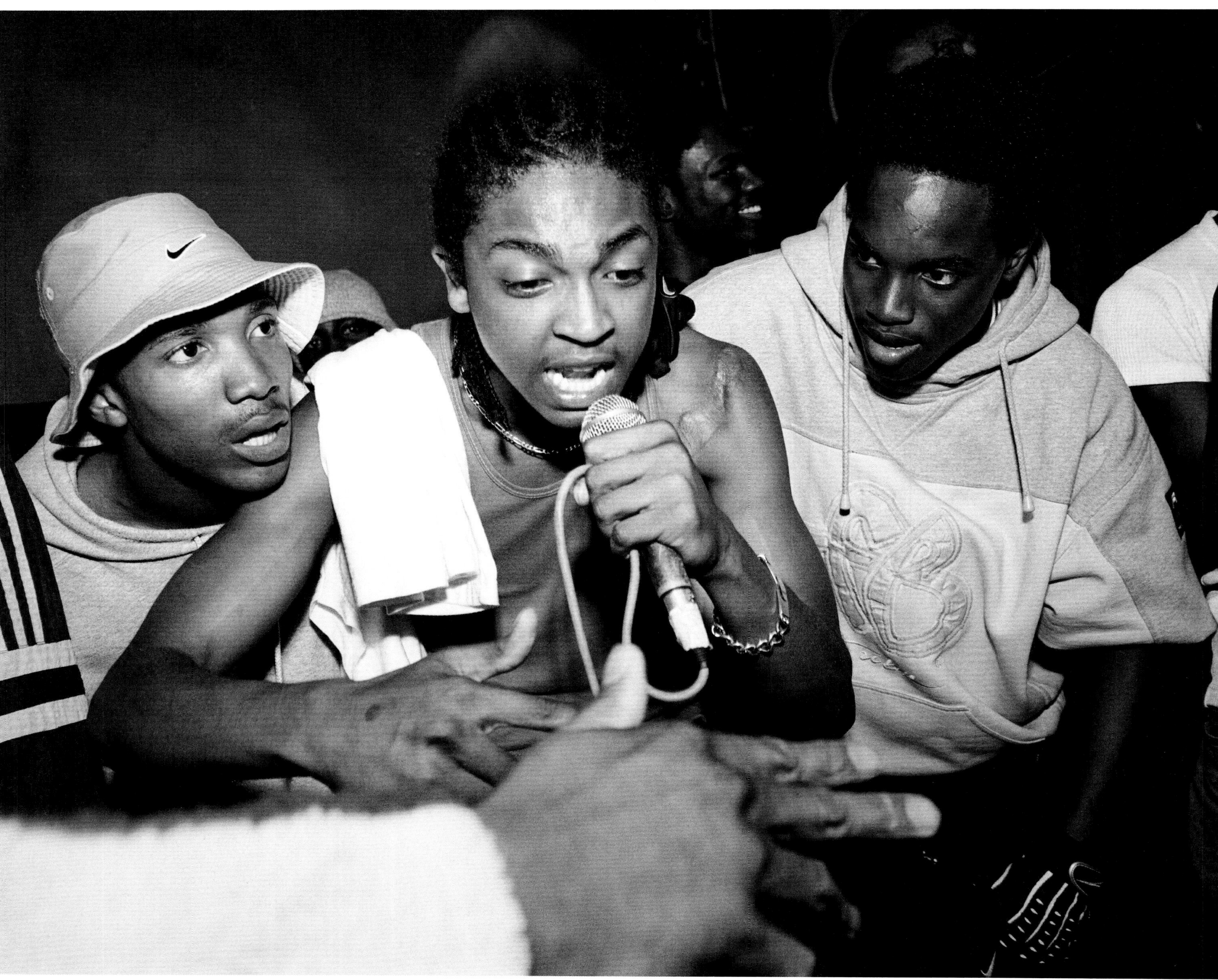

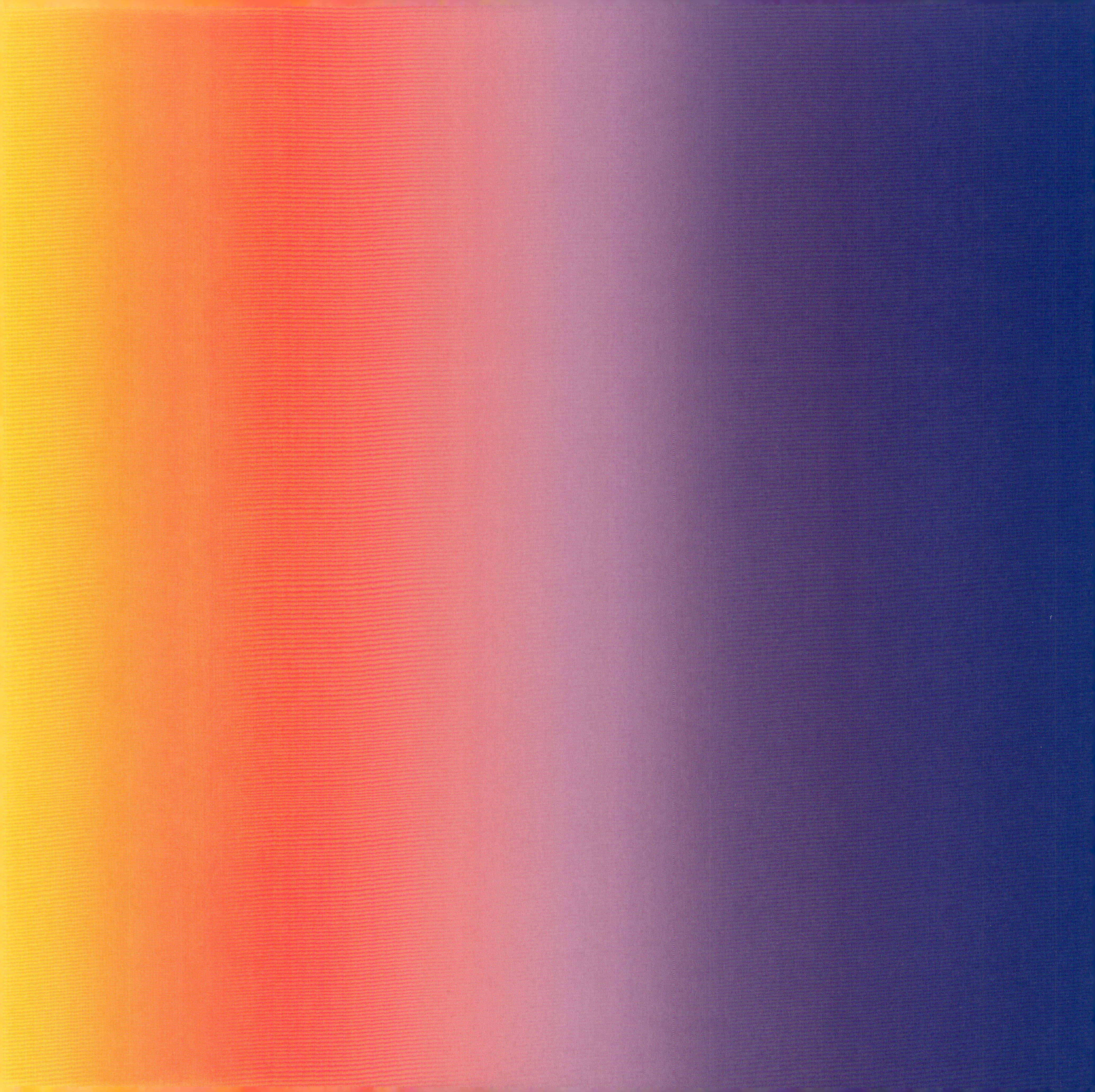

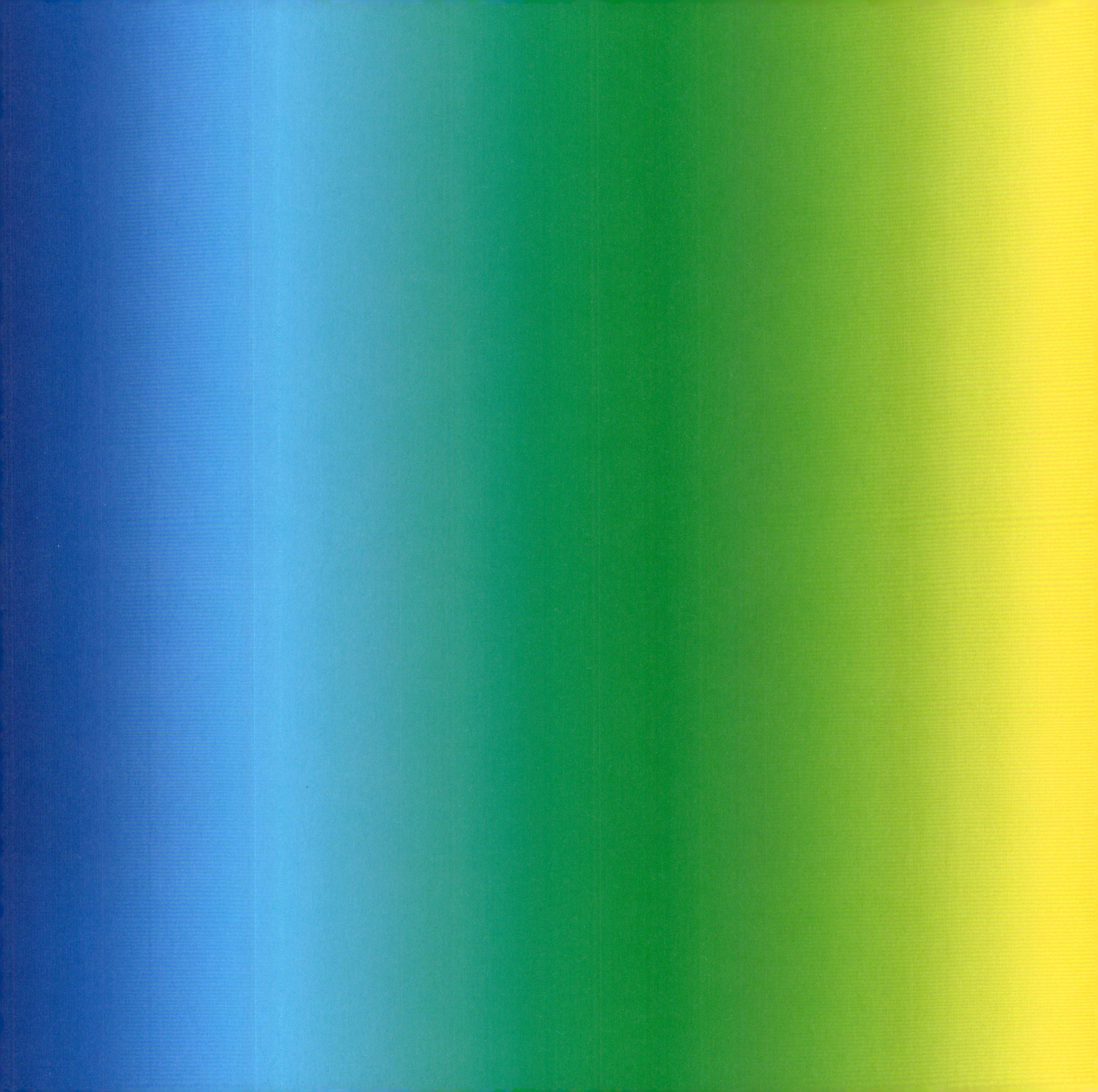

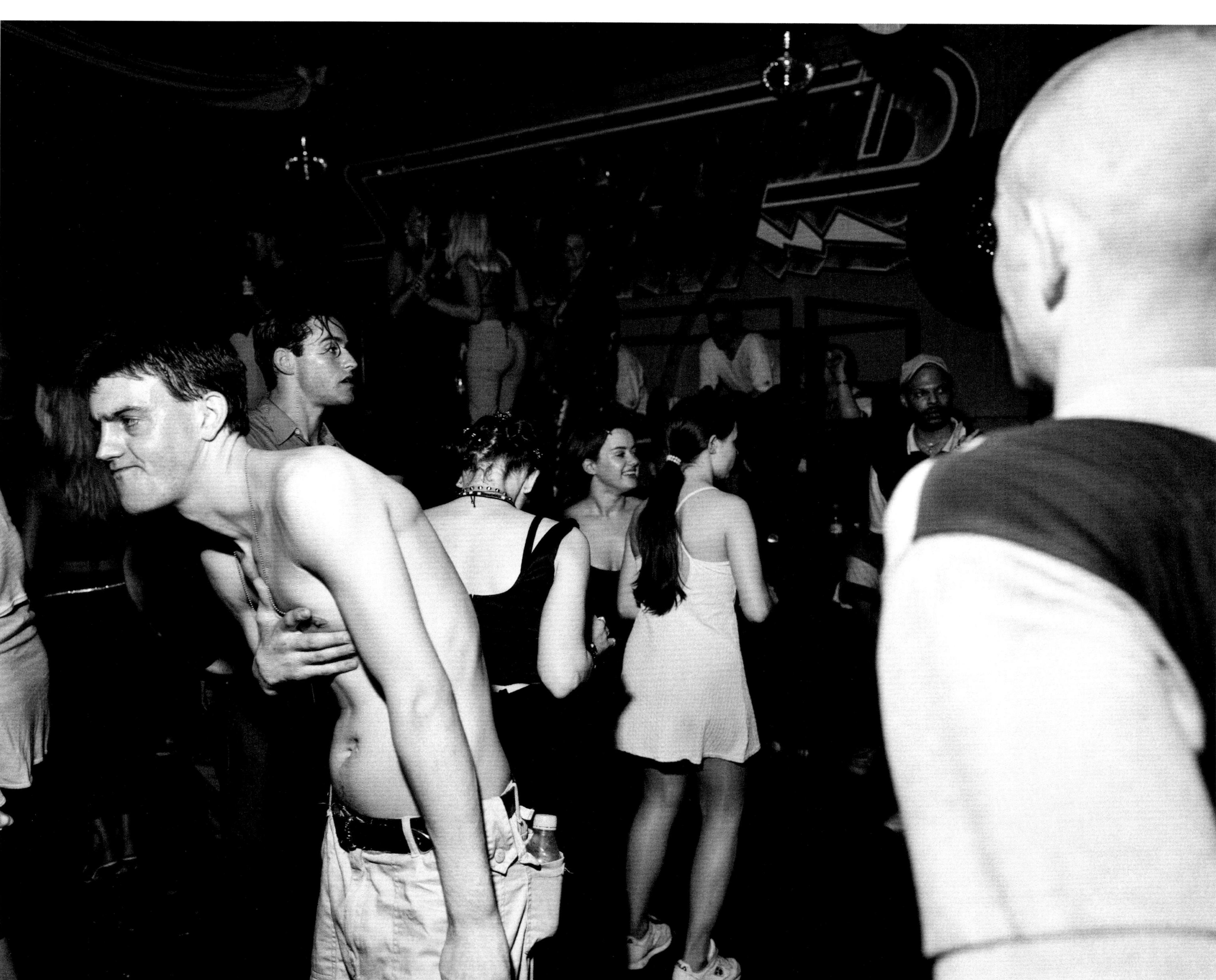

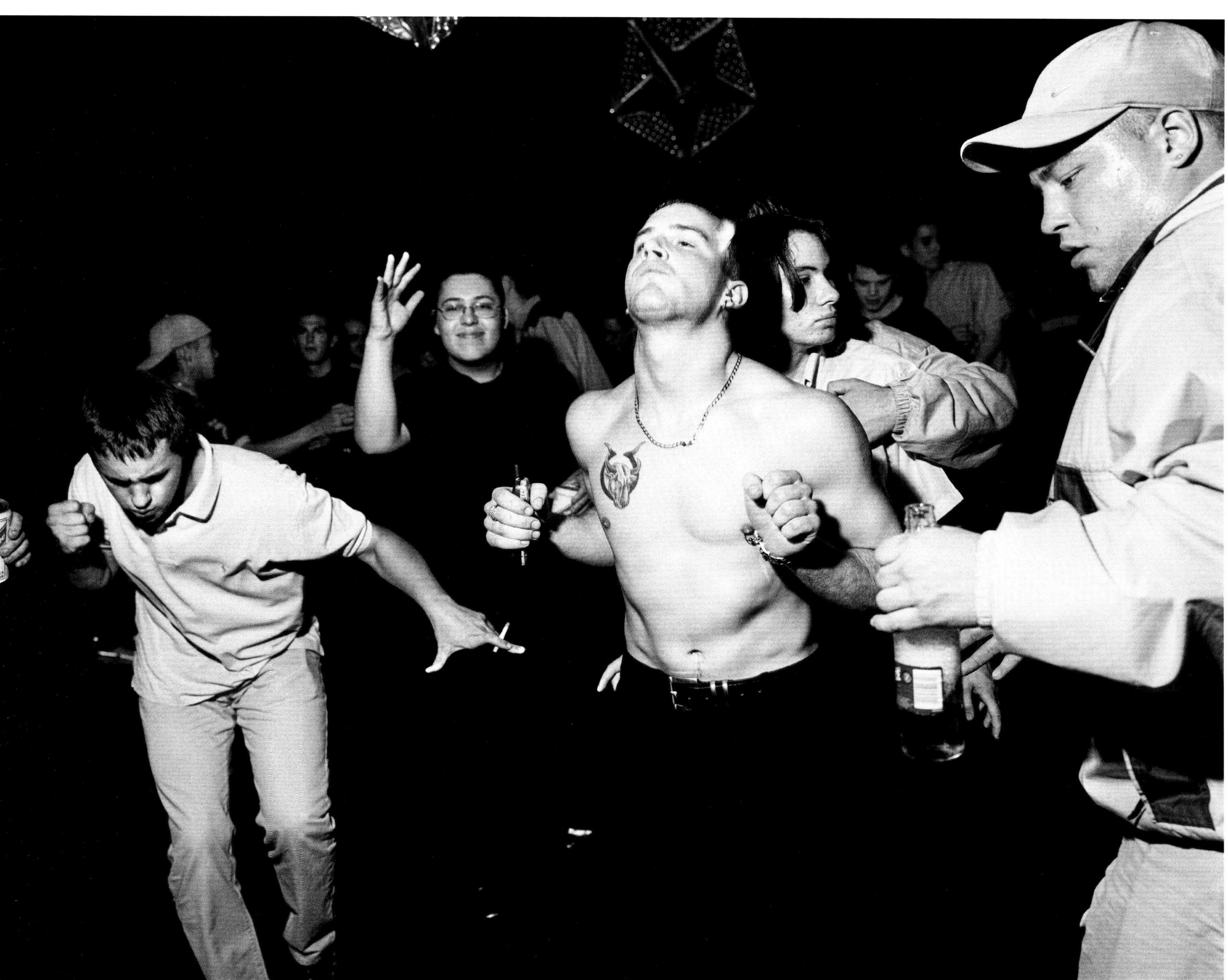

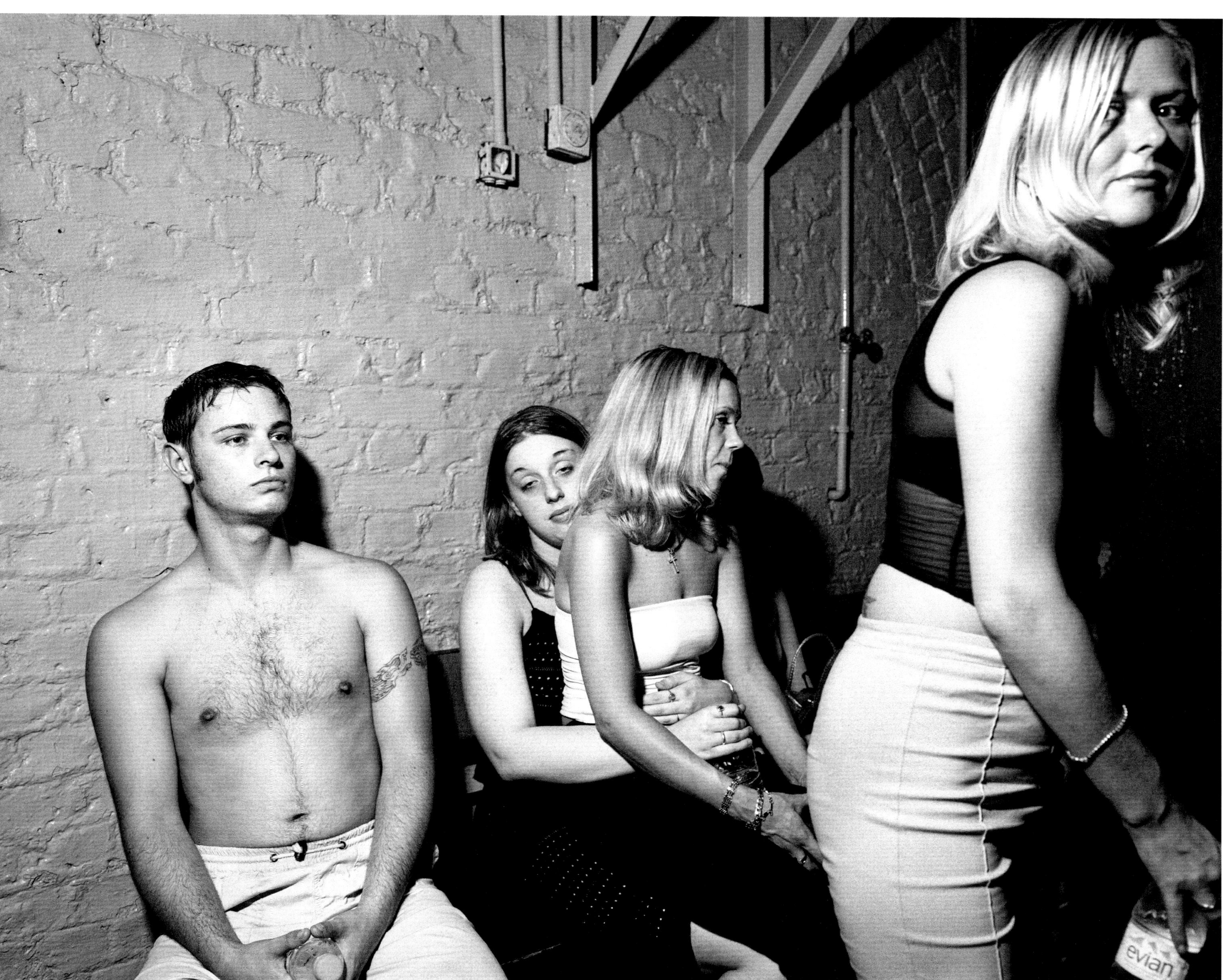
evian

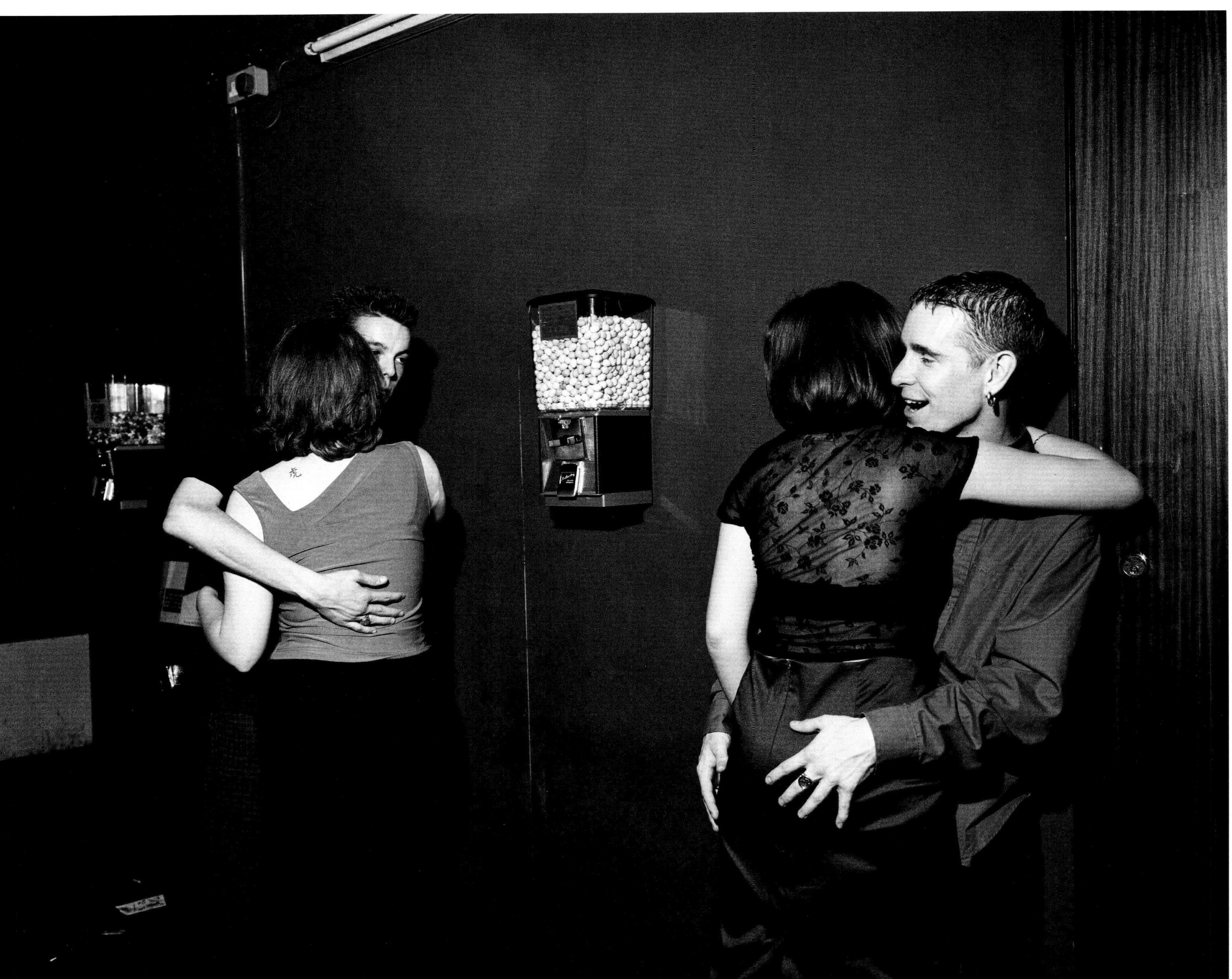

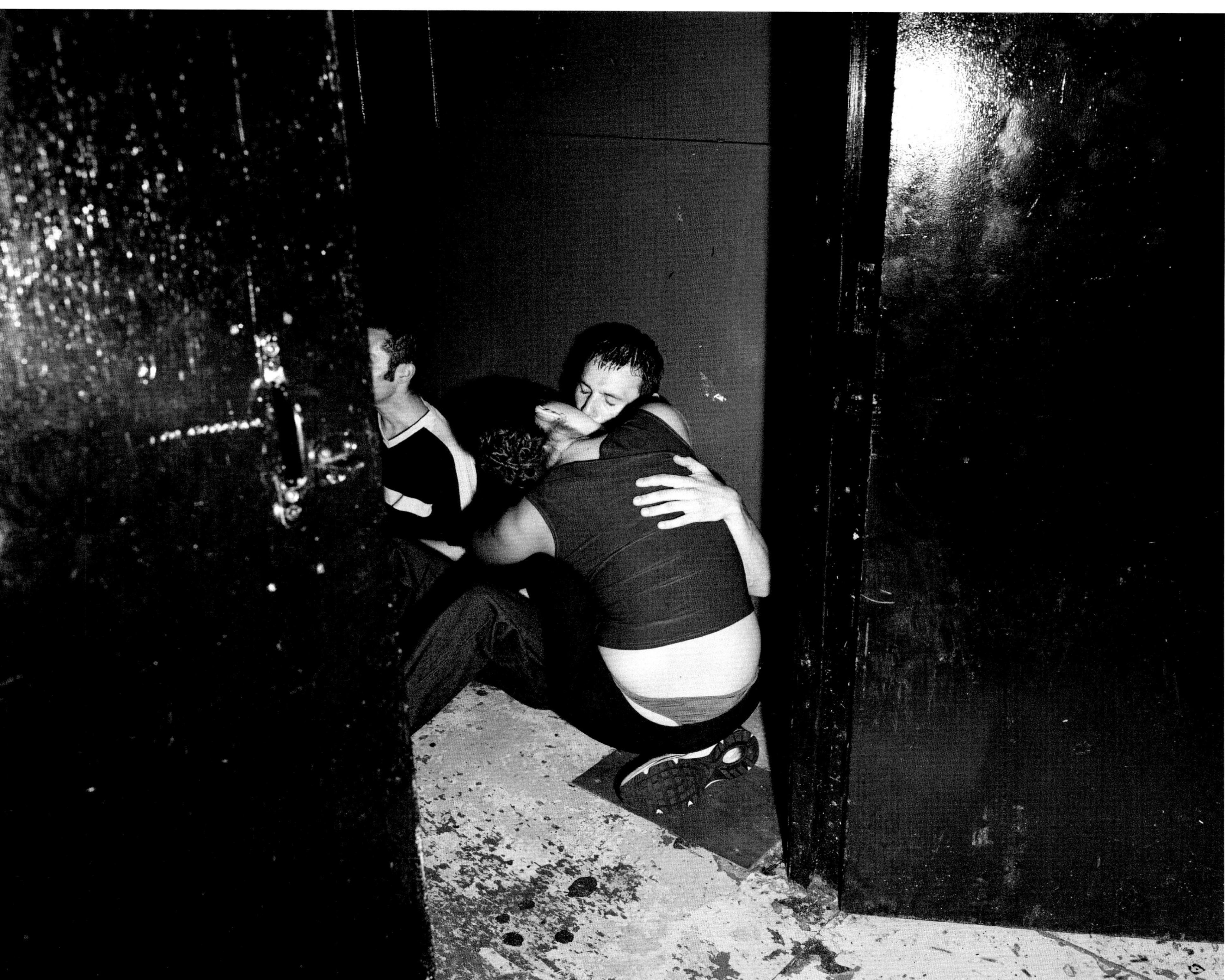

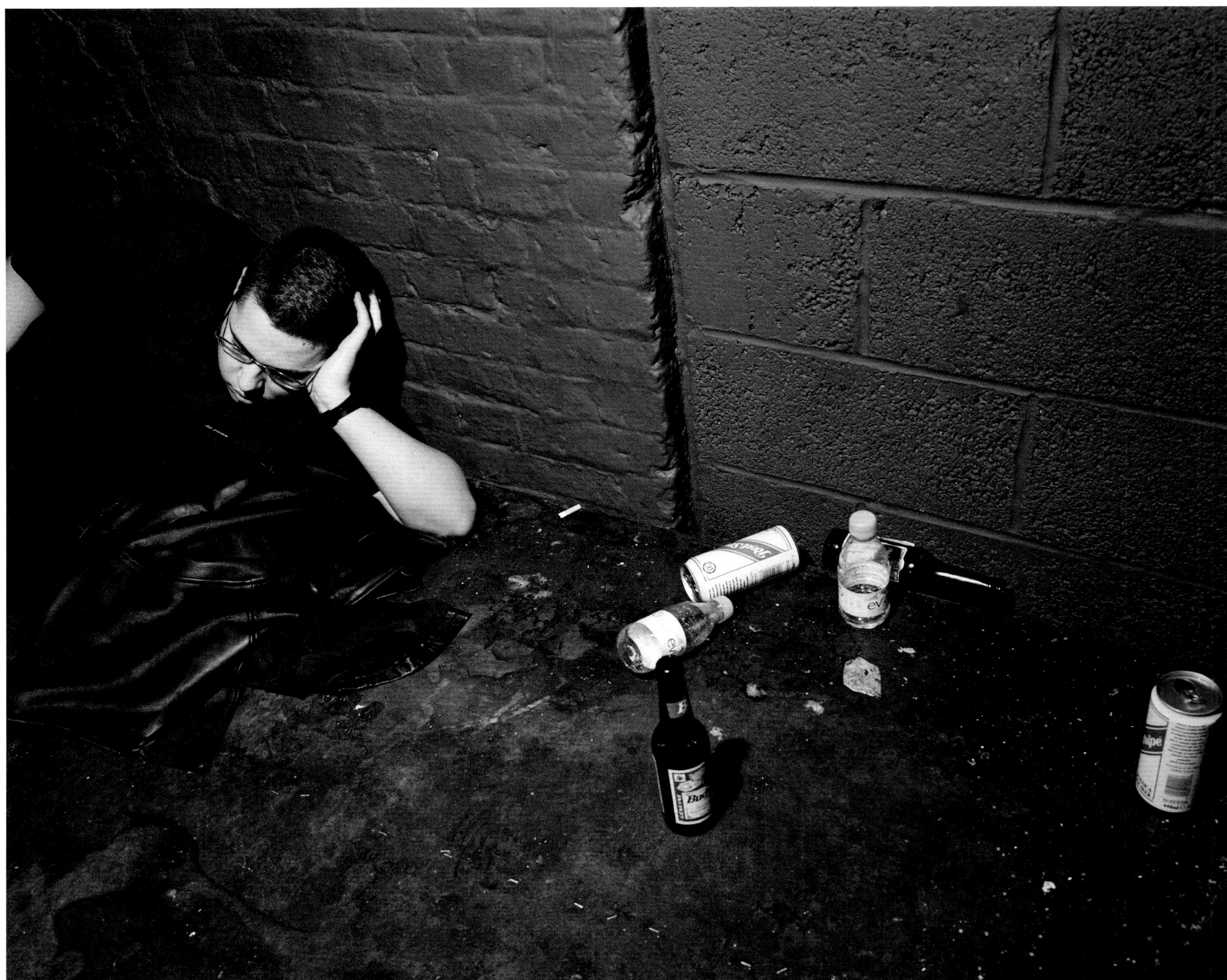

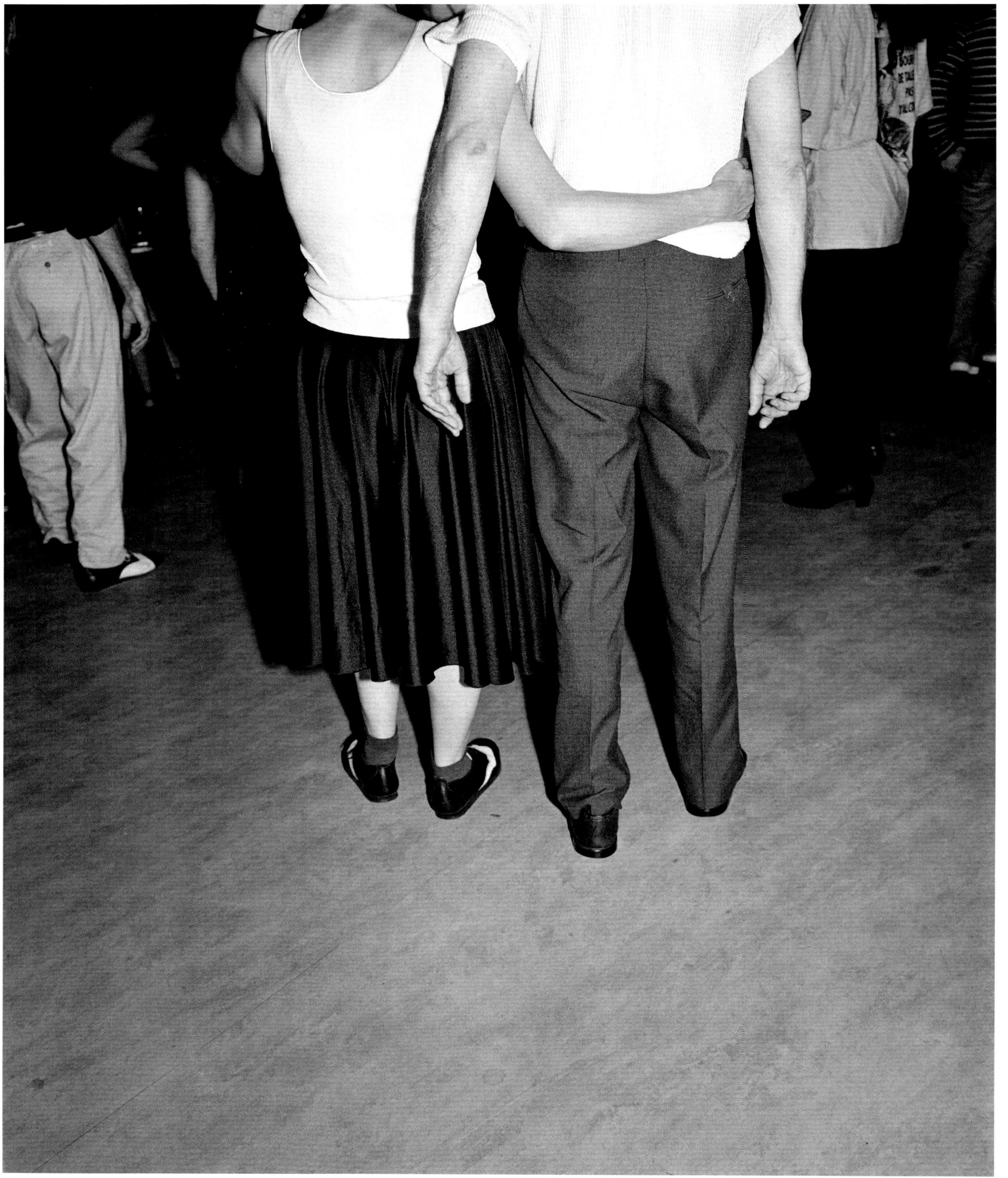

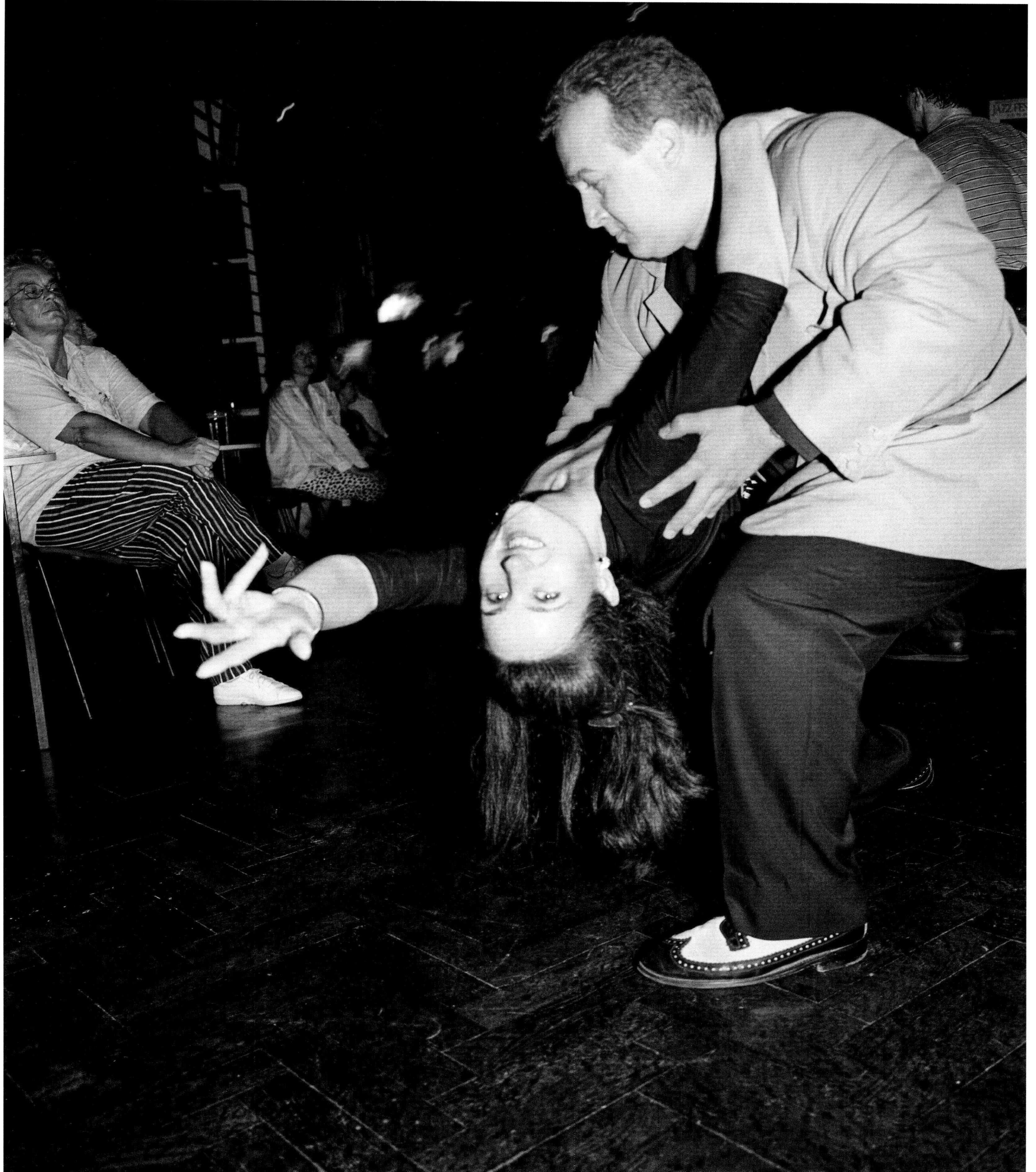

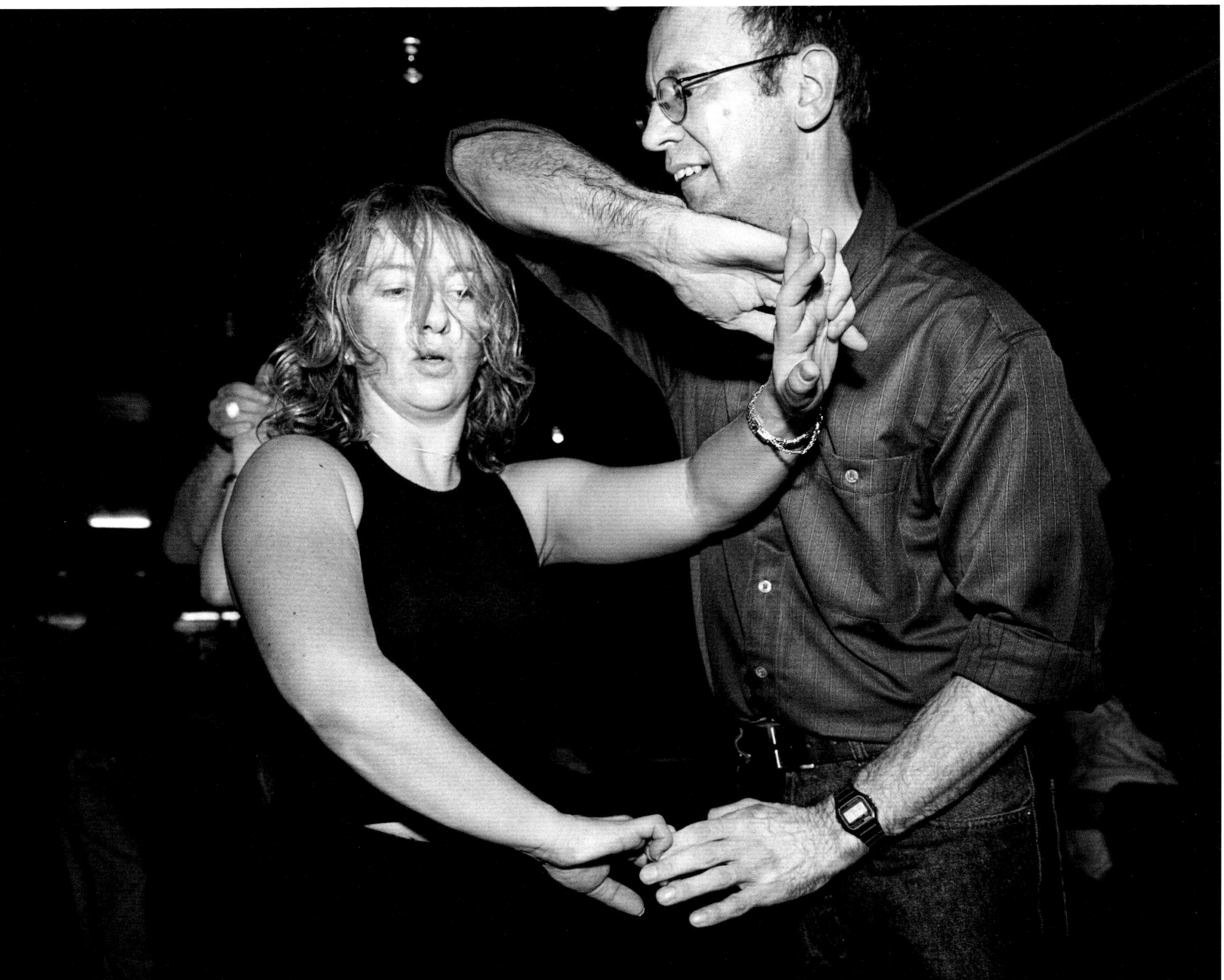

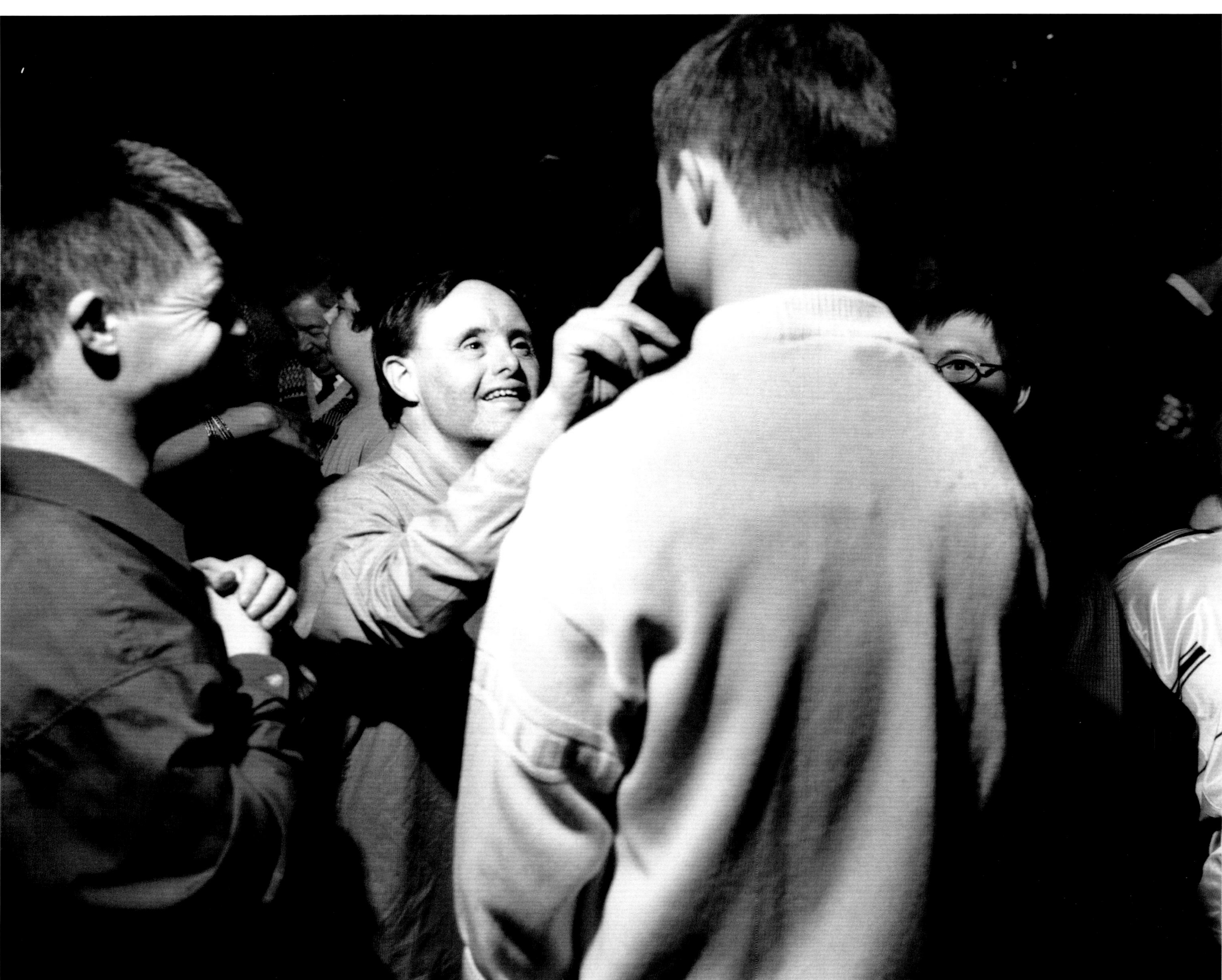

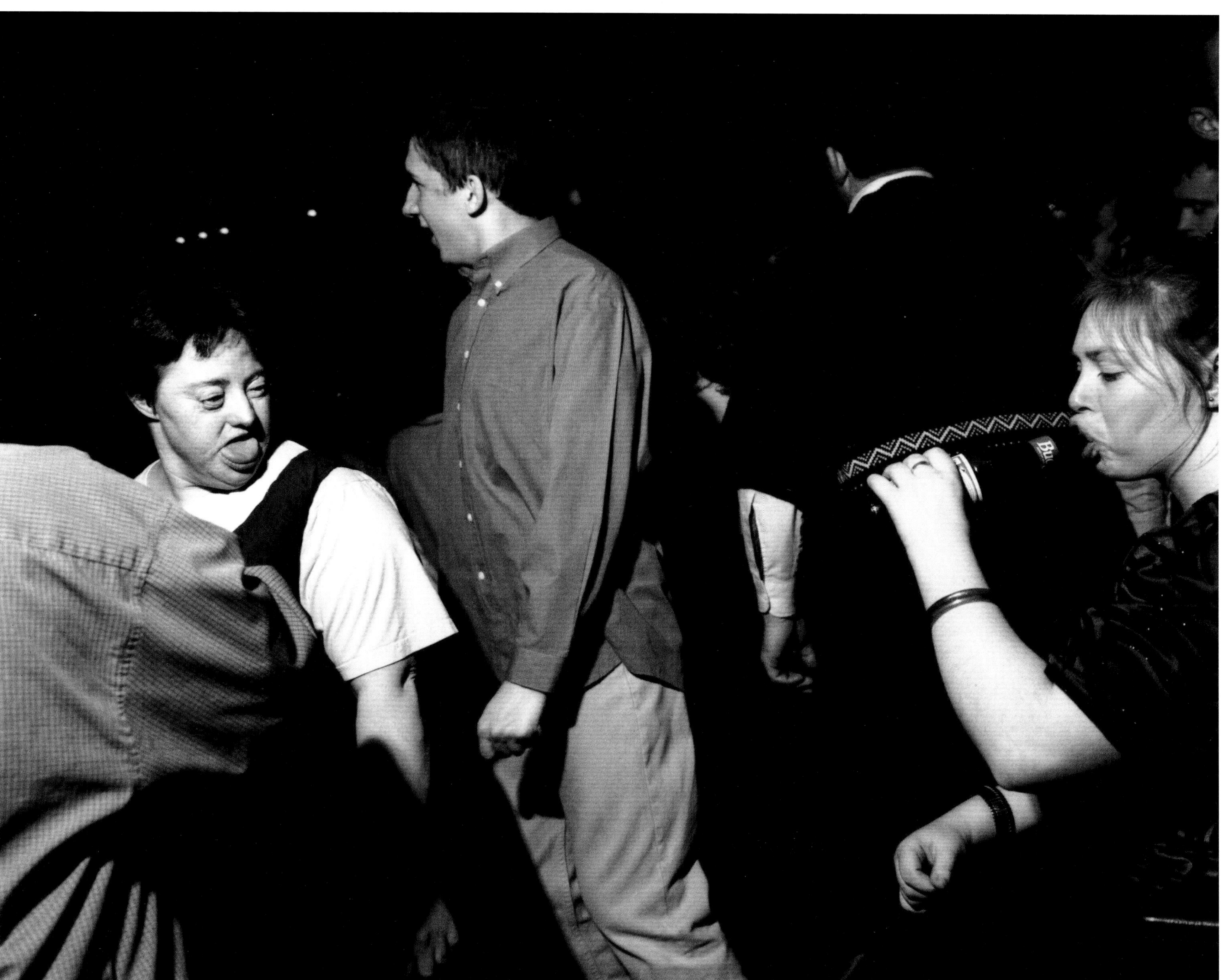

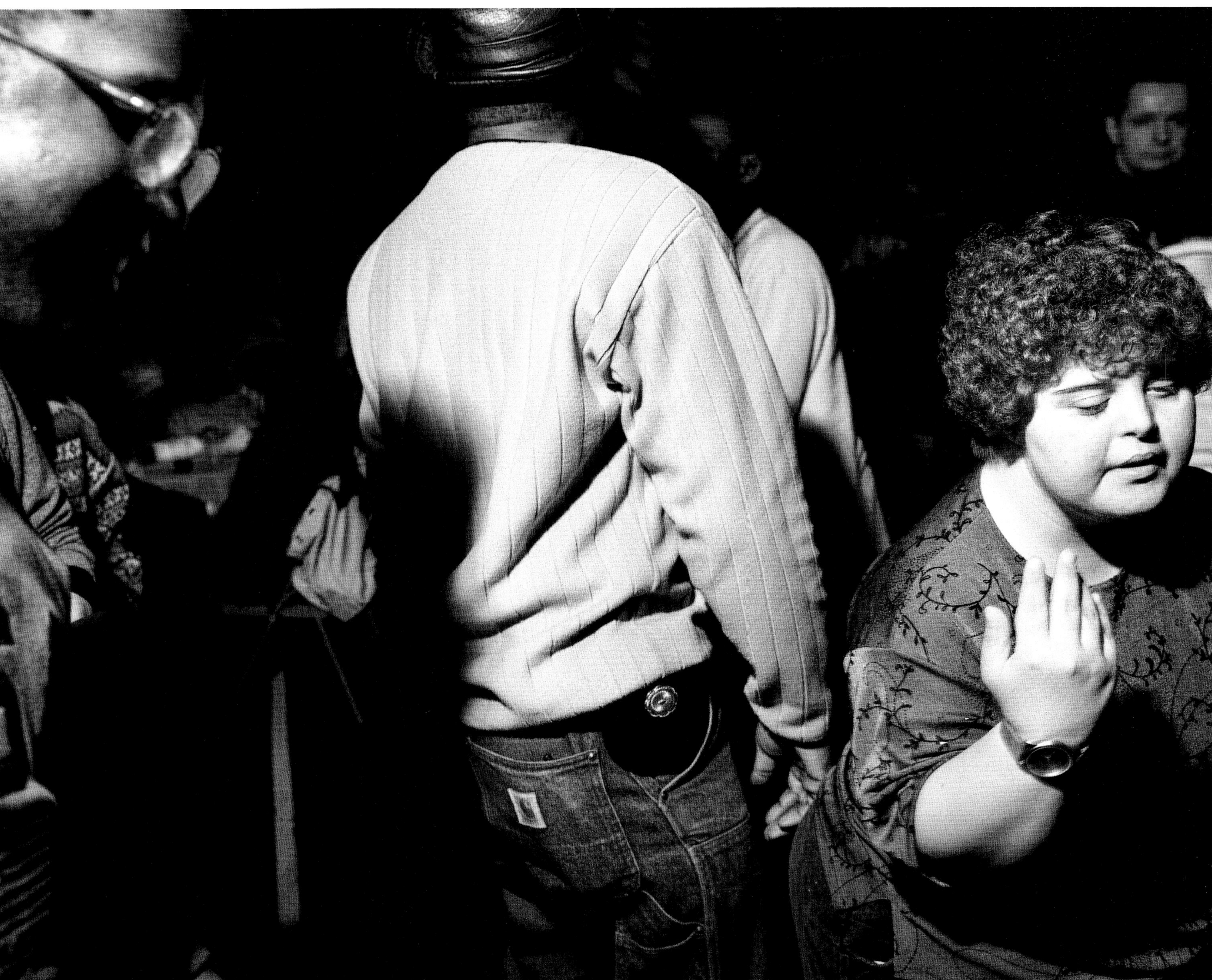

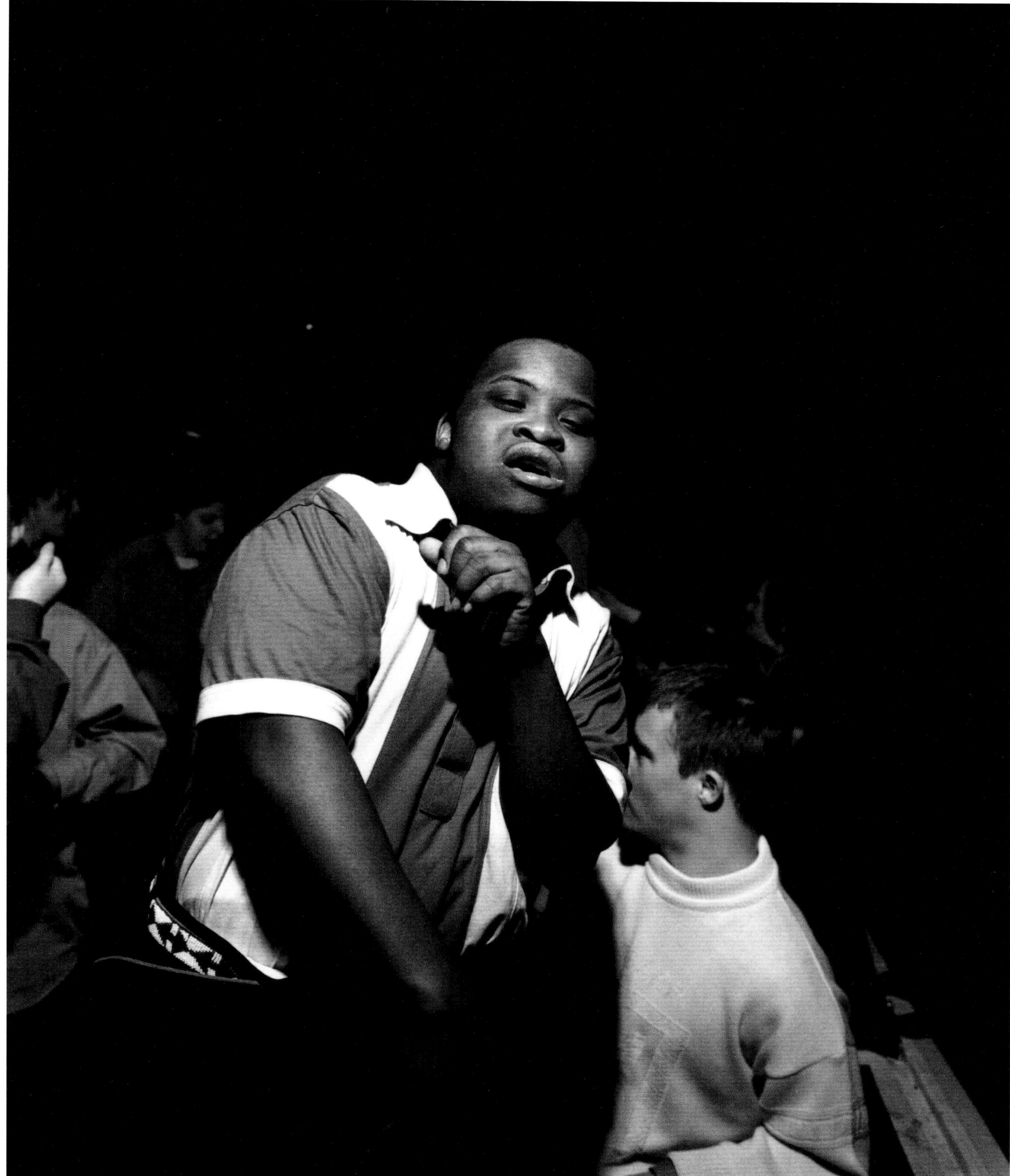

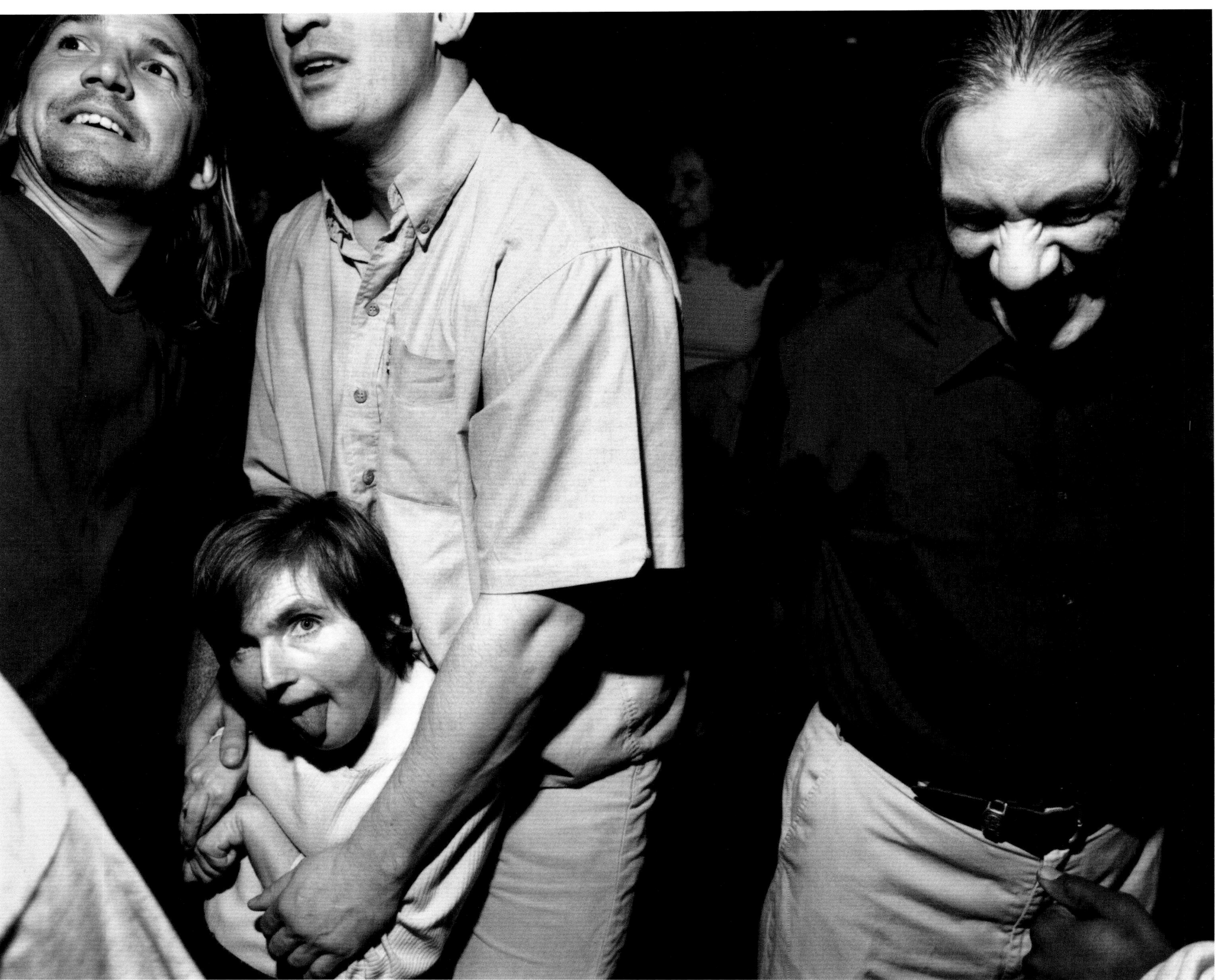

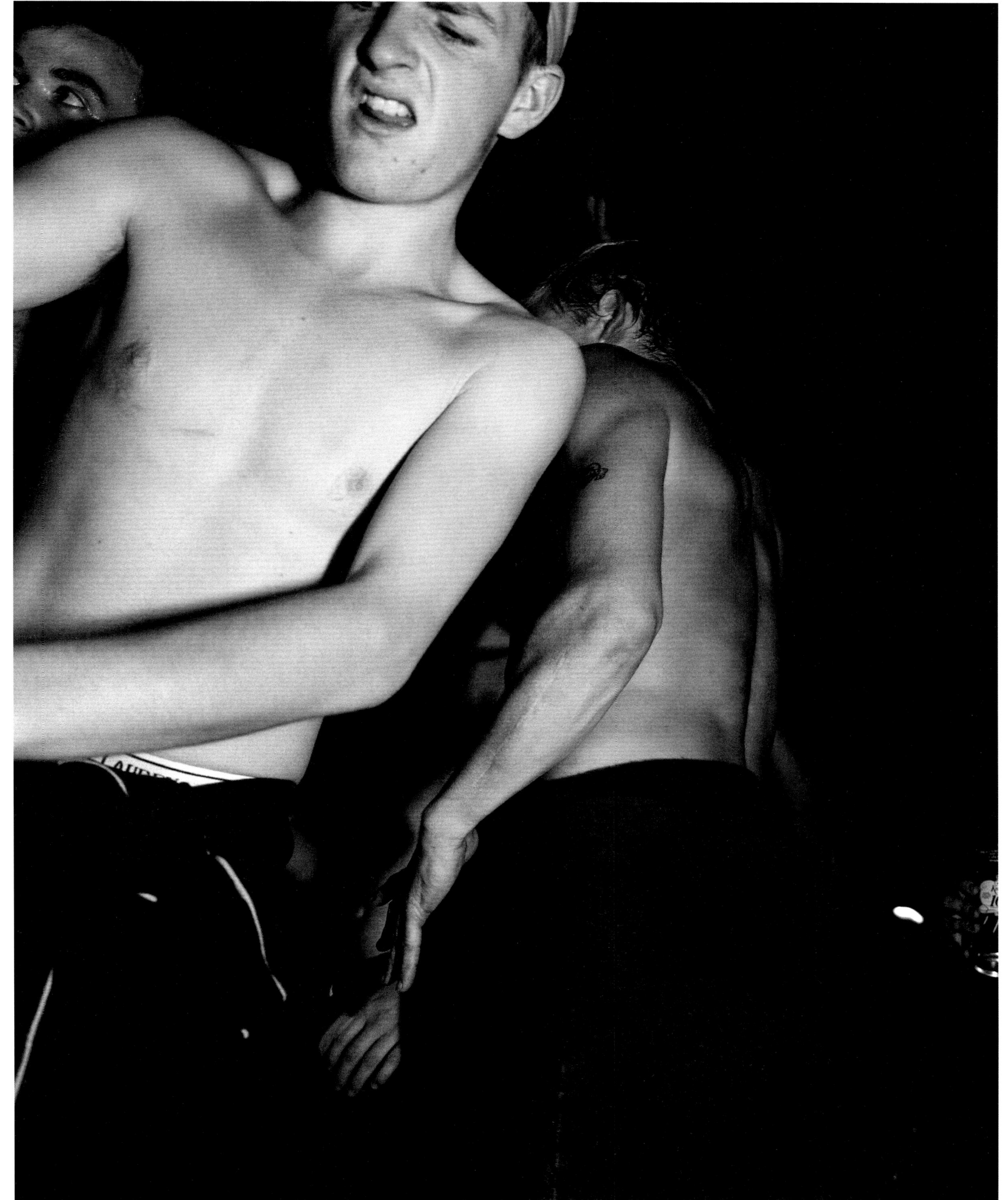

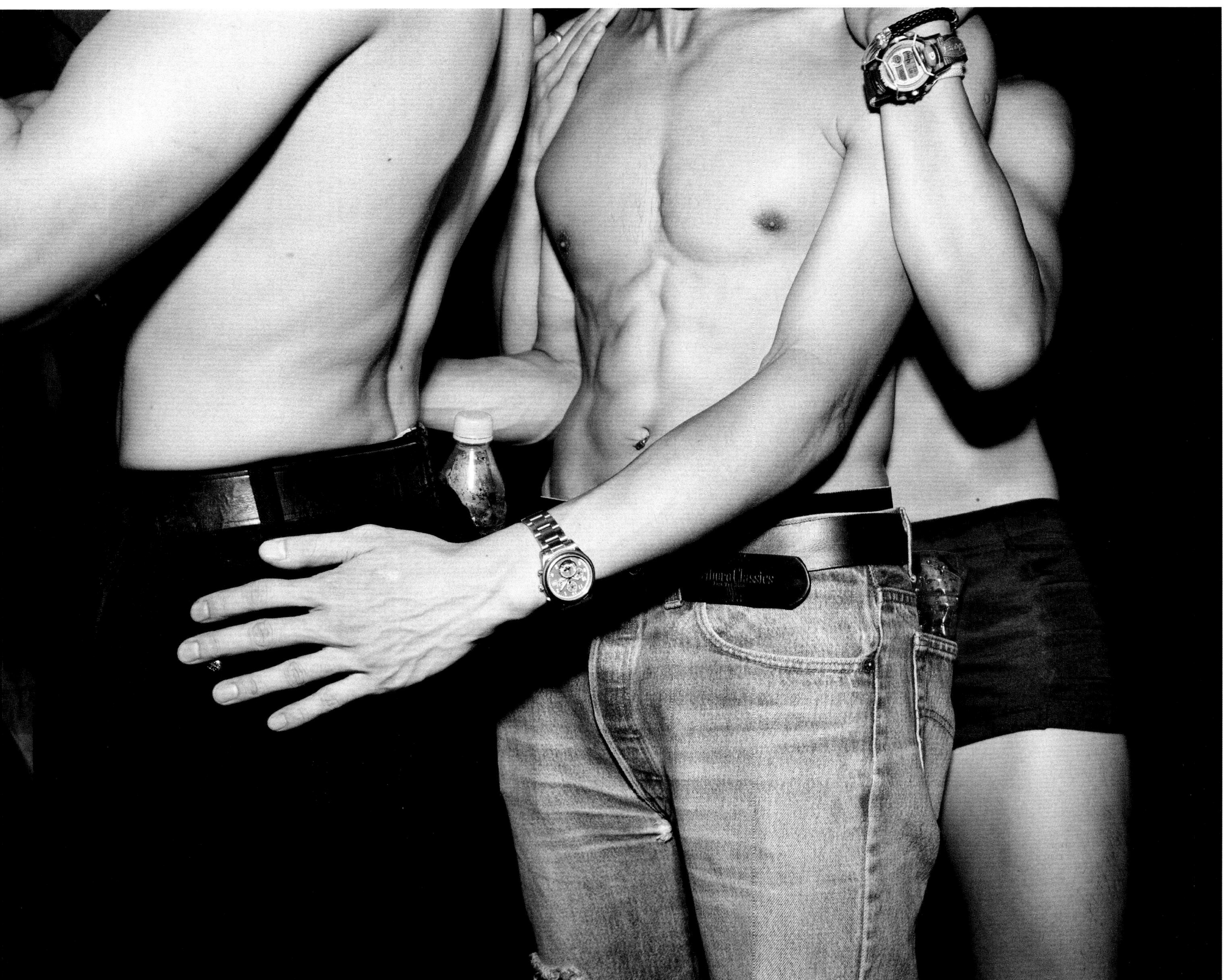
Classics

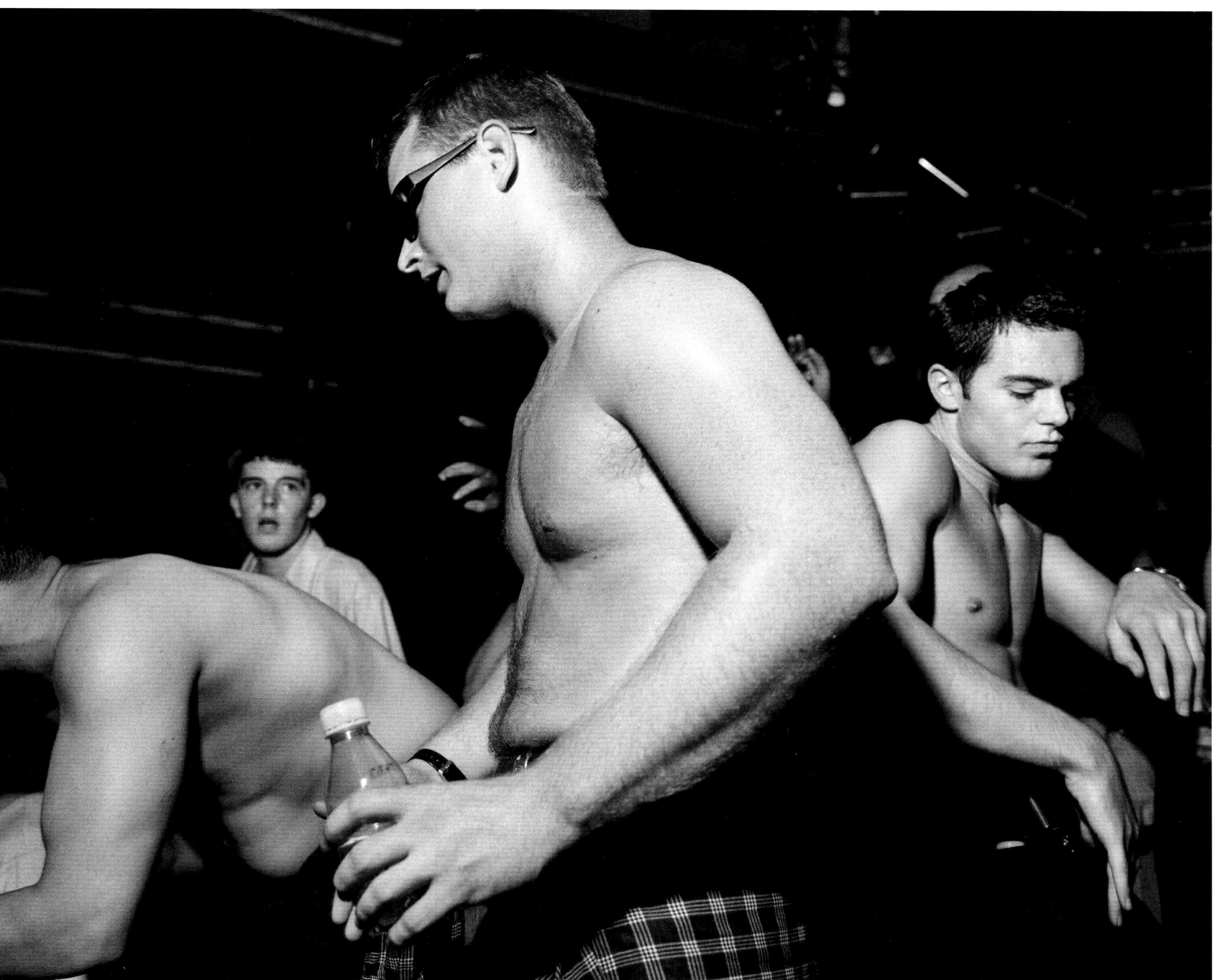

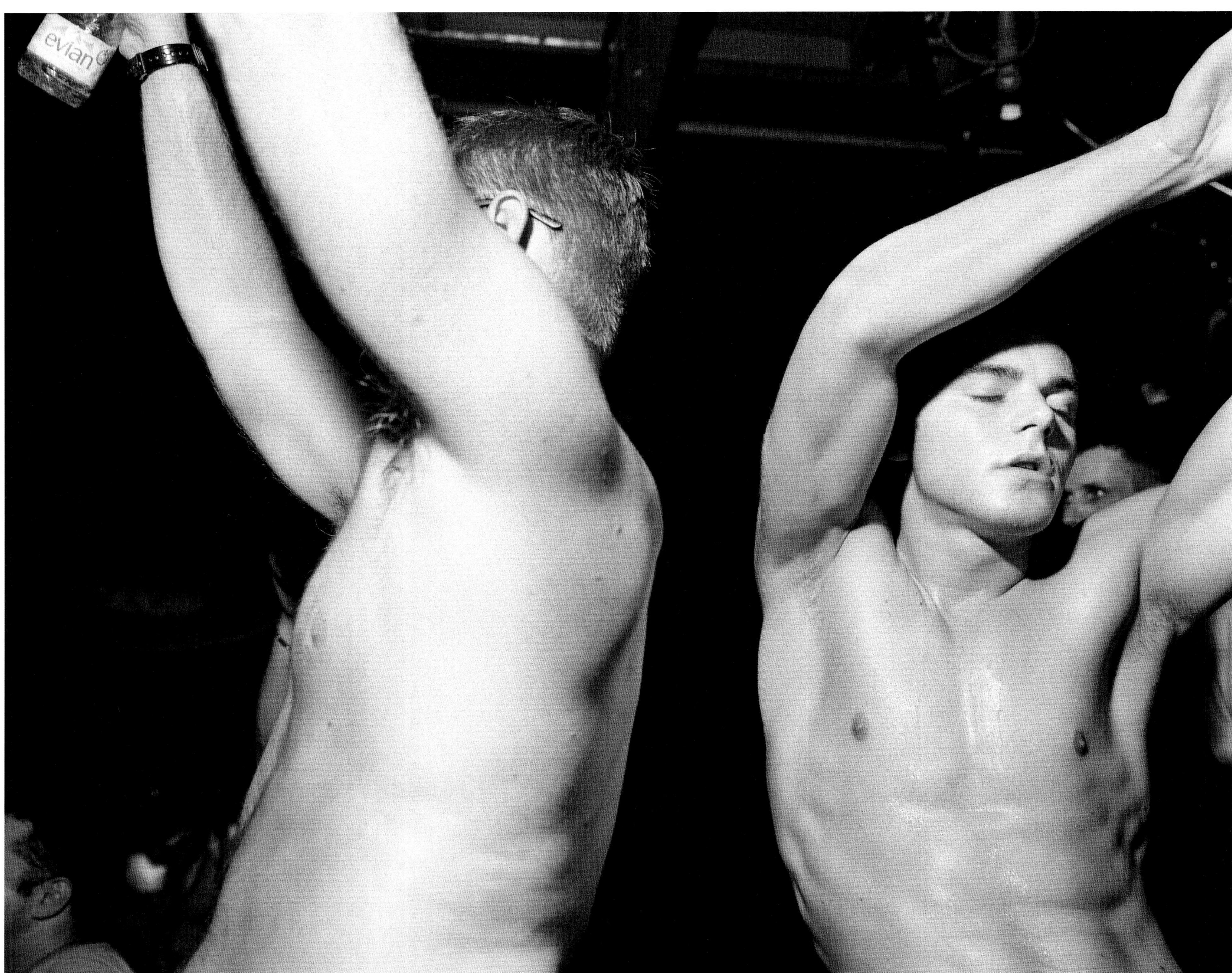
evian

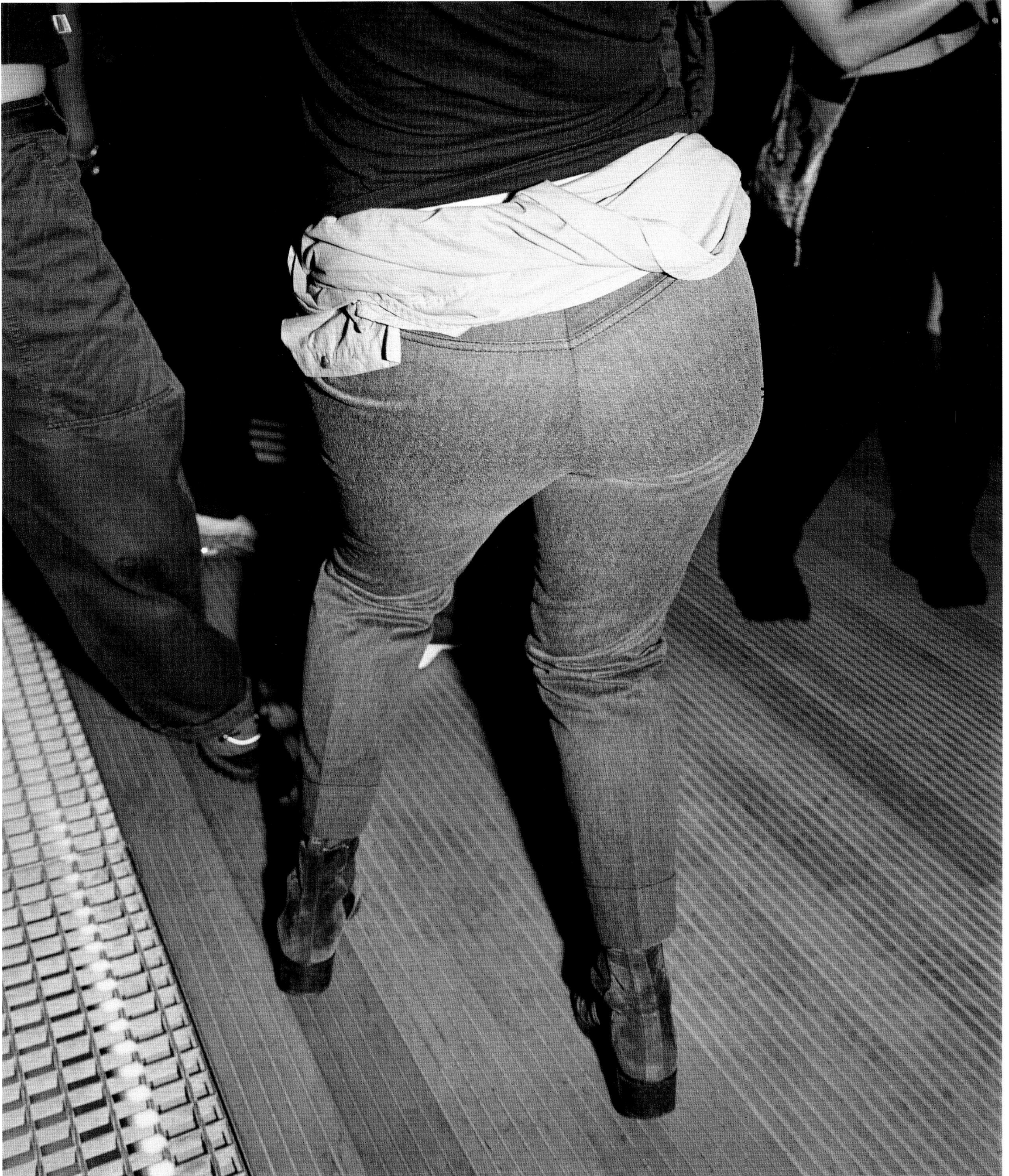

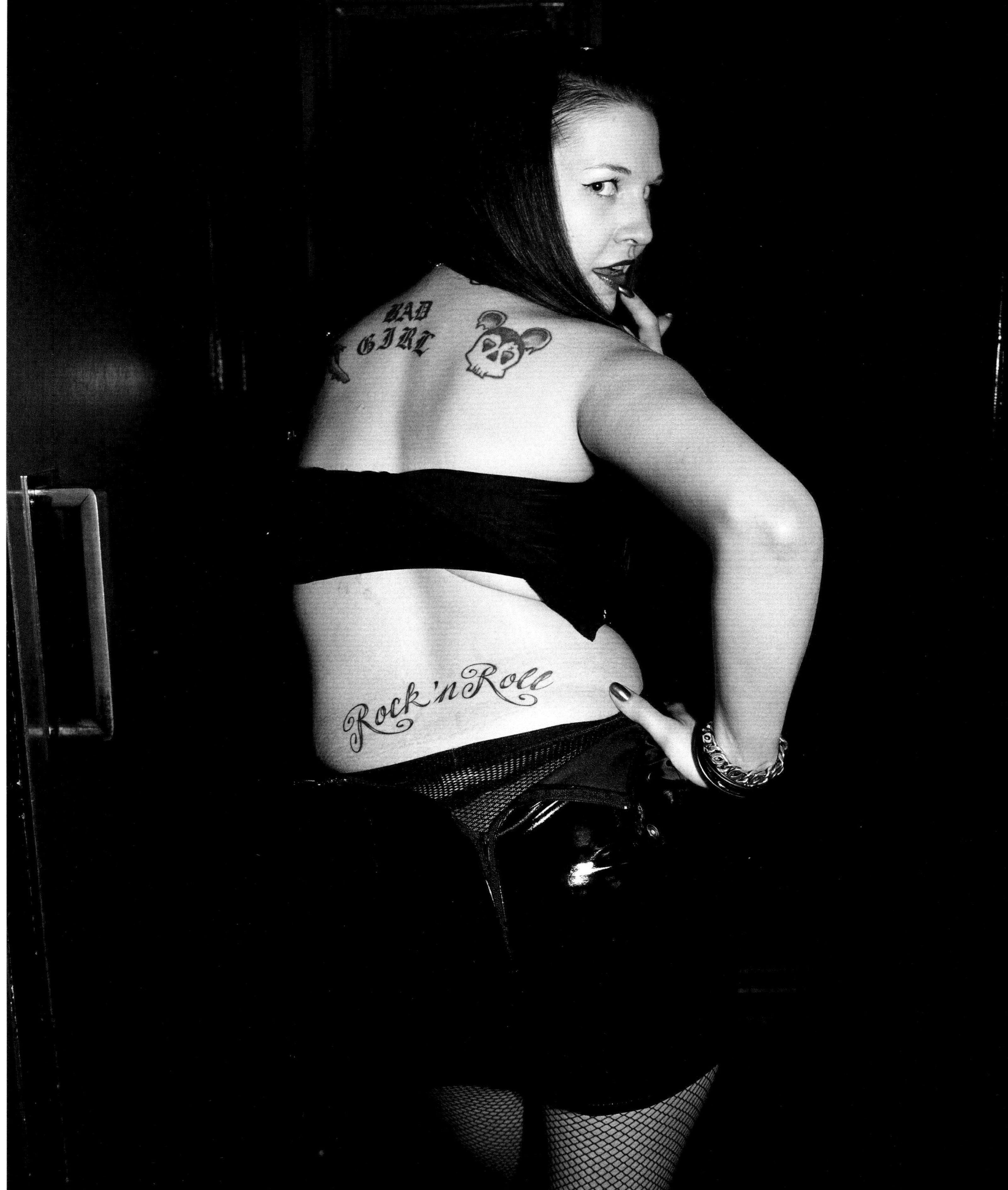
BAD
GIRL
Rock'n Roll

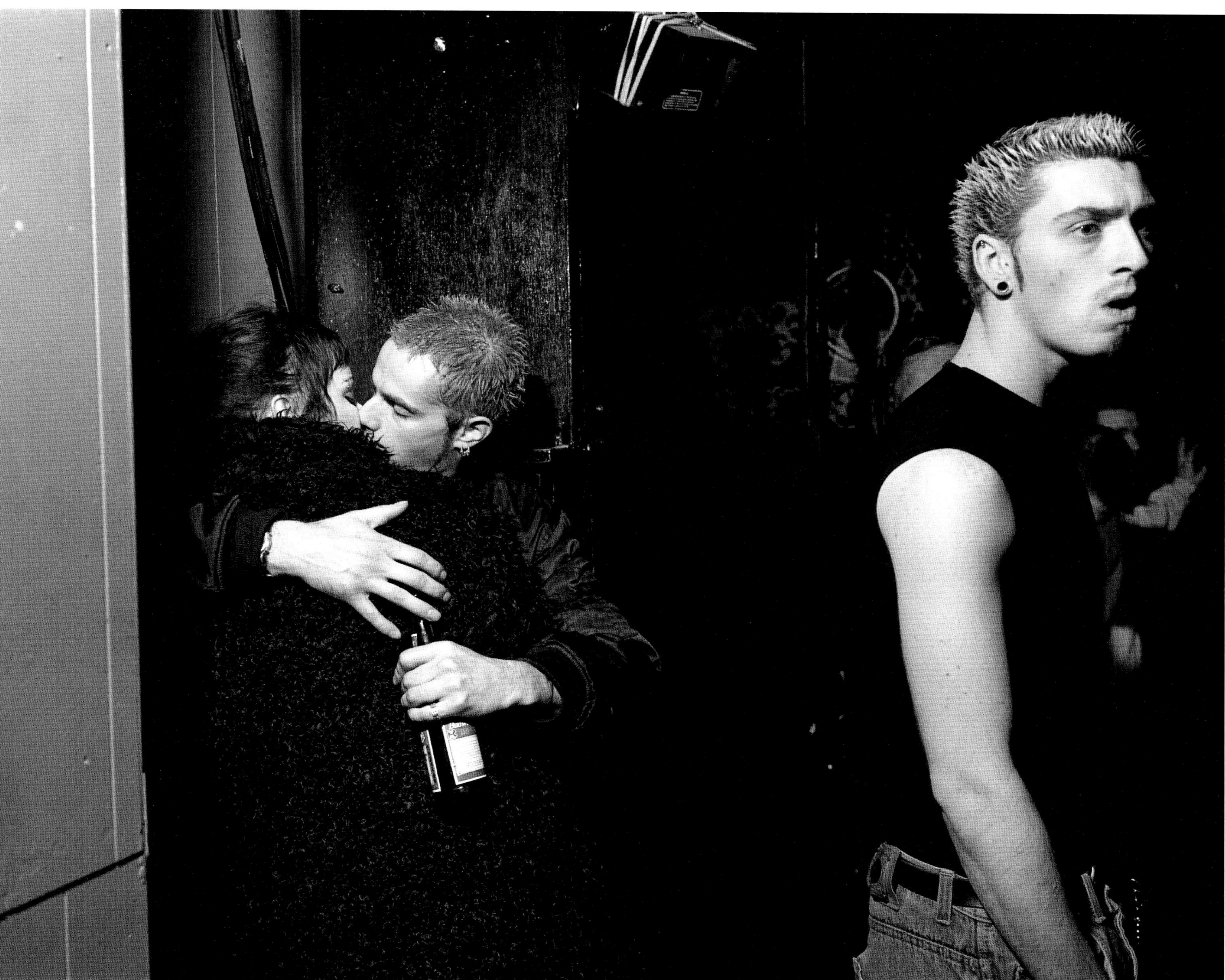

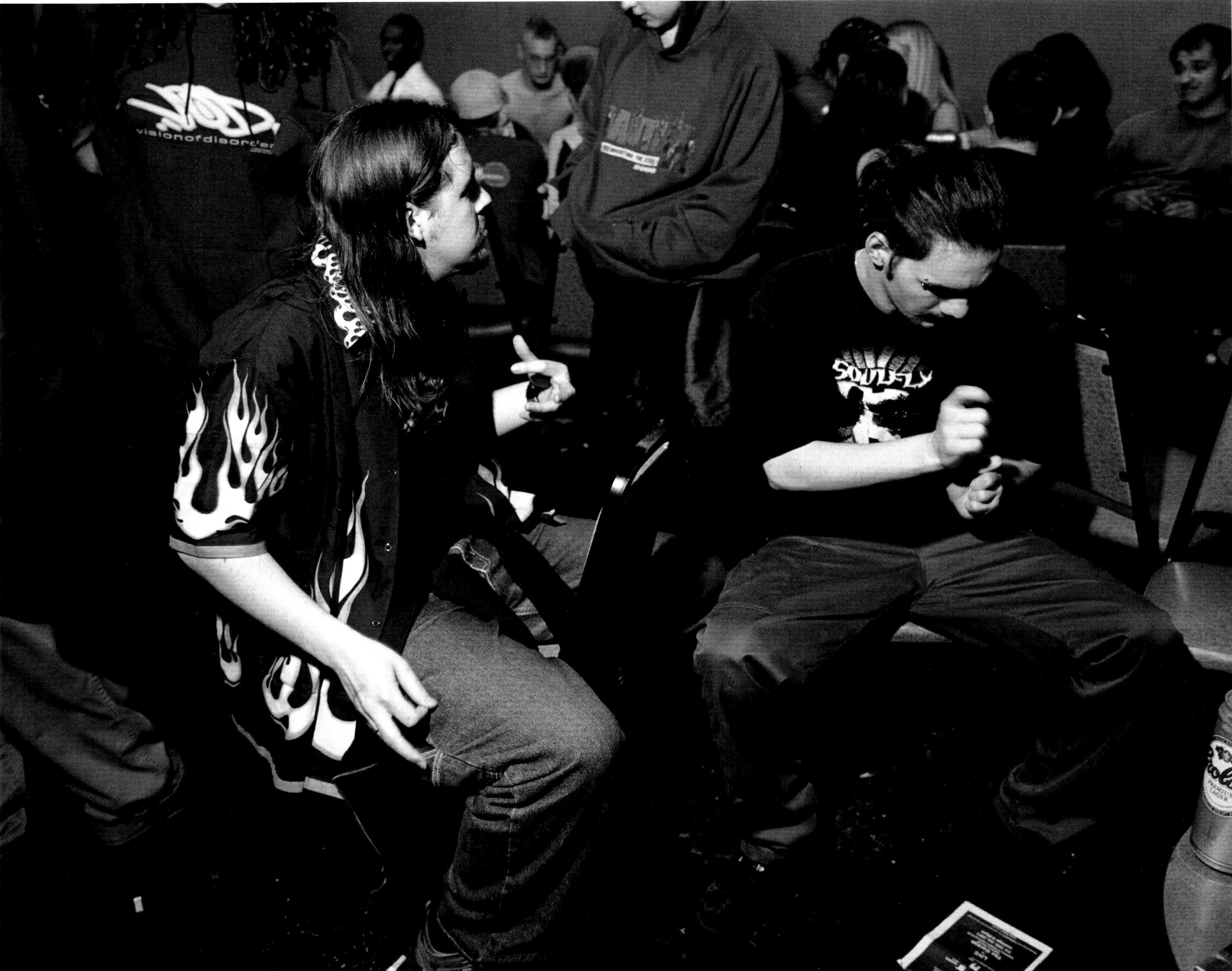
visionofdisorder
SOULFLY

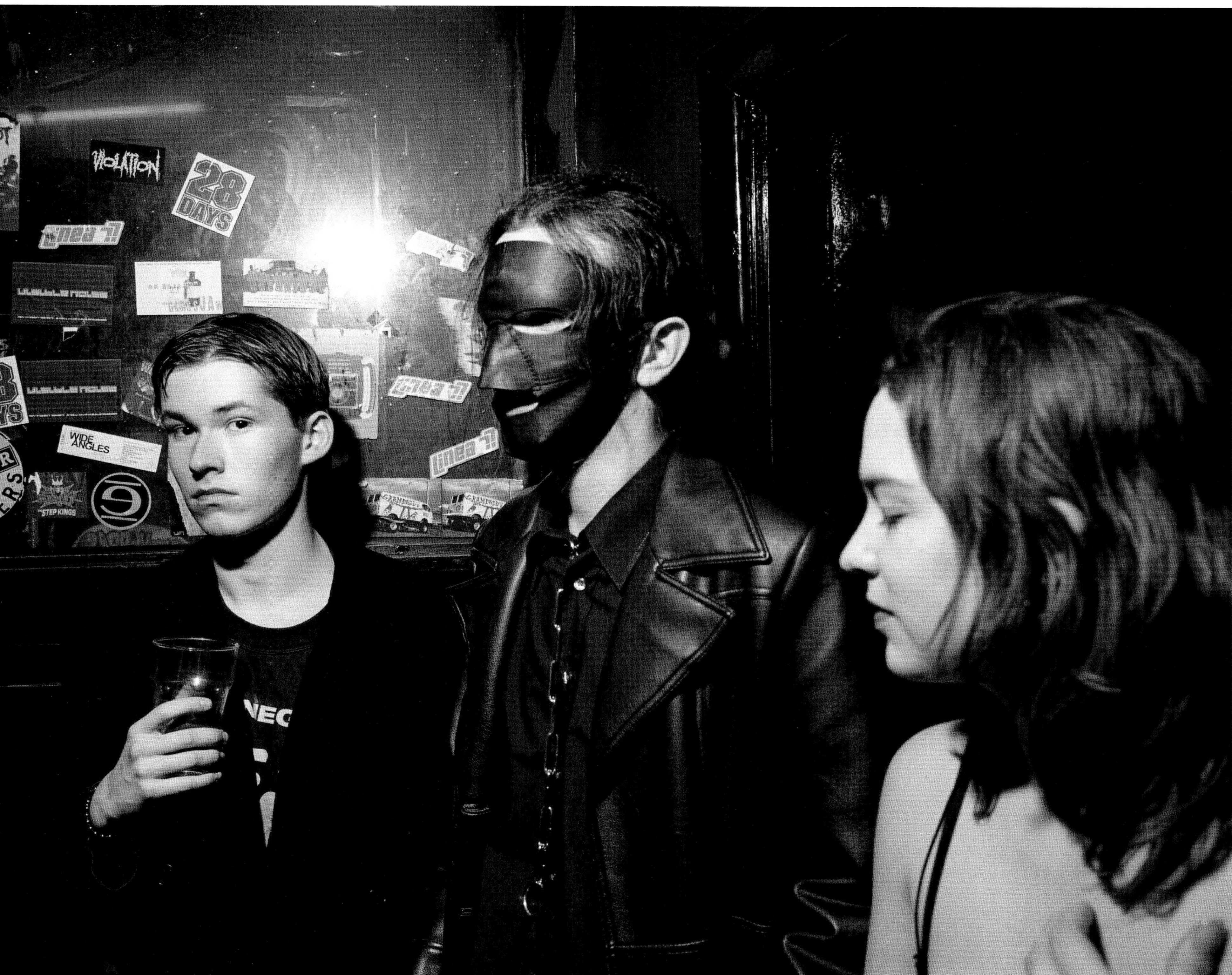
VIOLATION
28 DAYS
WIDE ANGLES
STEP KINGS

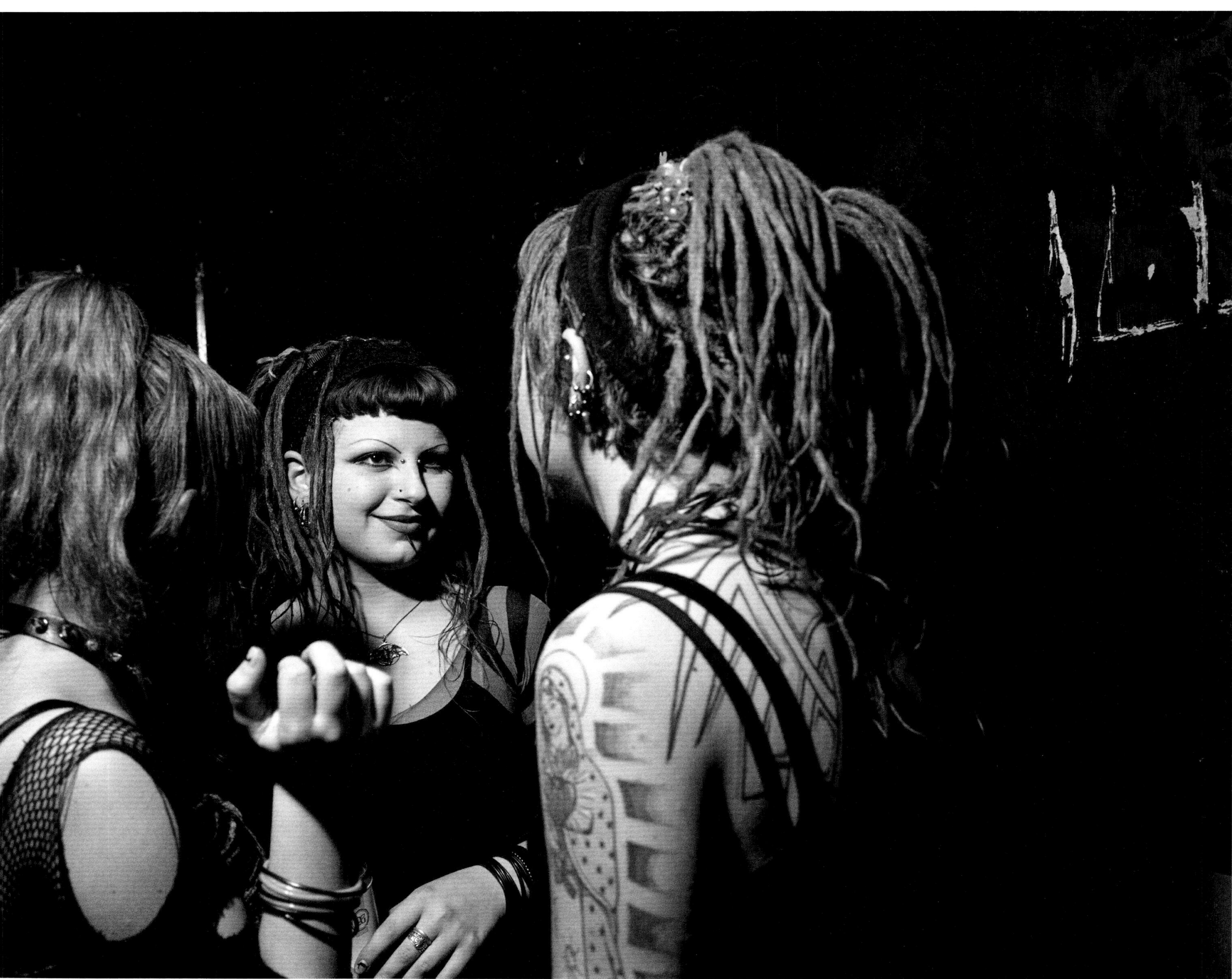

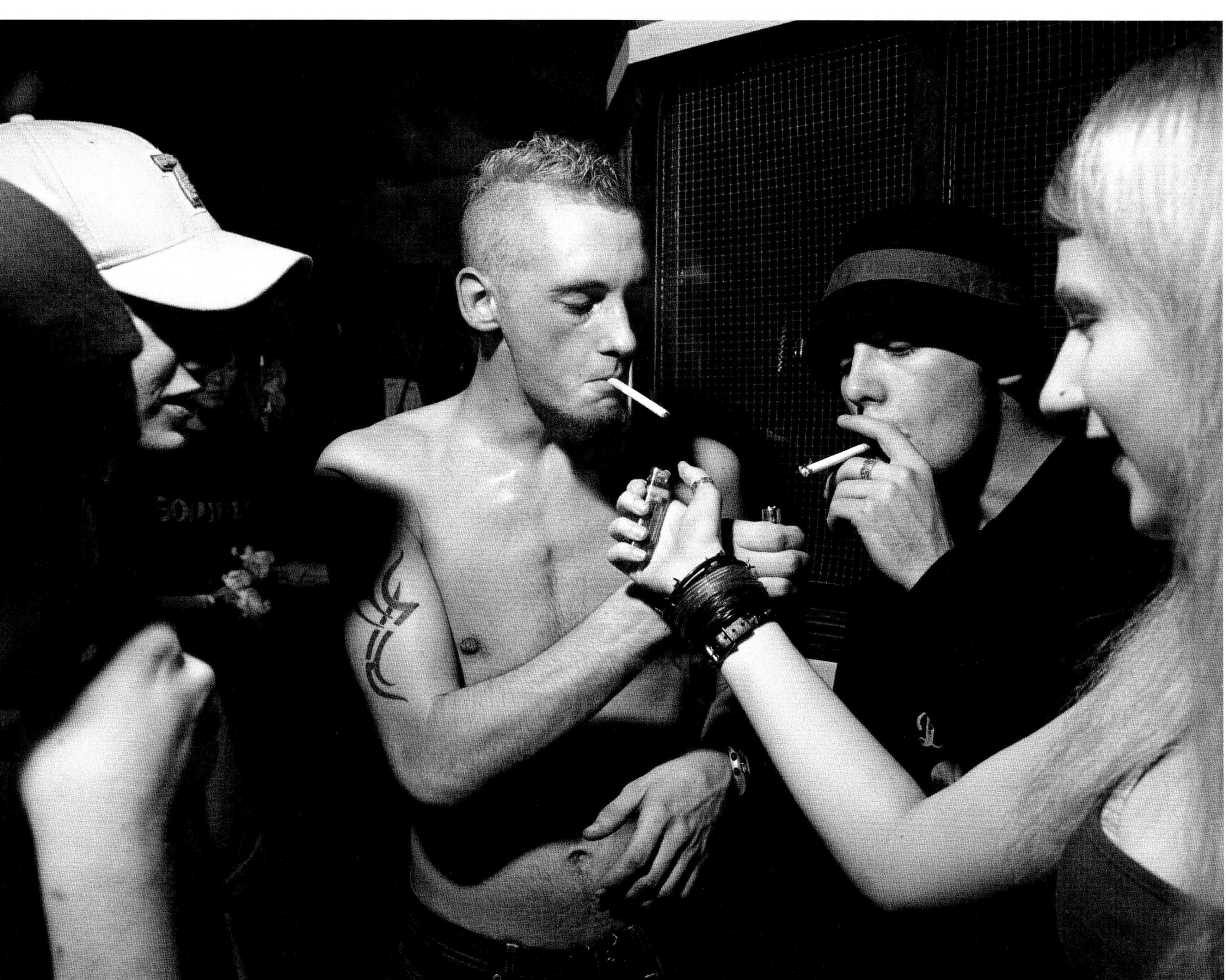

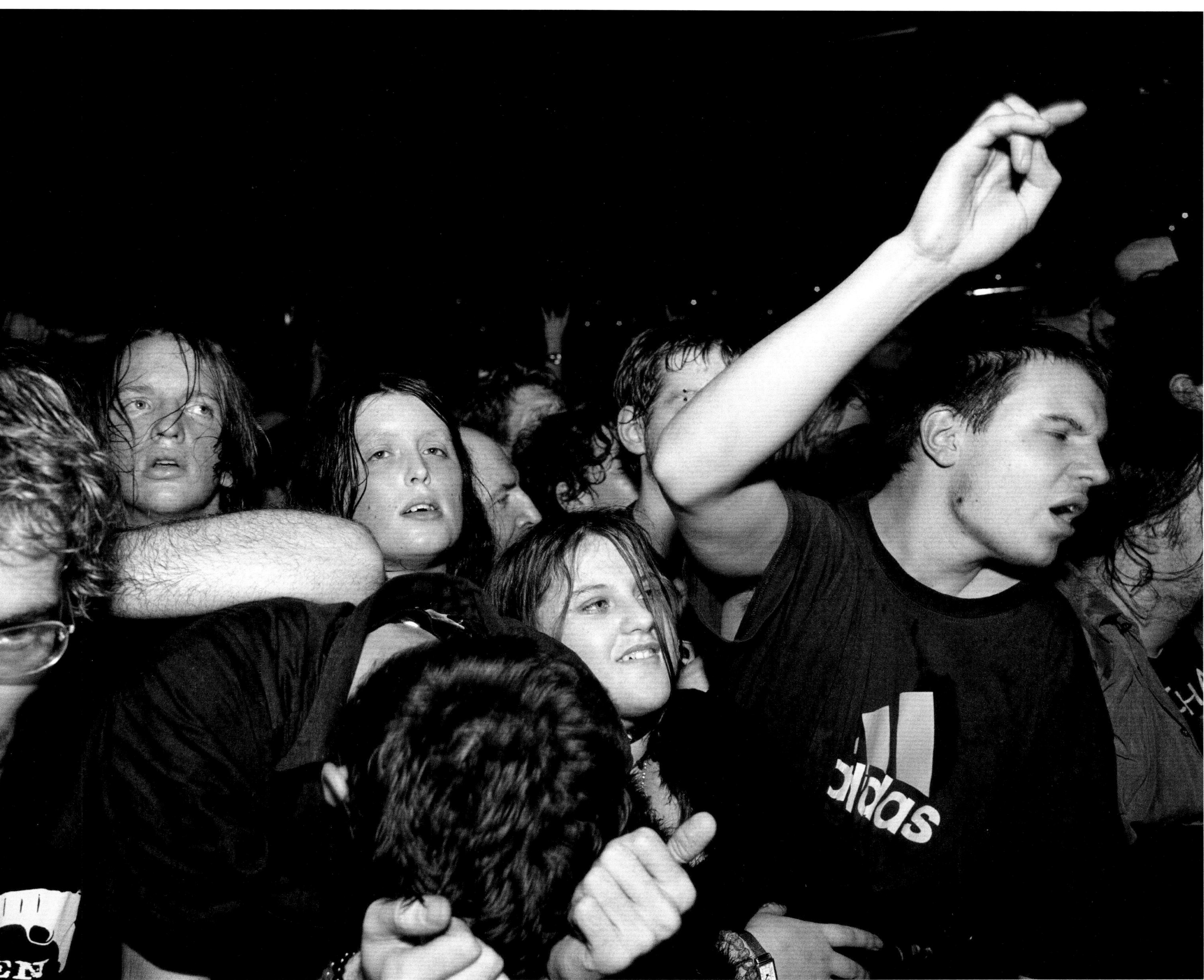

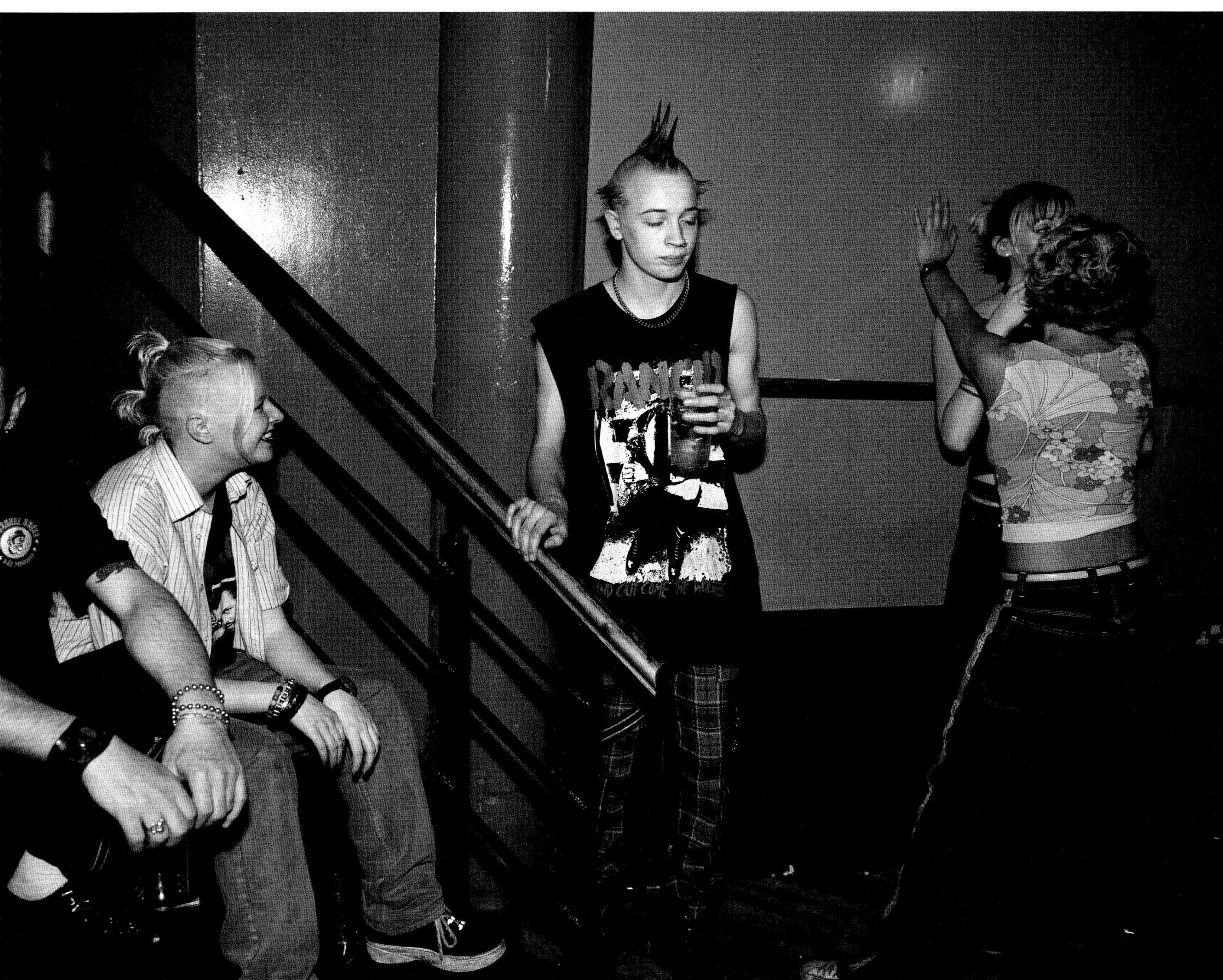
AND OUT COME THE WOLVES

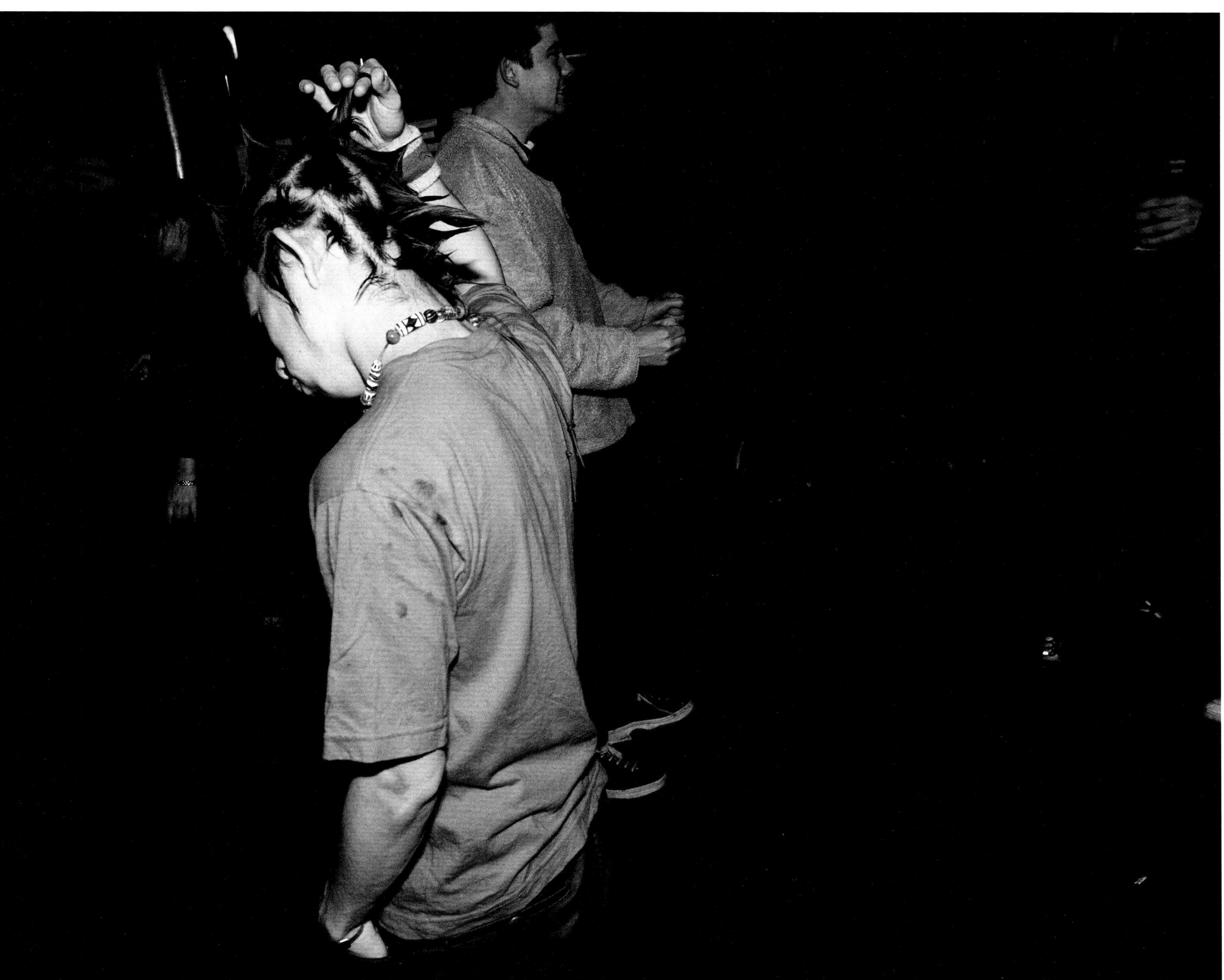

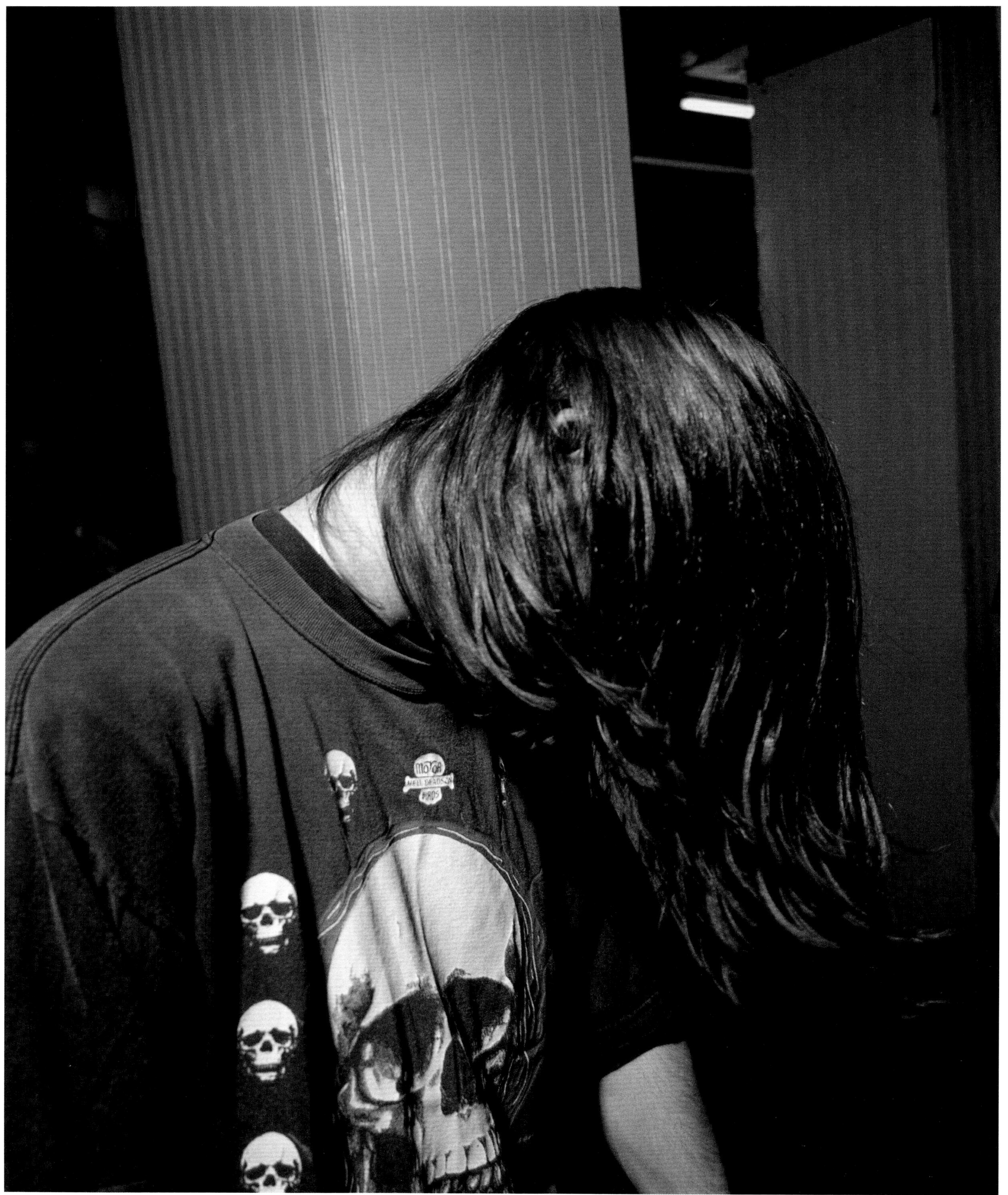

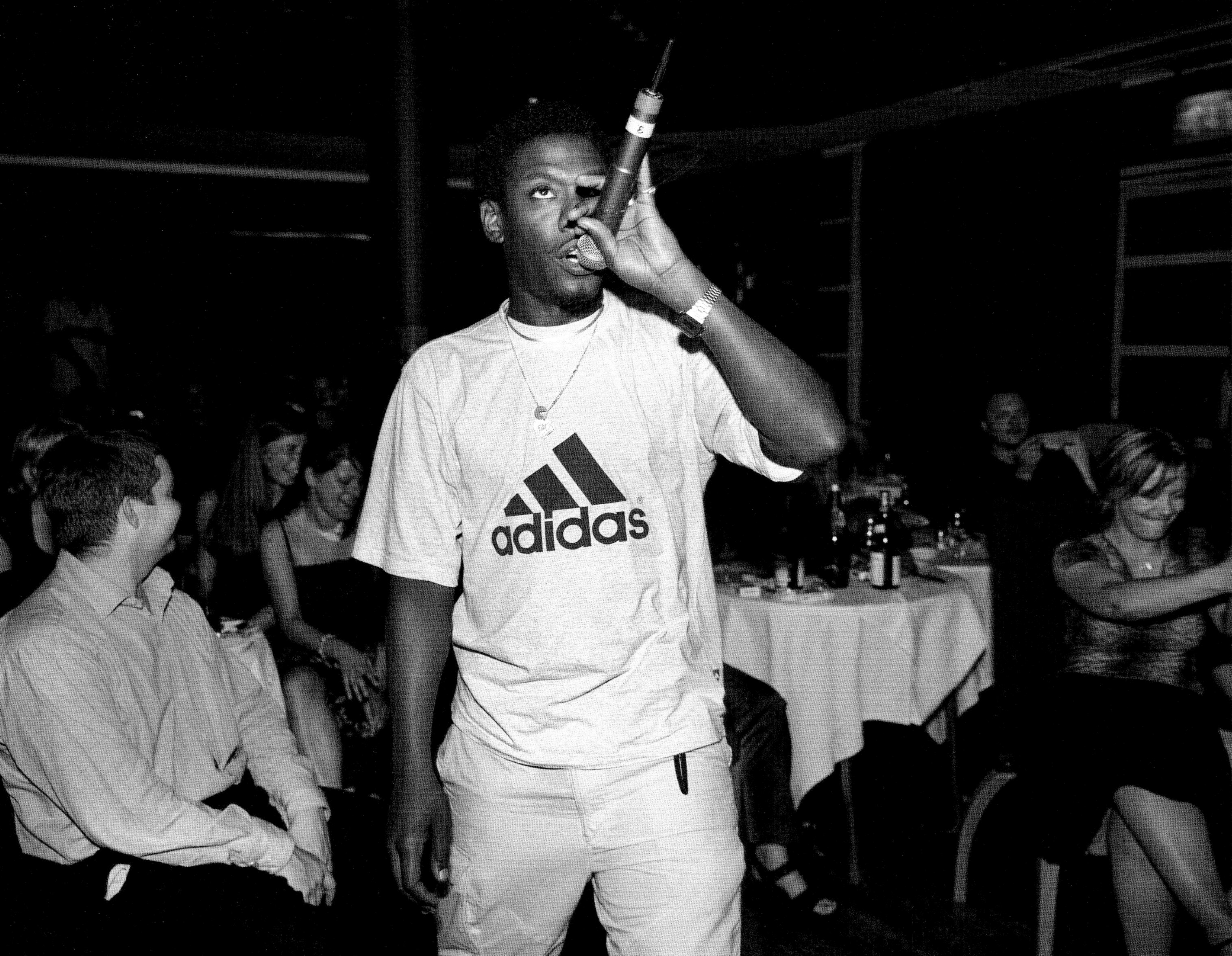
adidas

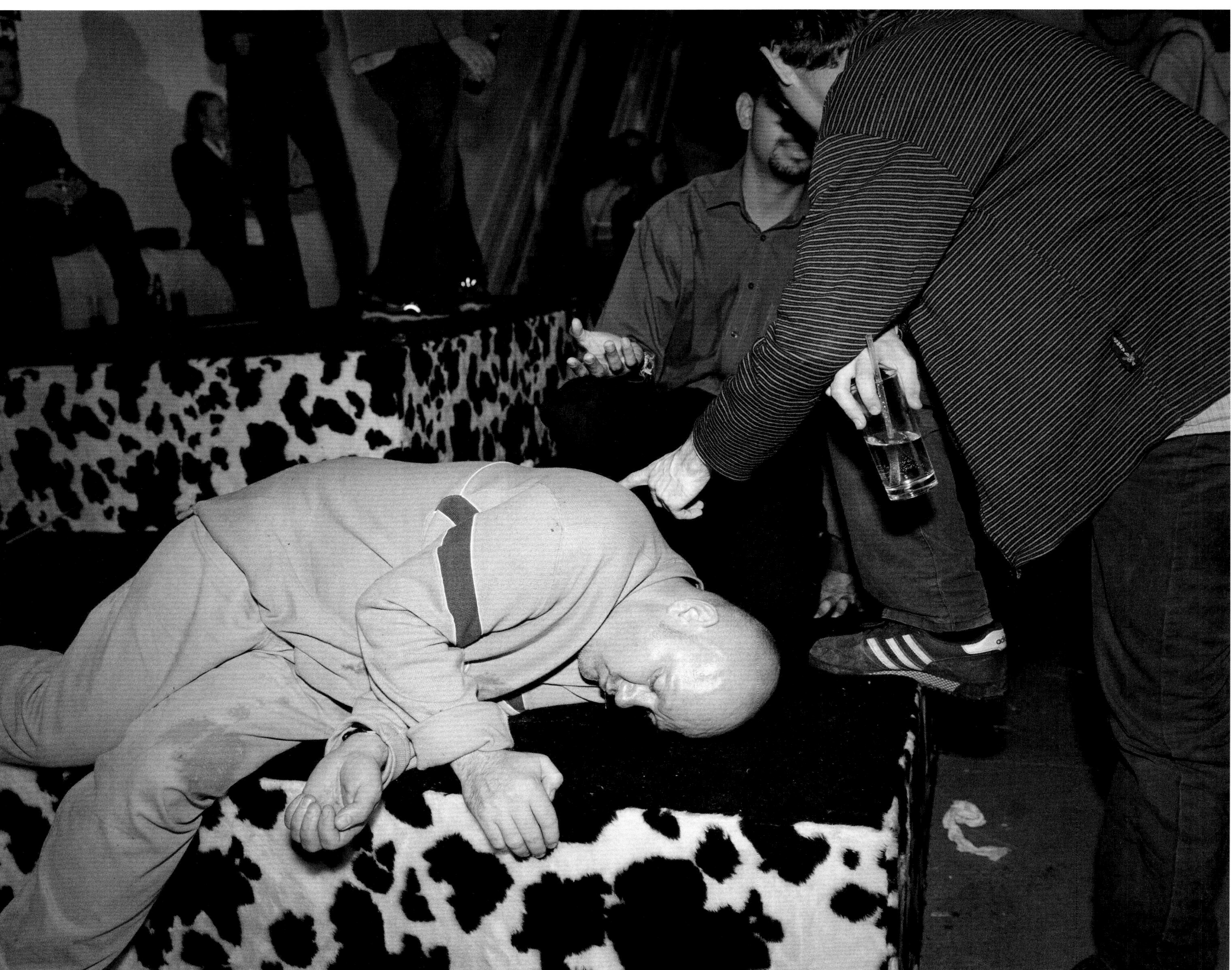

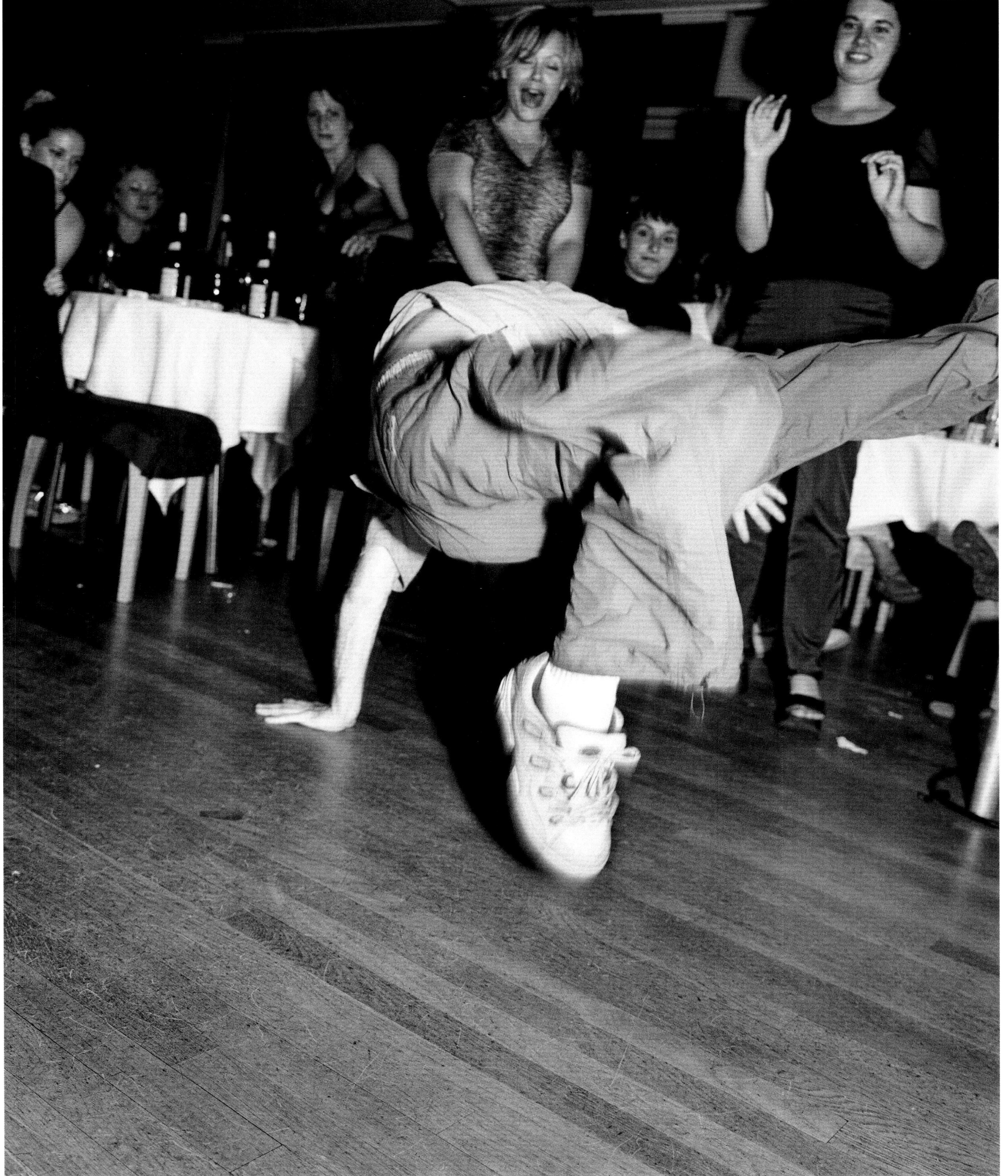

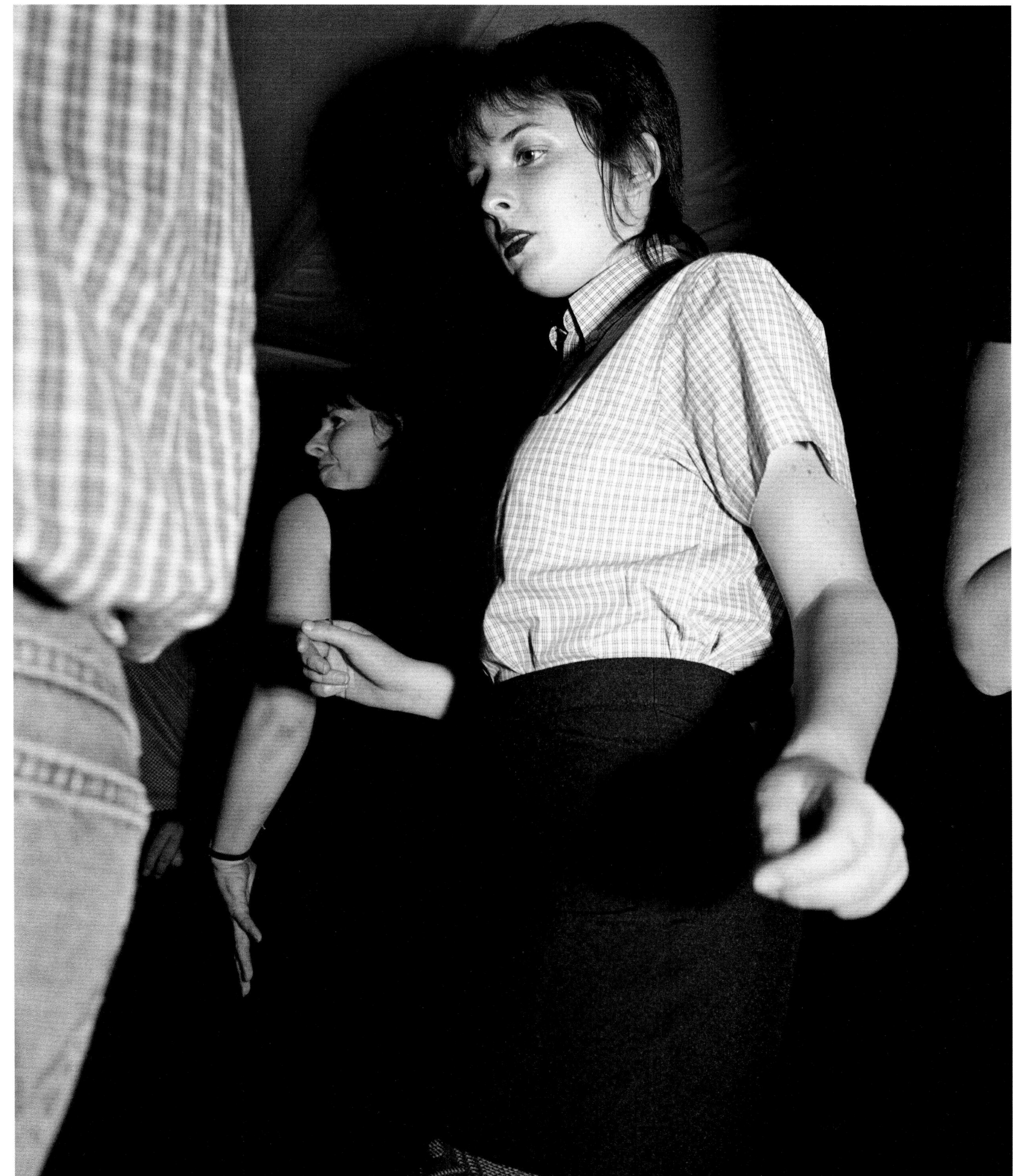

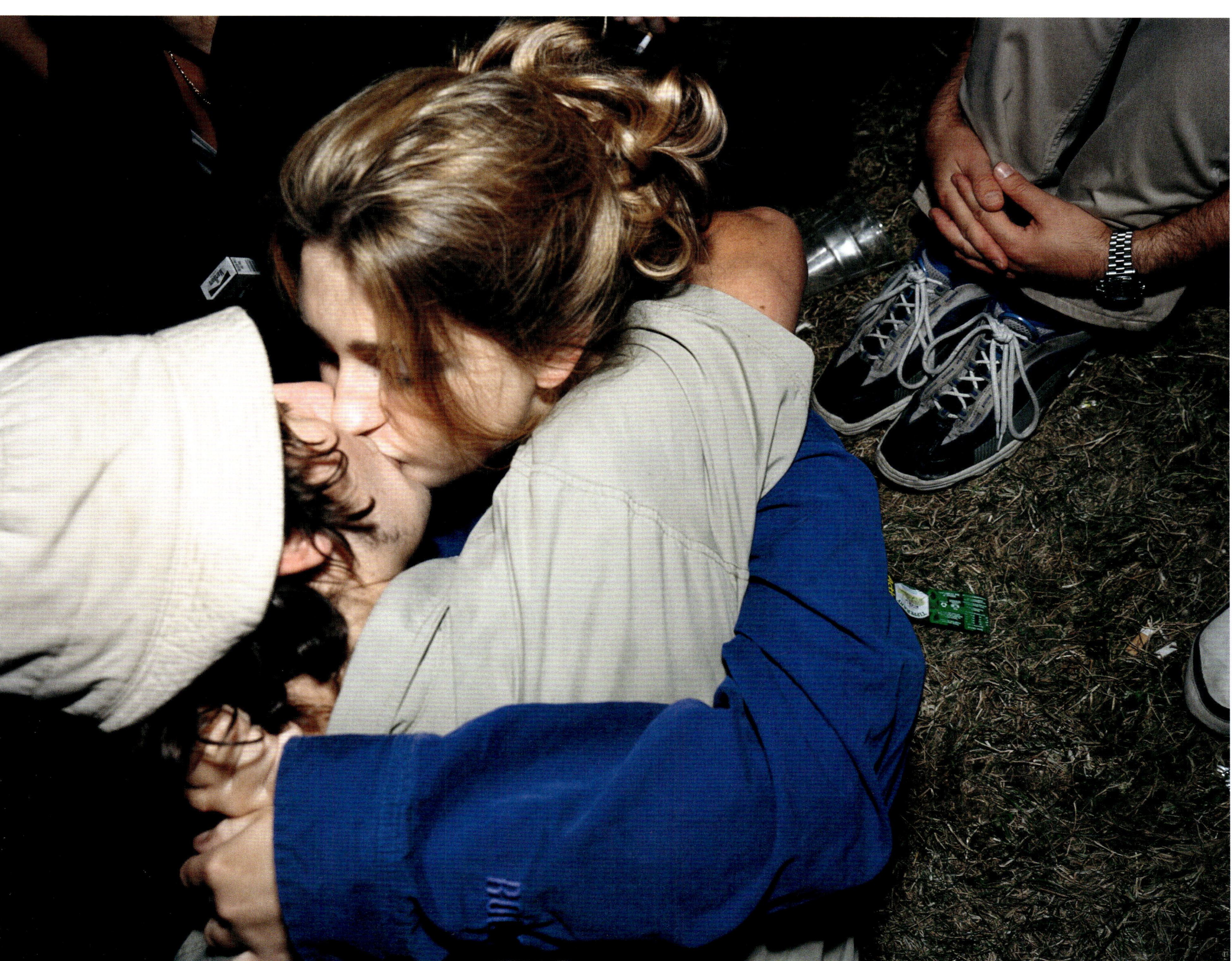

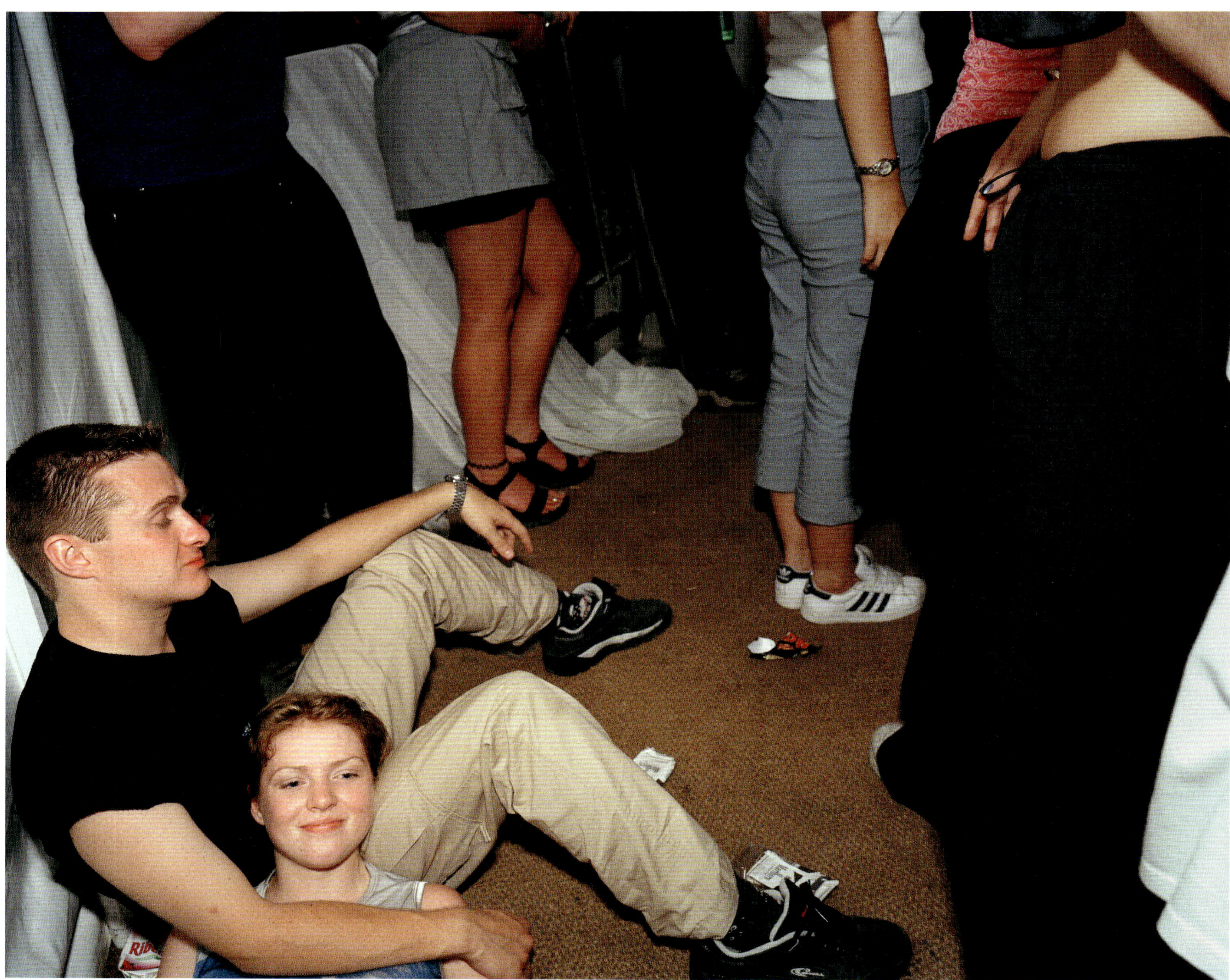

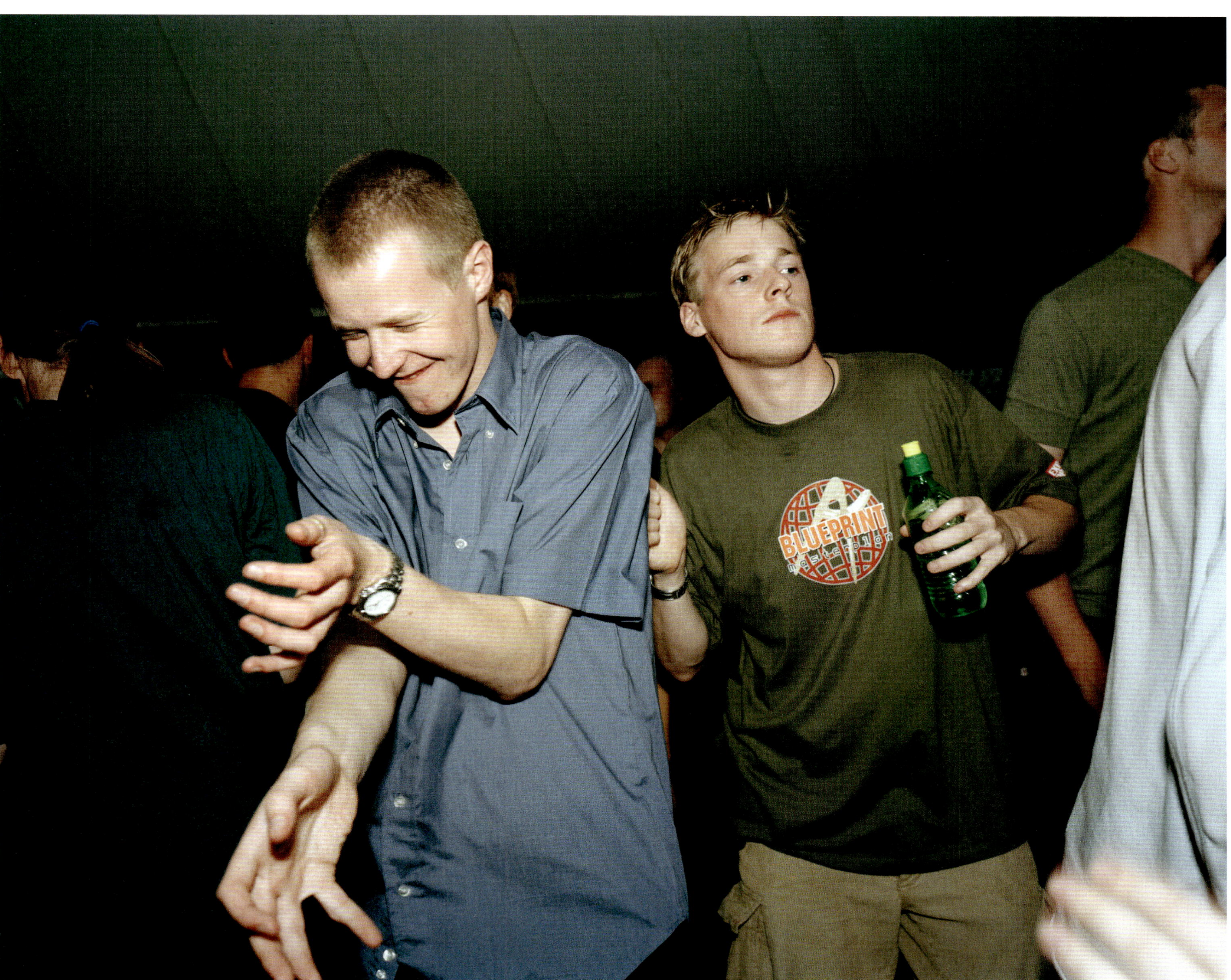
BLUEPRINT
masterplan

WHILE YOU WERE SLEEPING

Ewen Spencer in conversation with Justin Quirk

I first met Ewen Spencer in 1999 when I was working as the staff writer on Sleazenation, a small independent style magazine based in Shoreditch. The area was then in the process of transforming from a derelict post-industrial pocket of east London to the new creative centre of the Capital. Ewen was one of the regular photographers who worked across the title shooting portraits and documentary stories, but most notably contributing a series of stark, black and white images each month that accompanied the club listings in the back of the magazine. Made everywhere from run-down pubs and taxi ranks to suburban megaclubs and warehouse parties, these pictures were the antithesis of what club photography then looked like. As the first wave of superclubs opened in the capital, these instead showed a side of British life that was strange, absurd, vibrant, surreal and often very messy. The photographs from that time form the basis of this book and capture the last moments in London before life went online and digital culture took hold. It was a strange, exciting, cautiously optimistic time to be alive, and a lot of people overdid it a bit. Some of them are in these pictures **Justin Quirk, 2021**

Justin Quirk: So let's start with why we're talking today about these pictures.

Ewen Spencer: The reason really was just to try and jog my memory, I might be able to jog yours, I don't know. But the exercise really is not to be too nostalgic

Of course.

I speak to a lot of people who have a real kind of apprehension towards nostalgia. And it seems to be a common feeling amongst people of our age [laughs]. But I just like to think of it as an honest, factual series of pictures.

So let's go back to how this period of making pictures started.

These were a continuation of pictures that I'd made whilst I was at Brighton School of Art. I quickly realised that I can go off and make photographs in, say, a service station along the M4 and turn that into a photographic project – it's about a society, people being trapped in a little chasm for 20 minutes while they're having a break from the motorway, and all kinds of things are played out there. So as a photographer I found those places interesting.

There's a similarity with clubs I guess – quite strange, confined spaces, separate from normal life with their own rhythm. Were you shooting nightclubs as well then?

Yeah – while I was at Art School I was still going to Northern Soul all-nighters. But I realised that I should maybe start making photographs there – it was actually more interesting to me because it was something I loved. So I took those photographs from the all-nighters to Sleazenation magazine when I graduated. And that's when someone at the magazine said, 'Oh, you should go and make photographs of these other nightclub moments, these other subcultures'. And I was sent off with a bag of film to photograph these people and places.

So just to get a bit of context on time, that was '97, '98?

Yeah, that was '97 – I graduated in '97 and they were the first people I went to see because I really liked the magazine. And it felt like personal work that I was doing anyway, but it was to be published in a magazine.

Were you living in London at that point?

I was in Brighton, actually. I was living in Brighton in '97, '98. '99 I moved to London for about a year and then moved back again to Brighton

So where were you professionally at that point?

I was literally working for Sleazenation and that was it. Otherwise I'd occasionally pick up work at these contract publishers doing the magazines for inflights, or Virgin Trains or whatever. So there were those places that you could earn a living. You certainly couldn't earn a living working at Sleazenation. They'd cover your costs as it were in terms of film and processing, which was good because that's a great expense. You weren't getting paid much – but I was proud of them being in there. And it felt like a good place for my pictures to live because of the rest of the subject matter and

content in the magazine was very much aligned with how I was feeling, and the pictures made sense in there.

How did the connection with the magazine originally come about?

The office address was printed in the back, so I just went in – I'd sent in some promo cards of my Northern Soul pictures from my graduation show at Brighton and I'd targeted other specific creatives who I wanted to work with. They were up behind Kings Cross, so I just turned up and I remember bumping into (founding editor) Steve Beale in a similar way to you, and he's like, 'Oh, great, yeah, I think I know who you are', and he just took me through to see Steve Lazarides (photographic director).

Steve Lazarides recollected the Northern Soul pictures. He said, 'You know what? You should go out and make some pictures for us'. And it seemed logical – I targeted him and I got the response I wanted. He gave me a bag of Kodak 120 film in a see-through carrier, just pulled it out of a drawer.

How did you find him on that first meeting?

He was quite a verbose, charismatic individual… I mean, they all were, really, at that time. It's difficult to express, really, the sorts of people they were. They were quite extreme people to meet and be around. And I loved it, I thought it was brilliant, because they were pretty uncompromising.

I don't think I fully appreciated at the time that it was quite a strange environment to be working in.

Yeah, I was expecting something different – some people who were probably fashionable, sartorially, you know? But these guys didn't really give much of a shit for all of that. They were just very into stuff, they were into things. They were enthusiasts, they had opinions, it was exciting. It was good to be a part of.

One thing I think I was aware of even then was how little they seemed to be influenced by or bothered by what anyone else was doing.

I remember as the magazine grew momentum and notoriety and its visual identity, Steve Lazarides was approached by lots of established photographers and artists, and he knocked most of them back. He was like, 'I don't want to work with those people, we're making our own language', and it was that attitude. I was really impressed by that.

In terms of how you viewed your own work at that point, were you conscious of that new style emerging then?

I felt quite confident about the Northern Soul pictures, I was really happy with those – they made sense to me and I felt I had arrived somewhere technically. But I also realised that photographing something I was passionate about made more sense and the pictures were more successful if I was photographing something I was into and that related to me. And I think he understood that straight away.

Did you tend to hit the same clubs again and again or did you do somewhere once and then move on?

I would do probably two or three parties a night. Some of them would be things that Sleazenation had pre-arranged, because my pictures were used alongside a couple of other photographers to illustrate the listings pages. And the listings pages became quite infamous, because they were quite slanderous. They were pretty brutal. And to be perfectly honest, some of the clubs and parties deserved it.

What sort of places were around in that early Shoreditch period?

I was sent quite often to things like the 333 (on Old Street). That seemed to be somewhere that was very popular with a very small crowd of painfully hip people who were playing ironic heavy metal records and that sort of thing, which was quite good fun to photograph. But straight away I was wanting to try other things. My brother lived in Clapham, and so I would find myself back there late at night. I would do things like go to the local disco there, and I would literally blag my way in. They'd just let you in because you had a camera.

What was that like by comparison to Shoreditch?

It was a fucking dive, but it was great because that sort of place was full of just working-class people wanting a good night, who were just really shitfaced. To go somewhere where people were clubbing for a different reason was a release. And I understood and recognised that because of where I am from in Newcastle and how people like to party up there. They party

for the same reason, they partied because they want a release. They work hard and play hard.

What were you working with in terms of the camera back then?

It was a Mamiya 6. A rangefinder, sort of like a 'press camera' people used to call them. Which isn't factually correct, but that's what they were called.

What was your hit rate like at that point?

You'd get 12 exposures and my hit rate was pretty solid because I was quite conservative with my film. Because I didn't just want to go to the clubs that they'd arranged for me to go to. I wanted to go to other places and push the envelope a little bit, so I'd be quite thrifty with the film that he (Lazarides) gave me and I'd make sure that I could spread it across quite a few events in one evening. And I think that's maybe why I have such a range of places and scenes, and those different pockets of subcultural happenings. I'd even photograph on the night bus that I was on and in the street.

And in terms of how people were interacting with you, I think that would probably be one of the big differences if you went out and were shooting again now. I don't know if people are more or less self-conscious nowadays, but it wasn't a common thing to see someone walking around with a big, professional camera in those days

The camera was quite stealthy because, it was just entirely black with a little black handheld flashgun. I used to tape up the logo, which was white, so you couldn't see it. So I did work quite stealthily, but I manouvered myself around these places to make sure that I would be... Not invisible, but a part of what was going on. I think I made it clear that I wanted it to be a more observational moment, rather than people smiling at the camera in a fluffy bra like you saw in Ministry or Mixmag

That was the thing that hit me as a reader when I first picked up Sleazenation, because the clubbing photography I was used to at the time was the total opposite of what they were publishing.

At that particular institution in Brighton, we had very much come out of that school of British documentary photography, people like Chris Killip and Graham Smith. My lecturers were Paul Reas and Mark Power, who were both at the time very established – Paul's a very well-regarded educator, went onto the University of Wales to teach and become head of course there, and Mark Power became a member of Magnum. And they were very much steeped in that tradition of documentary. When we arrived there the Sunday Times Magazine idea of a heroic figure in photography was dwindling. Our generation probably didn't like the idea of 'I'm the guy going off to war,' anyway. We were taught to look at what's around you in your immediate surroundings. And I was very interested with that idea. 'What did you love?', 'What was your world'? And therefore it became a reflection of you, it became autobiographical.

And I guess those worlds of nightlife were completely familiar to you at that point.

They were to all of us at that time because we'd just experienced the late '80s and early '90s, so that was all about self-expression through clubbing and that acknowledgement of one another's appearance – the sartorial codes, how they nodded to a taste in music, and what you might be into. All those things were more important, I guess, to us as students going through that degree course, rather than being an 'heroic' type of photographer or artist of some kind.

I think there's a perception of the late '90s that there was a lot of euphoria and optimism. I remember that period fondly myself, but looking at those photos, there's something quite melancholic about a lot of them. You often pick out someone iso ated in a crowd, and there's something quite dingy about the surroundings – I forgot how rundown London was. What's your memory of that time?

I think people were having a lot of fun at a time when there wasn't perhaps an awful lot available to them. And if you put that through the prism of today, things can certainly be more clinical and sanitised, a lot safer. At that time people were still making nightlife out of areas that had been disused or forgotten, so the environments were pretty grubby. And it might be a room above a pub somewhere, that has become a popular spot for about 250 people every fortnight. And that becomes a destination for those people. And it grows. And there's little moments where it's growing and the popularity is just going sky-high. And what happens is you have people in these dingy little places – that aren't intended for that kind of capacity or concentration of people – and what you get, I guess, is an overflow. And at the time you had a lot of people really going hard on being quite hedonistic, taking a lot of pills, coke was becoming hugely popular at that time.

Was finding people in that state significant for the pictures do you think?

I wasn't always looking for wasted people, I was looking for characters. People that would be standing out, because you're going to get good pictures with those people. And people gravitate towards those people in social situations. You're looking for the big characters – it might be three girls that are having the best night ever and you just start working around them in terms of pictures. When they condone what you're doing, then the rest of the place gathers around. Sometimes it'd be about photographing the hardest-looking kid in there. Or you photograph DJ Spoony behind the decks or a kid MCing, and then everyone's like, 'Oh, he's down with the MC, that's fine'.

What do you think it is that dates the images? Were there things that surprised you looking back at them, things you'd forgotten or things you saw emerging out of them that you weren't aware of at the time?

There's no mobile phones. Smoking cigs. Massive variety in what people are drinking and some instances where you don't see any drinking going on. A lot more explicit necking, which I don't think you see as much now because people are more conscious that they're going to be photographed and immediately put onto social media of some description and humiliated through that. Drunken embraces were, I think, more commonplace. And I think visually that's something that's really lovely, because people feel a loss of inhibition and feel comfortable to just be more demonstrative in public. Where now, I think people are more wrapped up and too self-conscious.

In terms of the project now, what was the impulse for collecting these images together? Is it a natural process of archiving or was there something that made you go back to them now?

We almost lost the archive at one point – It started to deteriorate and I had to get it rescued and backed up after a technical issue with a hard drive. So I did that during lockdown and it's all fine now, it's all healthy and safe. But I just started to go through everything and I

realised that there was this work that I'd always thought about from the very early days. And I started to look through them and consider them while I was working with my son, Kuba, and he was looking through and finding them really amusing. He was asking a little bit about what time this was, when this was occurring, these pictures, where they were made etc, all these questions. And I said, 'Well, while you were sleeping, you know? You were a little baby asleep in Brighton and I was coming back and spending the following day with you.' And so I think he found that also quite amusing – because obviously first and foremost he just sees me as his dad. But then there's this other side, which is this guy that goes into these strange places, photographing people that are probably a lot like him, really.

When you look back at them, how did that chime with what your son saw in them? What did he take from them?

People having fun, people being free. That's what he sees. He sees them as positive and celebratory images – which is how I see them. And hopefully, I think, without my influence, he was very much, like, 'Wow, look at that, that looks like an amazing time to be alive'.

Going back to Sleazenation, for such a tiny magazine, it feels like it formed its own style that has been very influential since. If you look at so many magazines now, I feel like you can trace back their visual language to that time. Is that overstating it, do you think?

Not at all, I think the language of Sleazenation at that time was unapologetically British and it was all about British values, there was a great pride in that as well. These photos, and the work that other contributors like Thom Murphy, Alasdair McLellan or Amber Rowlands were doing was very British. Obviously that's where they were from and that's what they knew, but they were definitely discussing their experience and that was clear visually. Whereas with other magazines at the time you would often have a kind of pseudo-American influence, or a Japanese influence, or this idea of a slightly detached European style etc. But in the main what we were doing at Sleaze was very British. It was a love of a very British, very working-class culture, and a play on that.

In terms of bookending that project, when did that work in the clubs come to an end?

Probably about 2000. I'd focused a bit more on the Garage scene and I started dedicating a bit more time to that. I was shooting that for The Face, and I went off to Ayia Napa to shoot for Arena magazine. And then The Face asked me to photograph a bit more exclusively for them – across the course of the year 2000 they asked me to go off with a writer called Kevin Braddock and photograph what was going on with kids in the UK at that time. I'd go off to Rock in Cornwall and photograph the very upper-middle-classes at play on the seaside. It was fascinating. And then the next month I'd go off and photograph a sixth-form disco in Rossendale in Lancashire. And then the following month I'd go off to Maidenhead, and photograph kids who were into Nu Metal. And so I spent a lot of time that year making a different set of photographs, and I started working predominantly in colour. I'd formed a look by then, so I wasn't really going to clubs much then at all. I was done with that a bit.

And by 2001 I was working with Mike Skinner, The Streets. We started to make those pictures that I'd been making over the last three or four years into something that was then a bit more constructed and set up – but to look and feel like the pictures that had been made that were more found, in clubs and on the street.

I always get the impression with you that as soon as anything goes overground, your interest starts waning.

It does, immediately. Something that a lot of people I know – and I think you could probably be included in this, so don't think you're any better than I am, or any worse – that as soon as something becomes a bit more sussed and a bit more obvious, it naturally becomes more mainstream and it becomes more pop. And therefore, for me, it became less interesting. Because what I was interested in visually, what I wanted was the manifestation of something, something that was happening. And you can't really replicate that excitement. It's those places where it's just kicking off, you know?

This is a transcript of a conversation that took place over two sessions in October 2021. For reasons of concision and clarity, both questions and answers were edited.

1998

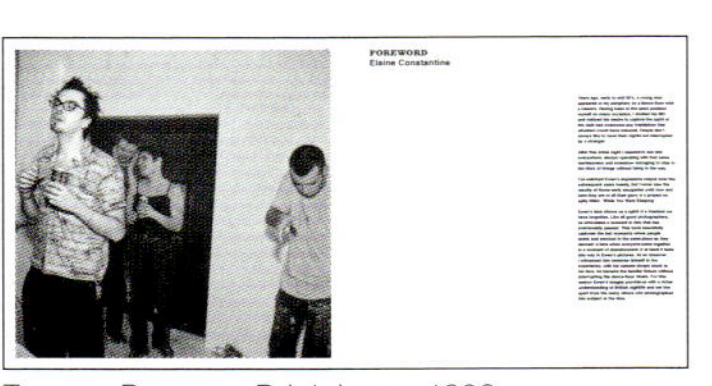
Truman Brewery, Brick Lane, 1998

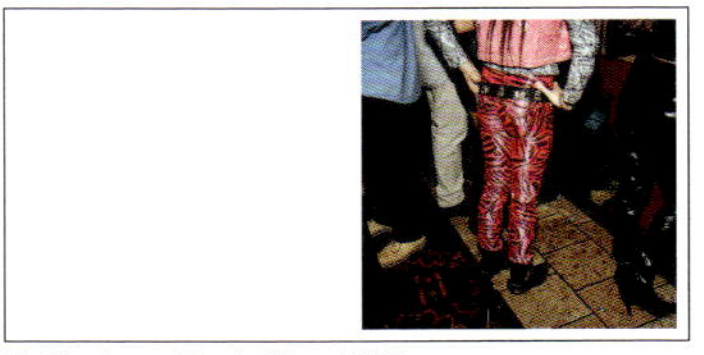
Nottingham Rock City, 1998

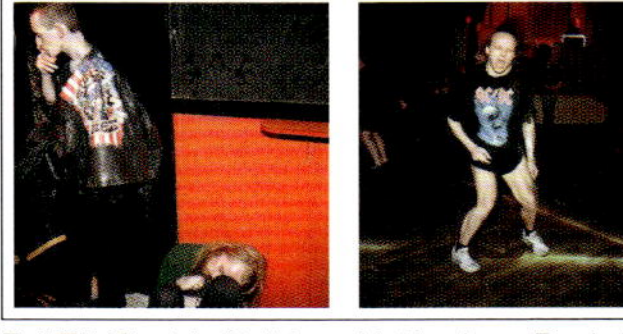
Full Tilt,Electric Ballri-oom, Camden, 1998 — Nottingham Rock City, 1998

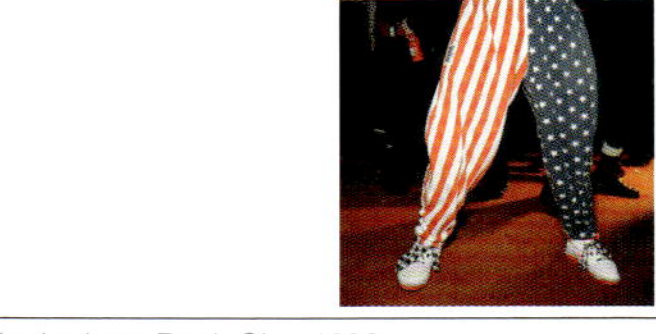
Nottingham Rock City, 1998

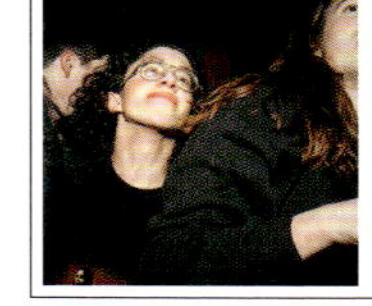
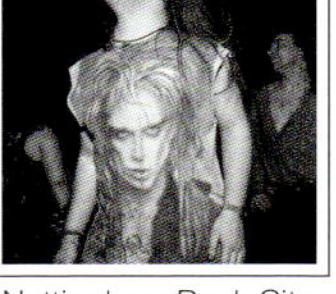
Full Tilt,Electric Ballri-oom, Camden, 1998 — Nottingham Rock City, 1998

Full Tilt,Electric Ballri-oom, Camden, 1998 — Nottingham Rock City, 1998

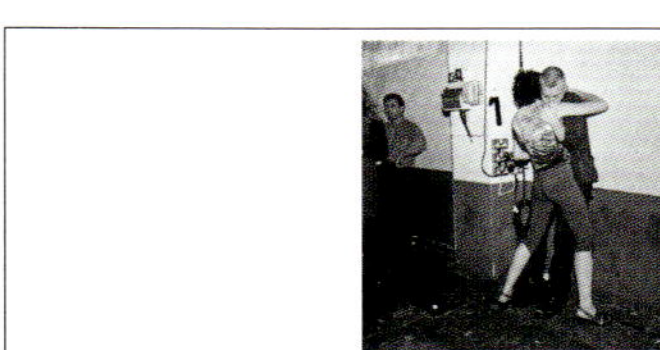
Sonik Mook Experiment, 333, Old Street, 1998

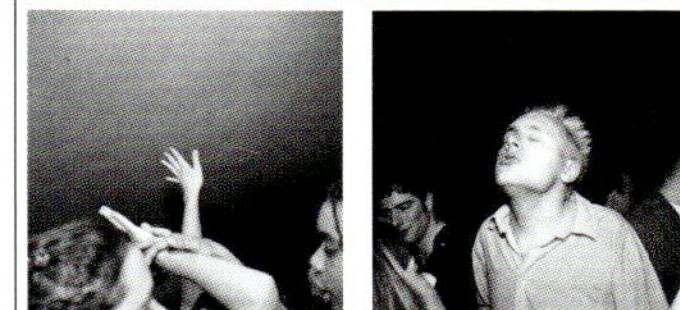
Sonik Mook Experiment, 333, Old Street, 1998

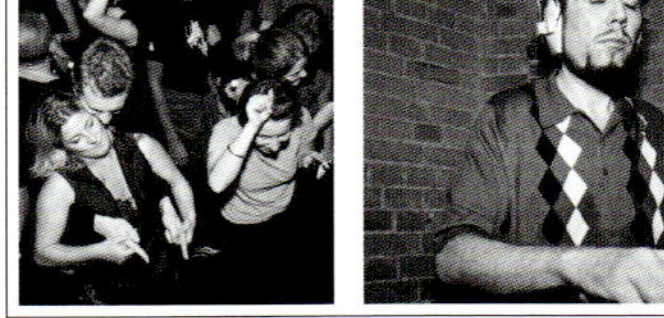
Sonik Mook Experiment, 333, Old Street, 1998

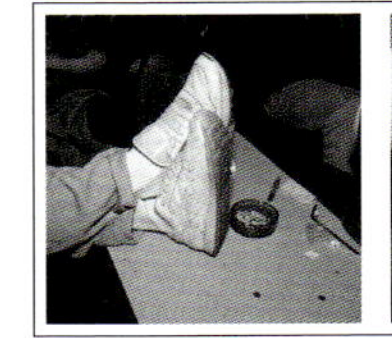
Sonik Mook Experiment, 333, Old Street, 1998

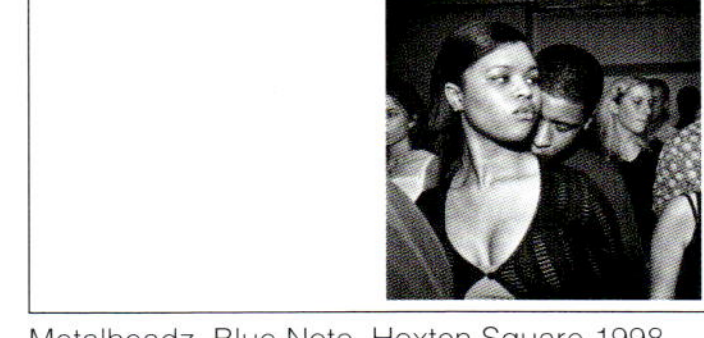
Metalheadz, Blue Note, Hoxton Square,1998

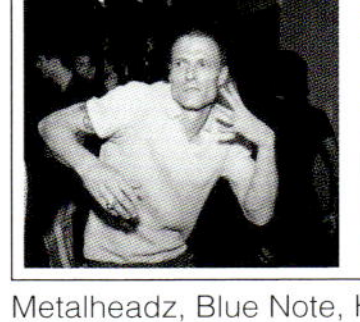
Metalheadz, Blue Note, Hoxton Square,1998

Metalheadz, Blue Note, Hoxton Square,1998

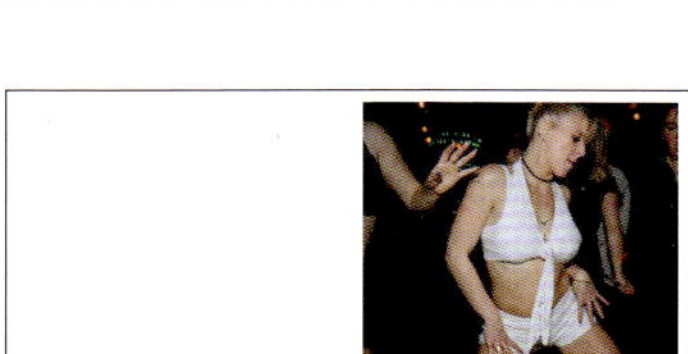
Infernos, Clapham High Street,1998

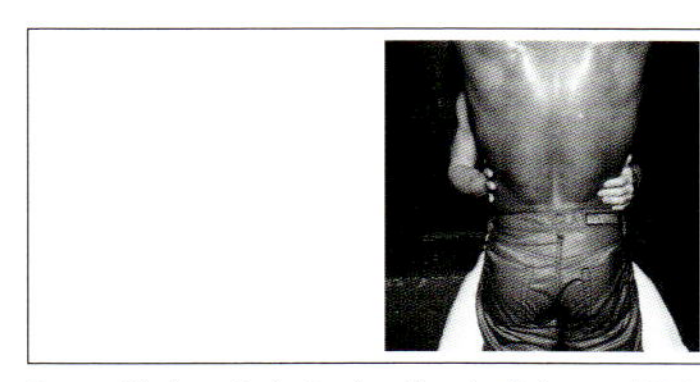
Queer Nation, Sub Station South, Brixton, 1998

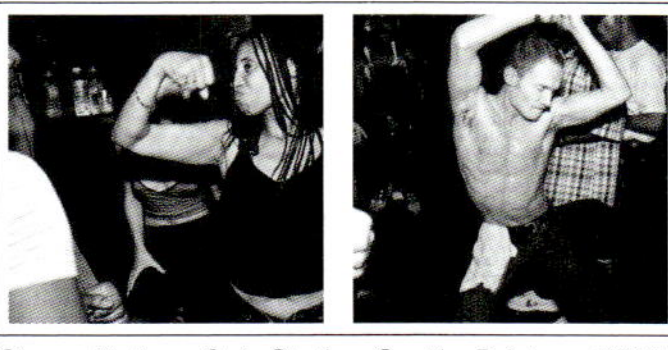
Queer Nation, Sub Station South, Brixton, 1998

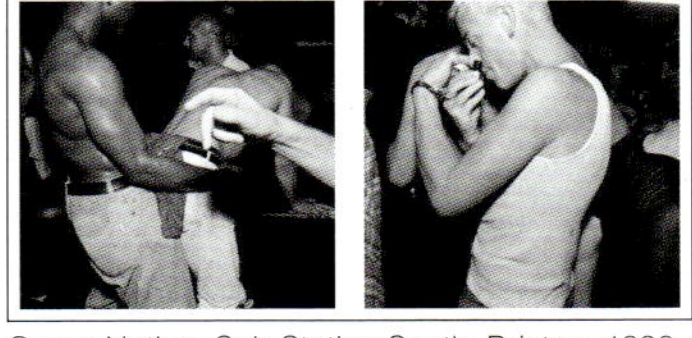
Queer Nation, Sub Station South, Brixton, 1998

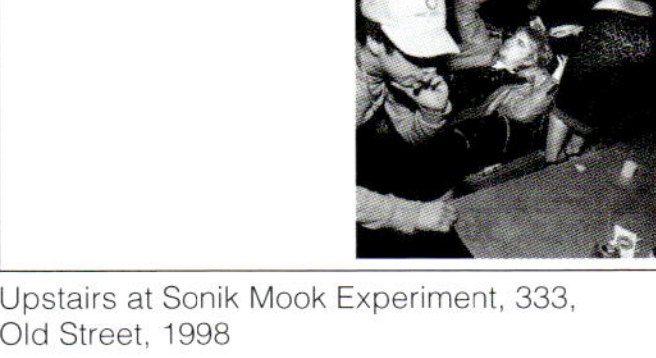
Upstairs at Sonik Mook Experiment, 333, Old Street, 1998

Upstairs at Sonik Mook Experiment, 333, Old Street, 1998

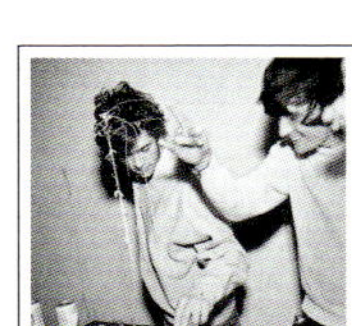
Upstairs at Sonik Mook Experiment, 333, Old Street, 1998

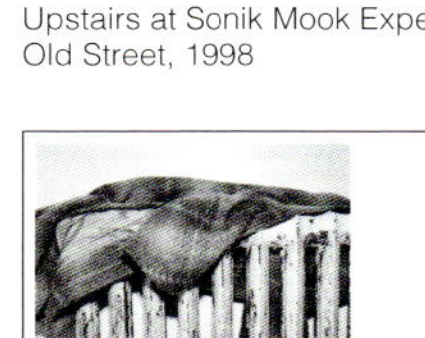
Upstairs at Sonik Mook Experiment, 333, Old Street, 1998

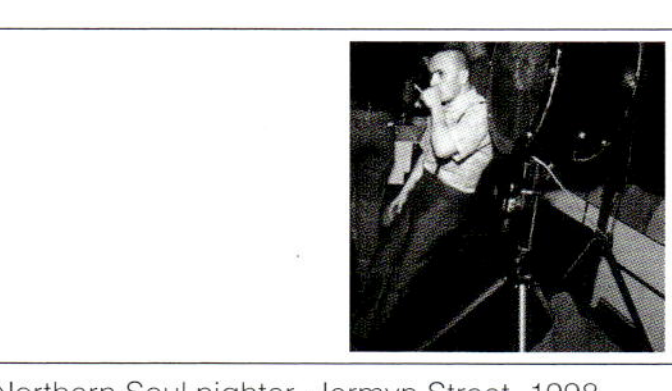
Northern Soul nighter, Jermyn Street, 1998

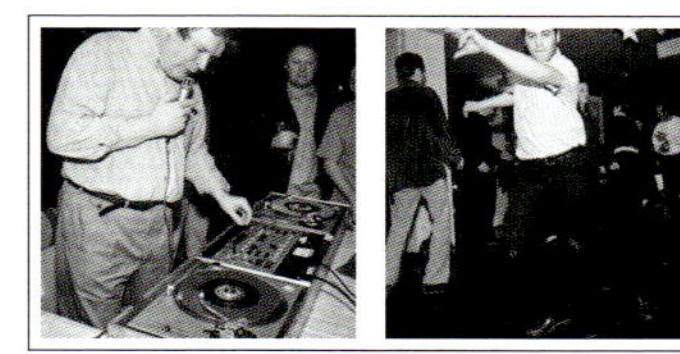
Northern Soul nighter, Jermyn Street, 1998

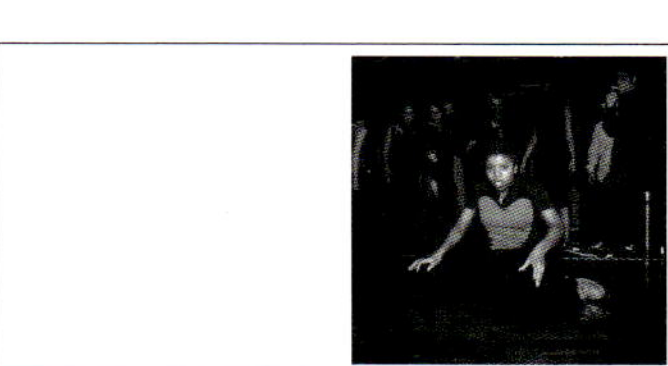
Deep Funk, Madame JoJos, Soho, 1998

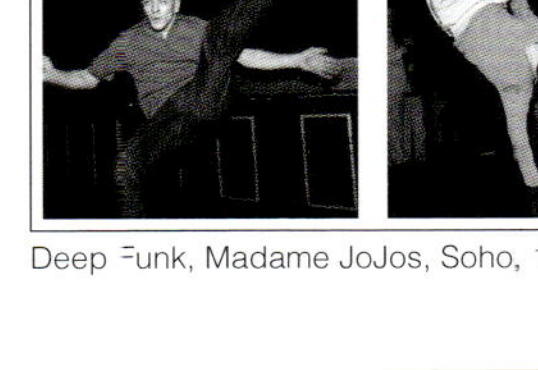
Deep Funk, Madame JoJos, Soho, 1998

Wild Fruit, Brighton, 1998

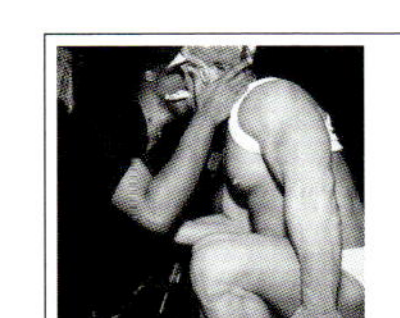
Wild Fruit, Brighton, 1998

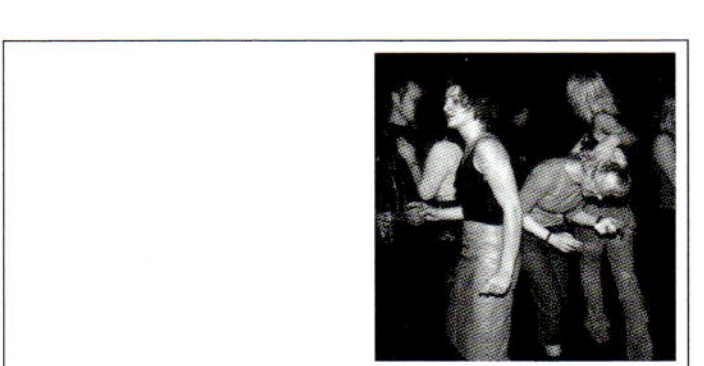
ICA all dayer, London, 1998

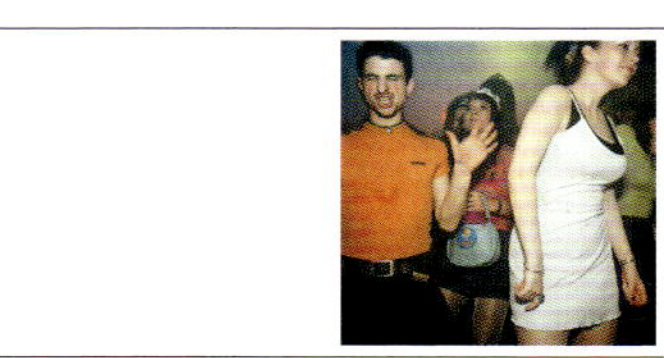
Zapp Club, Brighton, 1998

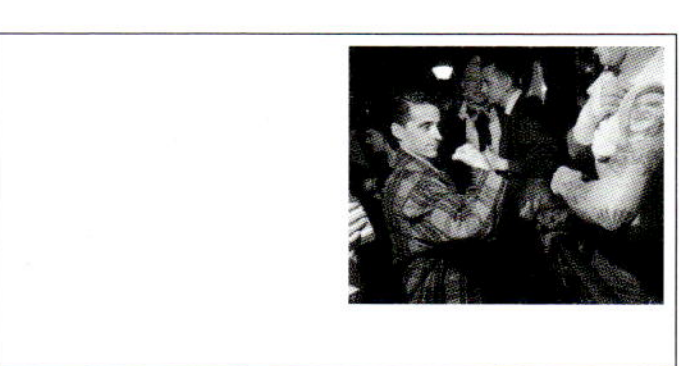
Elephants Head, Camden, 1998

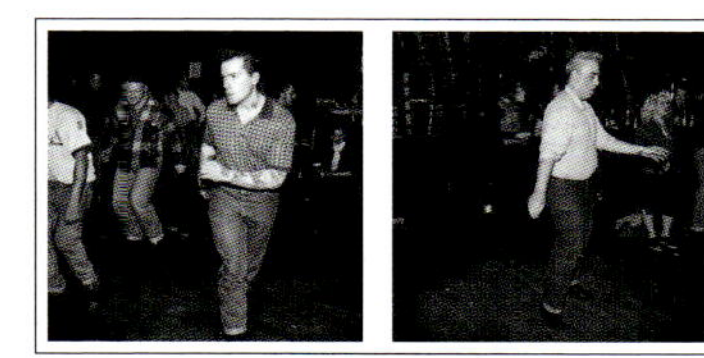
Elephants Head, Camden, 1998
Dingwalls, Camden, 1998

1999

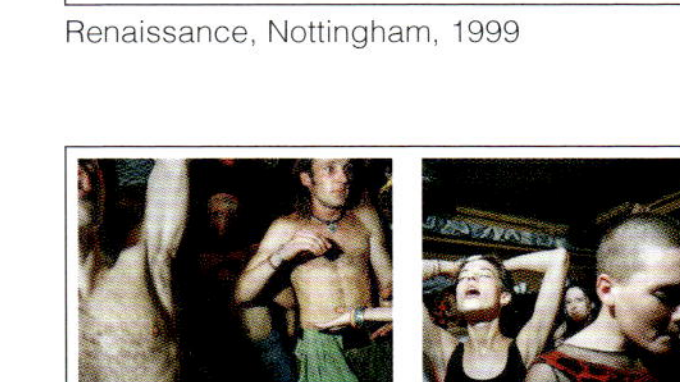
Renaissance, Nottingham, 1999

Trance Raves, Brixton, 1999

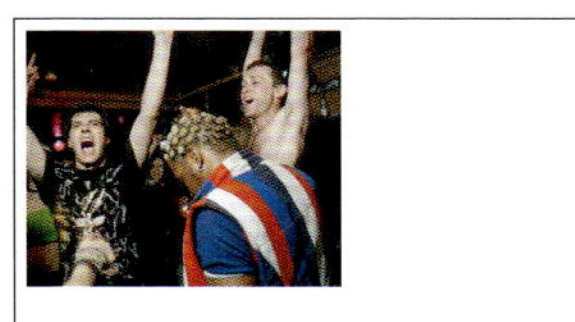
Trance Raves, Brixton, 1999

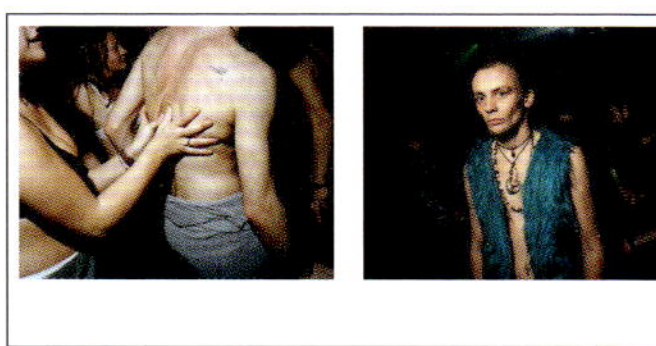
Trance Raves, Brixton, 1999

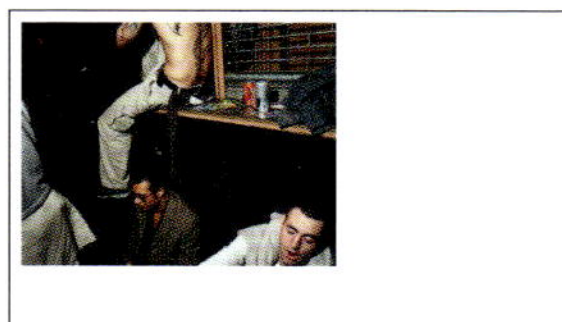
Trance Raves, Brixton, 1999

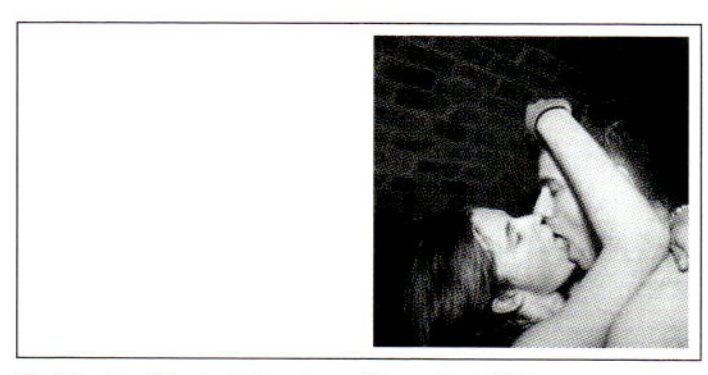
St Moritz Club, Wardour Street, 1999.

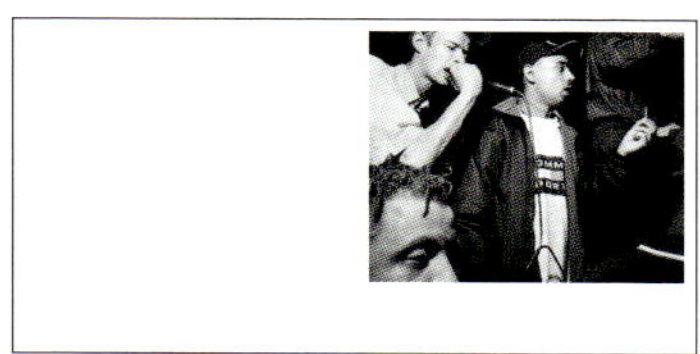
UK Garage Rave, Old Kent Road, 1999

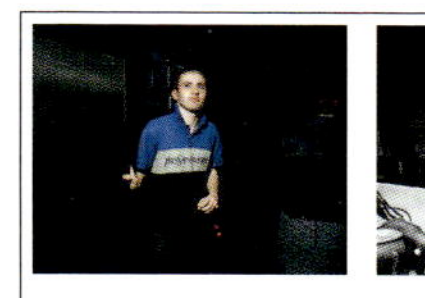
UK Garage Rave, London, 1999 — DJ Spoony, Twice as Nice, The End, 1999

2000

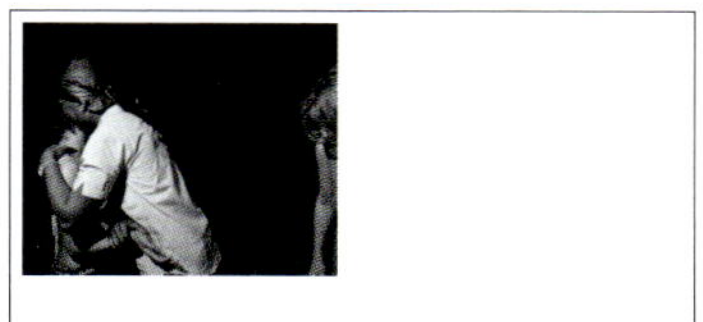
Twice as Nice, The End, 1999

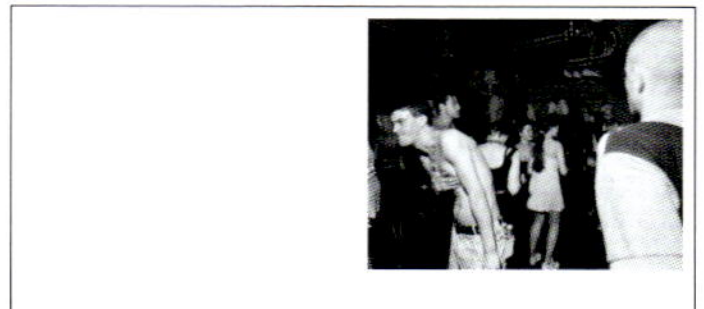
The Cross, Coal Drops Yard, Kings Cross, 2000

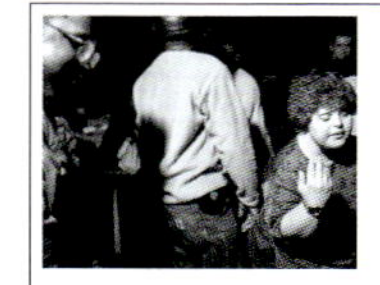
The Beautiful Octopus Club, New Cross, 2000

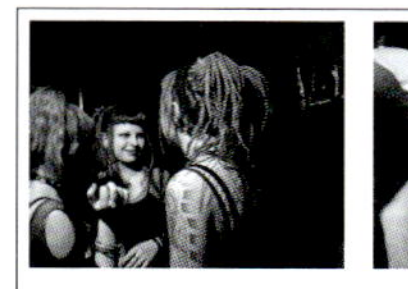
Club Metro, Oxford Street, 2000

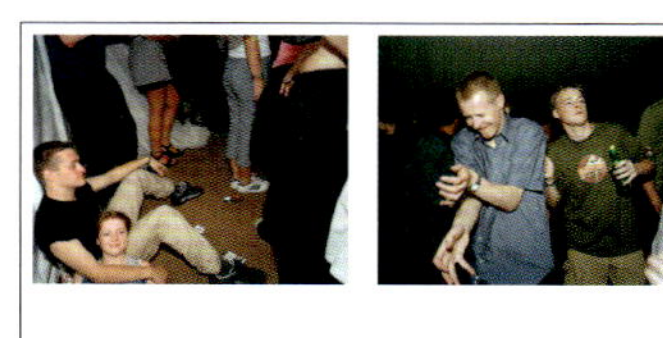
NY Sushi, Sheffield, 2000

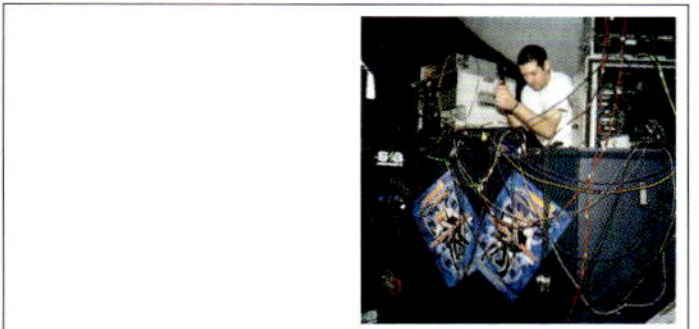
2wentys Holiday Reunion, Prestayn, 1999

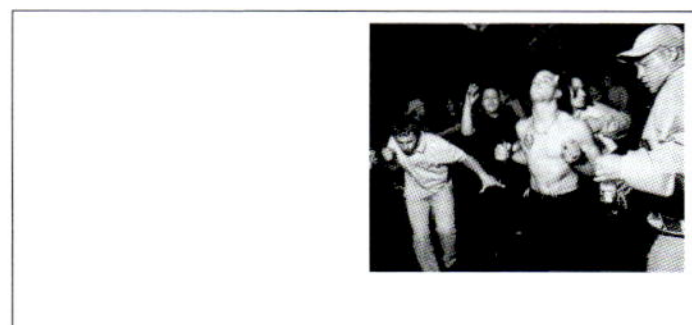
The Cross, Coal Drops Yard, Kings Cross, 2000

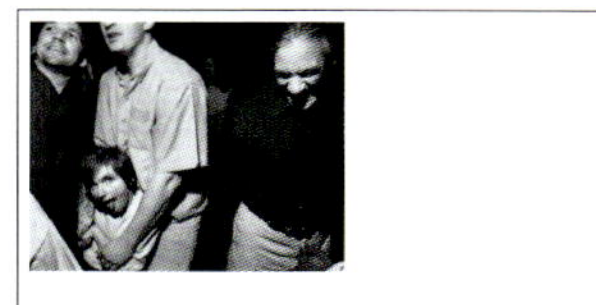
The Beautiful Octopus Club, New Cross, 2000

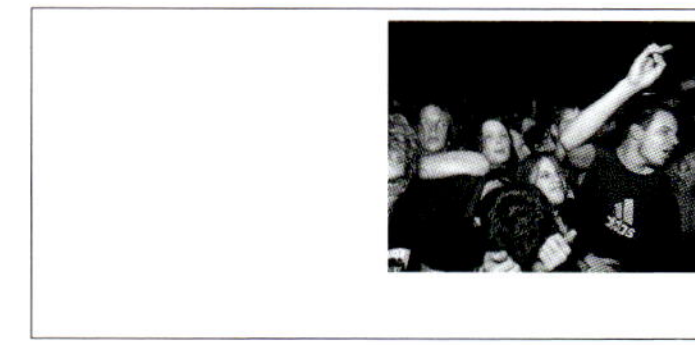
Slipknot, London Astoria, 2000

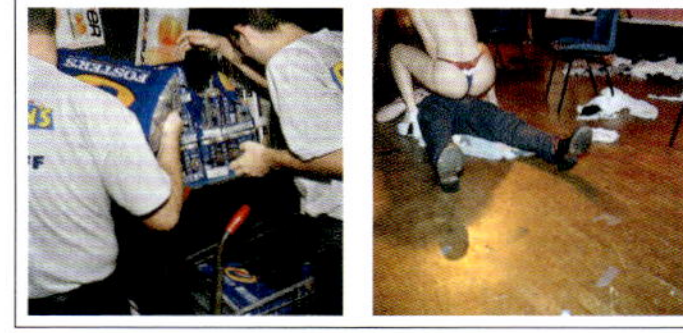
2wentys Holiday Reunion, Prestayn, 1999

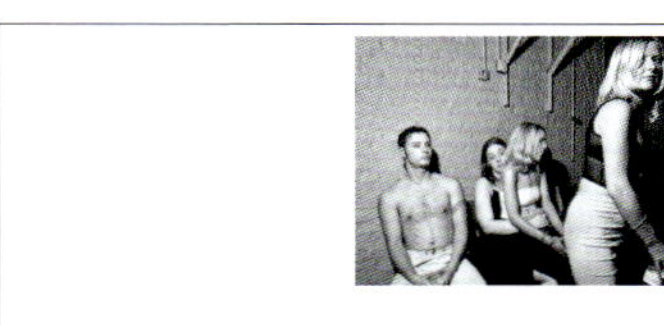
The Cross, Coal Drops Yard, Kings Cross, 2000

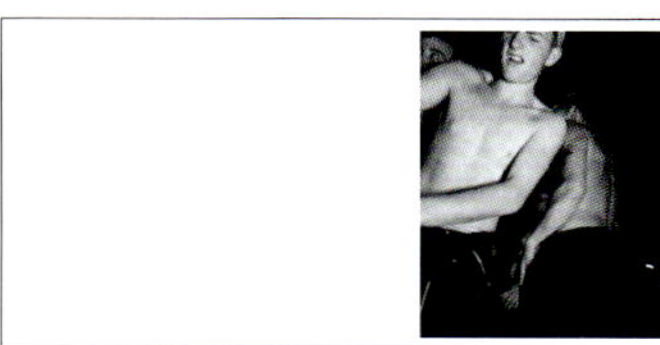
Summer Rave, Manchester 2000

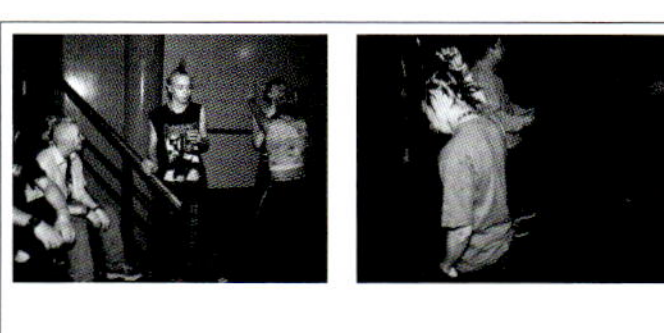
The Sanctuary, Camden, 2000

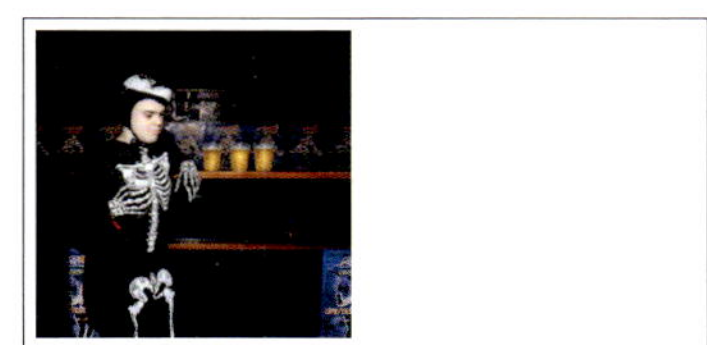
2wentys Holiday Reunion, Prestayn, 1999

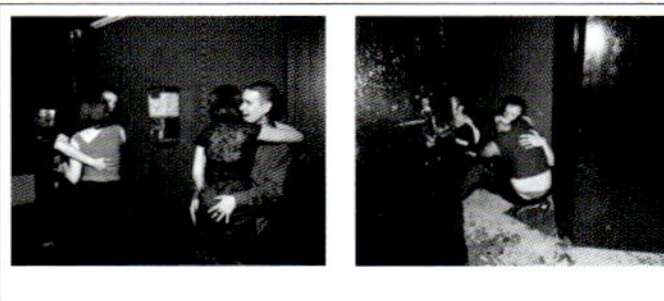
The Cross, Coal Drops Yard, Kings Cross, 2000

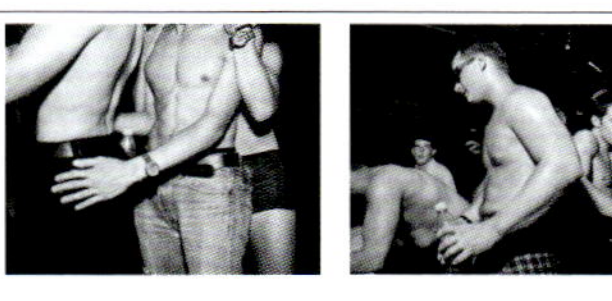
Crossings, Charring Cross Road, 2000

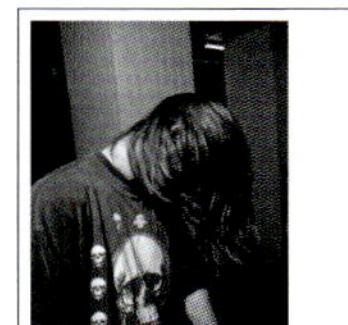
The Sanctuary, Camden, 2000

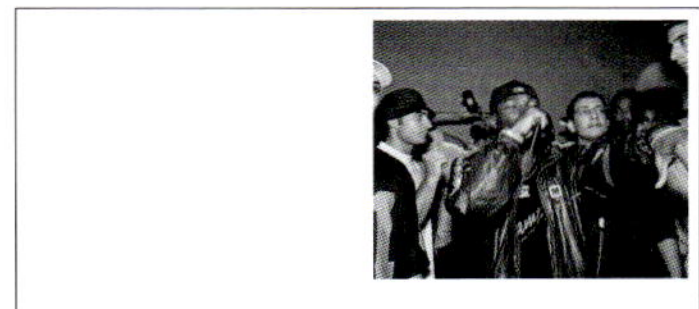
WKD, Kentish Town, 1999

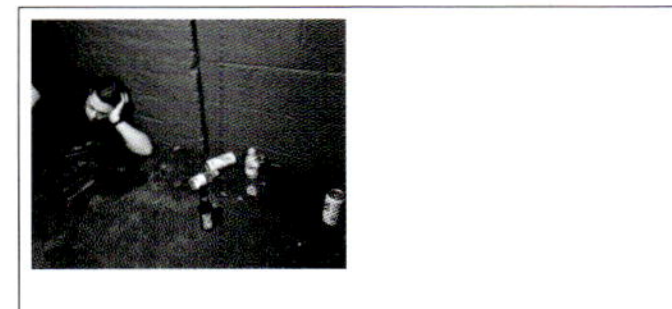
The Cross, Coal Drops Yard, Kings Cross, 2000

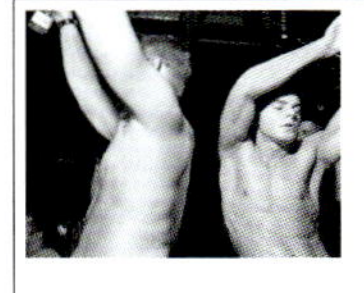
Crossings, Charring Cross Road, 2000

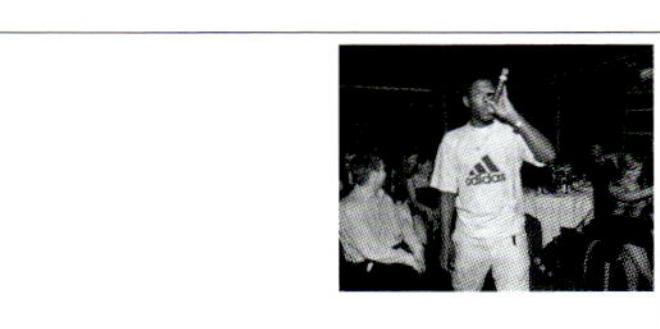
Roots Manuva, Clapham 2000

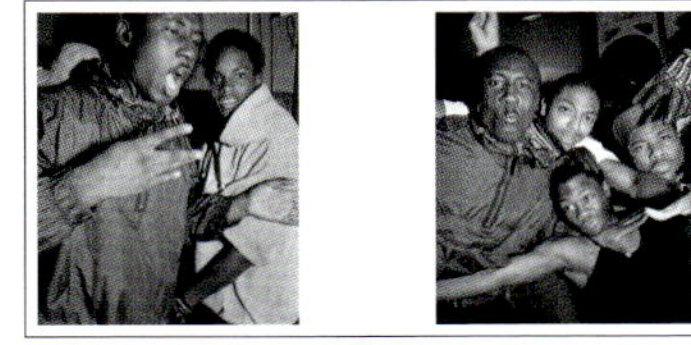
WKD, Kentish Town, 1999.

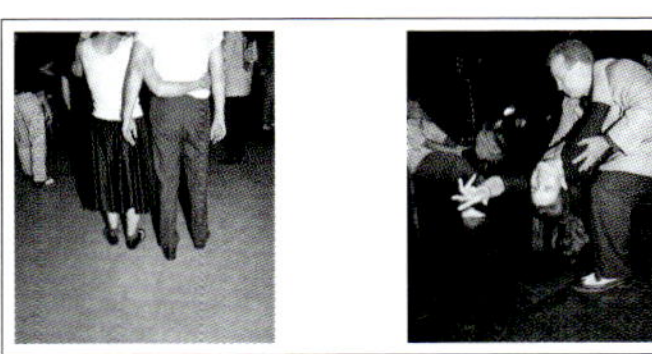
Le Jive, 100 Club, Oxford Street, 2000

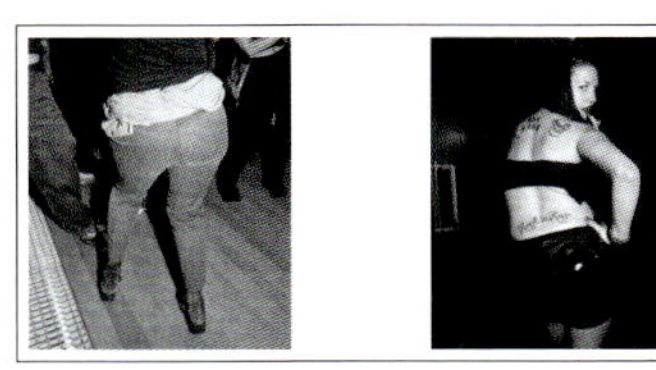
Madame JoJos, Soho, 2000

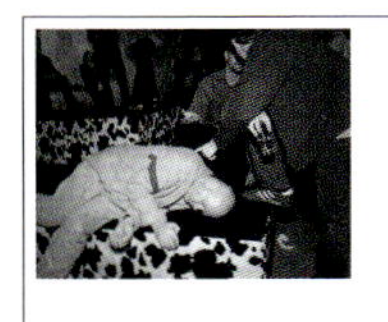
Truman Brewery, Brick Lane, 2000

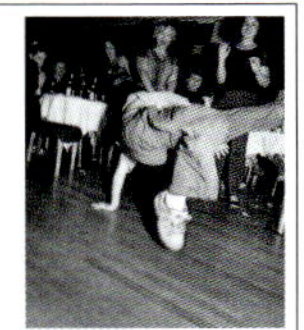
Roots Manuva, Clapham, 2000

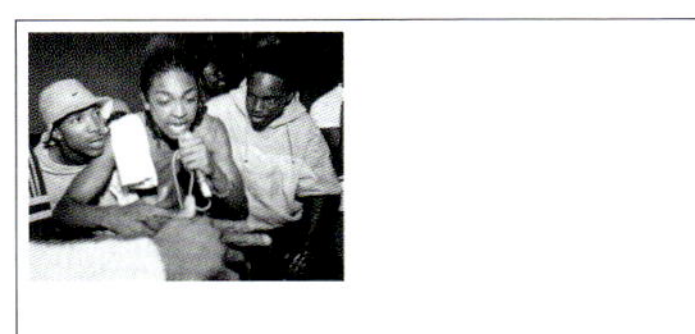
WKD, Kentish Town, 1999.

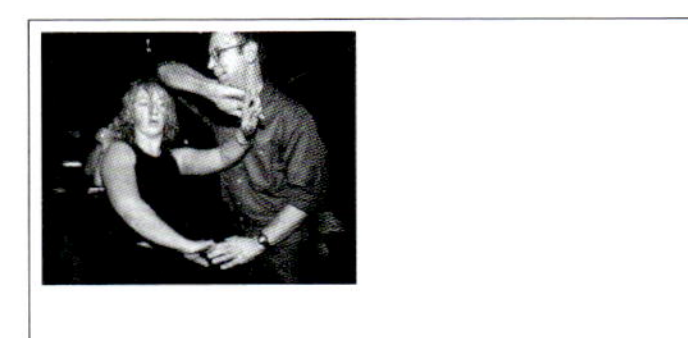
Le Jive, 100 Club, Oxford Street, 2000

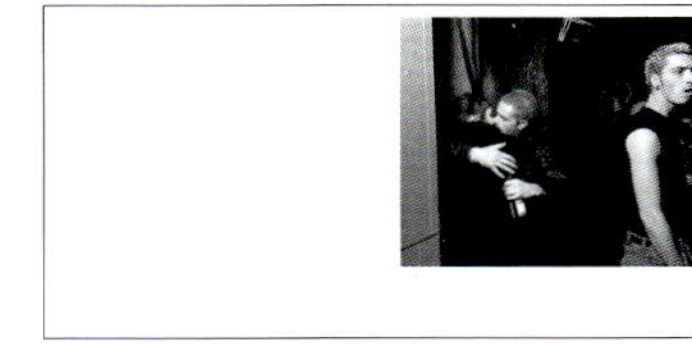
Club Metro, Oxford Street, 2000

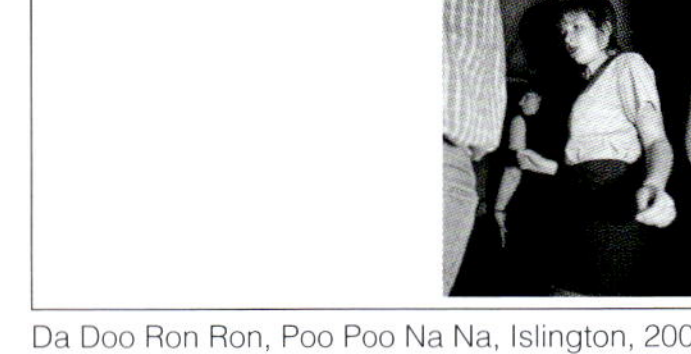
Da Doo Ron Ron, Poo Poo Na Na, Islington, 2000

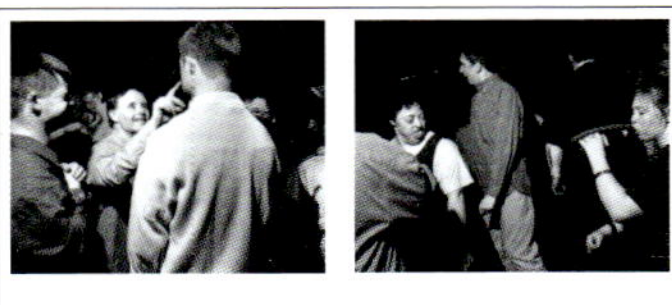
The Beautiful Octopus Club, New Cross, 2000

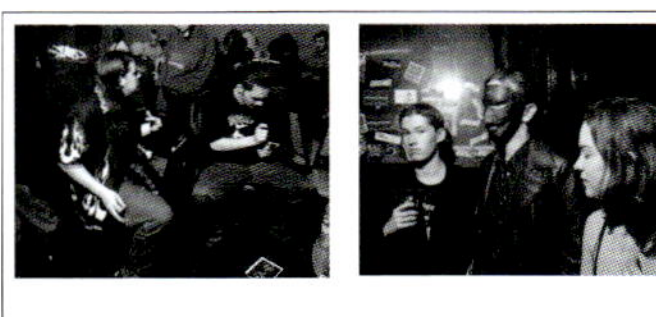
Club Metro, Oxford Street, 2000

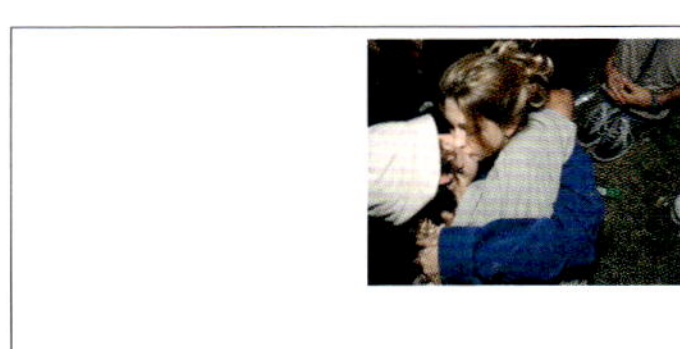
NY Sushi, Sheffield, 2000

Kind Thanks to my brother Cass for letting me crash at his place in St Lukes Ave, Clapham circa 97-99 and to Bruce and Danny Alder. Big Thanks to Steves Laz and Beale for repeatedly sending me out into the night.
Thanks to Glenn and Craig for helping instigate these pictures coming to press 25 years later. Who knew?
Huge thanks to Scott King and JQ for being involved and being so supportive in the process and to the best there is, Elaine Constantine.

Ewen Spencer
WHILE YOU WERE SLEEPING

Art Director: Scott King
Retouch: Jonathan Broadbent

Published by Damiani
info@damianieditore.com
www.damianieditore.com

Printed in December 2021, Italy

ISBN 978-88-6208-769-8